FASTEN IT, FIX IT, MEND IT, MAKE IT

Be your own best handyman with this practical, easy-to-use homeowners' guide. Filled with ready information and problem-solving advice, it's the handbook you need to keep your house in tip-top shape, inside and out.

MAN AND HIS HOME

By Daniel J. Albert & Norman Spector

POPULAR LIBRARY · TORONTO

ALL POPULAR LIBRARY books are carefully selected by the POPULAR LIBRARY Editorial Board and represent titles by the world's greatest authors.

POPULAR LIBRARY EDITION

Copyright © 1972 Daniel J. Albert & Norman Spector

PRINTED IN CANADA

All Rights Reserved

CONTENTS

Common Problems ... Uneven Temperatures ... Poor Combustion ... Noisy Hot-Water Systems ... Pressurized Oil Burners ... Indoor Fuel Tanks

Room Fans ... Window Fans ... Attic-Fan Installation ... Room Airconditioners ... Airconditioner Maintenance ... Central Air-Conditioning Installation ... Cooling by Absorption ... Other Types of Cooling ... Air Dehumidifiers ... Electronic Air Cleaners

House Plumbing System ... Know Your Valves ... Till the Plumber Arrives ... Rusty Water ... Gurgling Noises ... Leaking Toilet Tanks ... Leaking Faucets ... Clogged Drains ... Cleaning Sink Traps ... Closet Augers ... Septic Tanks ... How to Purify Water

Insulation ... Fireplaces ... Chimney Troubles ... How to Light a Fire ... Water in Basement ... Draining a Flood ... Drainage ... Waterproofing ... Sticking Doors ... Sticking Windows ... Broken Sash Cords ... Replacing Windowpanes ... Sagging and Squeaky Floors ... Replacing a Lock ... Window Shades ... Cracks in Plaster

House Wiring System ... Electric Circuits ... Safety in Grounding ... Fuses and Circuit Breakers ... Splicing a Wire

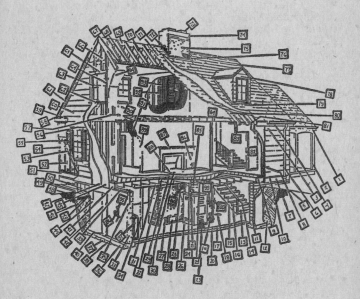

A HOUSE AND ITS PARTS

1. Porch Frieze Board
2. Corner Post
3. Frieze Board
4. Gornice
5. Top Soil
6. Rain Spout
7. Protective Weather Board

8. Rockwool Insulation
9. End Board for Joists
10. Anti Drip Molding
11. Foundation
12. Fill
13. Step
14. Railing

9

15. Stair Stringer
16. Riser
17. Concrete Floor Slab
18. Floor Drain
19. Support Post
20. Stone or Gravel Fill
21. Cold Water Line
22. Cross Members
23. Oil Burner
24. Floor Joists
25. Galvanized Collar
26. Oil Fired Furnace
27. Chimney
28. Chimney Cleanout
29. Floor Paper
30. Hard Wood Floor
31. Steel I Beam
32. Wood Sub-Floor
33. Concrete Foundation
34. Support Post
35. Anchor Bolts
36. Cement Footing
37. Tar Paper Joint Protection
38. French Tile
39. Bond Plate
40. Cement Trench
41. Joist Header
42. Stucco
43. Top Fill
44. Weather Proofing
45. Sheeting
46. Ground Fill
47. Tar Paper
48. Ground Level
49. Window Area Way
50. Casement Window
51. Joist Trimmer
52. Wall Studs
53. Diagonal Bracing
54. Corner Posts
55. Jalousies
56. Anti Drip Molding
57. Floor Plate
58. Eave Troughs
59. Cornice
60. Siding, Wood or Aluminum
61. Outside Gable Molding
62. Window Sill
63. Window Sash
64. Window Header
65. Window Frame
66. Gable Support
67. Attic Insulation
68. Ceiling Joists
69. Ridge Board
70. Roof Boards
71. Roof Rafters
72. Copper or Galvanized Flashing
73. Flue
74. Cement Cap
75. Brick Chimney
76. Flashing
77. Shingles or Slate
78. Dormer Window
79. Flashing
80. Roof Rafters
81. Top Plates
82. Partition Wall
83. Header
84. Partition
85. Expansion Tank
86. Wood Box
87. Marble Mantel
88. Hearth
89. Plaster Arch
90. Plaster
91. Lath
92. Furrings
93. Brickwork
94. Pointed Ceiling
95. Vent Pipe
96. Fill Pipe
97. Oil Tank
98. Draft Regulator
99. Hot Water Line
100. Hot Water Heater

Chapter 1

THE FOUR Ws

Everyone who lives in a house, whether as owner or tenant, knows his house needs constant care if it is to function in good working order. Added to the costs of mortgage interest, taxes, and utilities is a catch-all category called maintenance. Like a petulant child, a house—*any* house—keeps calling for help. It is the purpose of this book to show how to render that help and thereby accomplish two objectives.

A house that works well is a comfortable home; a run-down house is not. And a house that is properly maintained not only works well and comfortably, it costs less because heavy maintenance expenses are foreseen and by prompt action, avoided.

During more than a quarter-century in the fuel oil and heating equipment business on a large scale in Montreal, the authors inevitably found themselves in a second business: answering questions. When customers encountered problems concerned with home heating, they quite naturally turned to their fuel dealer as a presumptive expert.

We answered their questions and tried to solve the problems to the best of our ability. In the course of this we learned something ourselves.

During the period we are talking about, roughly since the end of World War II, questions from perplexed customers have seemed to increase in number every year. Seeking an explanation, we found it in the technological revolution of our time.

New equipment and structural techniques have made houses better and more livable, but they also make houses more complicated. A modern oil burner bears little resemblance to an old-fashioned coal furnace. An automatic washing machine is a far cry from a laundry tub with wringer. Houses built today are completely different from the old houses in every respect, not only in their mechanical contents but in their sophisticated compactness, weather-tightness, floor design, foundation, roof, walls—everything.

The transformation of housing with breathtaking speed placed a new premium on the handyman skills of the homeowner. Not only did he have more intricate mechanisms to deal with, but higher and higher labor costs whenever he called for the services of a plumber, an electrician, a carpenter, or a mason. The only way he could avoid heavy maintenance costs was to handle as many jobs as possible himself.

As dispensers of do-it-yourself advice to homeowners, we sought ways to do our job with less effort. An obvious solution was to reach a wider audience with each answer to a query, so that hundreds of persons rather than a single individual might gain access to a given home-saving idea. In 1967 a weekly newspaper in suburban Montreal accepted a regular column from us devoted to answering the queries of homeowning readers.

Originally entitled "The House Doctors," this weekly column grew steadily in popularity. Since 1969, renamed

"Man and His Home," it has appeared weekly in a large metropolitan daily, the *Montreal Gazette*.

What we learned was that many queries from readers—in fact, the majority of them—were concerned with identical problems, item by item and almost word for word. Readers would send in questions we had answered in the column not too many weeks before. Either they had missed that week's column or had read it only casually because the particular problem it covered did not materially affect them at the time of reading. We heard from quite a few people who clipped and saved our column regularly. Others asked if the articles had ever been put together in a permanent reference book.

This book is an outgrowth of our many years of answering questions and meeting the demands for how-to-do-it information from our customers and readers. You asked for it; here it is!

What Is Home Maintenance?

Despite the bewildering variety of jobs that a home handyman finds thrust upon him from one day to the next, those chores that demand a bit of special knowledge come in four major groups: Weather, Water, Workmanship, and Wear. We call them the four Ws of keeping a house in good working order.

Weather includes the measures every homeowner must take both inside and outside a house to remain snug despite any changes in the daily climate, no matter how severe. Heating, cooling, roofing, insulation, and certain other parts of the basic house structure come within this category.

Water means the supply of water, cold and hot, plumbing, drainage, and sewage disposal—the most important needs of a house next to four walls and a roof.

Workmanship has to do with the way a house is built: its design, basic structure, quality of construction work and materials. This "W" is especially important on the negative side, when the structure, wiring, insulation, etc., are found deficient in some important respect or when maintenance by a previous resident has been neglected or poorly executed.

Wear is the natural consequence of usage by people and the steady assault of the elements. Things do wear out, break, or break down. The older the house, the more important this factor becomes in an owner's maintenance program. Real estate experts recognize wear in financial terms through depreciation in value. If a property does not depreciate over a long period of years, it's because the land (not the house) has increased in worth.

About the Contents

The contents of this book are intended to help the reader in two ways: (1) quick fixes that he can take care of himself, and (2) more complicated jobs where he will need expert service, but which he should understand before he orders the work done. Admittedly the borderline between do-it-yourself and pay-someone-else is an arbitrary one. Just where the line is drawn depends a great deal upon the individual, his or her experience and skills.

We have simply assumed that most readers are not trained carpenters, plumbers, electricians, mechanics, or masons and we have made no attempt to give a complete course in any of those trades. Neither have we tried to tell anyone how to build a house.

What we have done is to try to impart what we know, in such a manner that anyone with common sense and proper tools can fix balky things so they work. Beyond that range we have not ventured, although in our own

14

field of home heating we have included far more than you are apt to find in other how-to-do-it books on home maintenance.

The reader is also referred to the guides and tables of materials and measurements that will be found of great value whenever the need comes to "look it up."

A Note on Ecology

Besides planning this book for its usefulness to the individual homeowner, the authors have also had in mind the importance of good home maintenance in protecting the environment. As fuel dealers more than twenty years ago, the authors were actively engaged in research on industrial, commercial, and residential processes where control of pollution could be developed and improved.

They were among the first to develop a program of replacing obsolete oil combustion equipment with more effective, lighter, and more efficient equipment. They also contributed to reeducating the consumer to the advantages of substituting lower sulfur content light fuel oil for heavy oils. Some of their conversion installations have been of demonstrable assistance in the reduction of air pollution in the Montreal central city.

Other pioneer efforts have been the introduction of a fail-safe oil gauge, high-velocity forced draft heating equipment, and evaporative type humidifiers. They were among the first proponents of the concept of complete comfort climate control—combining heating, air-conditioning, humidification, and electronic air cleaning into a totally controlled home environment.

An outgrowth of this work has been a prototype vehicle, one of the S. Albert & Co. Ltd. fleet, which may operate either on gasoline or liquefied propane gas. Current research on this vehicle is perfecting its operation on compressed natural gas or on a special blend of fuel called ND7. All of these alternatives to gasoline greatly reduce the pollutants in automobile exhaust.

ND7 is a derivative of ND53, a lead-free additive that has increased the efficiency of fuel oil combustion and has been used effectively to reduce pollution emissions from smokestacks. In the ultimate vehicle the motorist would be able to select the fuel most suitable for environmental requirements, simply by flipping a selector switch like the channel selector on a TV.

But these are digressions; if this book helps to improve *your* environment as well as the community's, we will be happy and content.

Daniel J. Albert
Norman Spector

Chapter 2

HAVE THESE HANDY

If you intend to do any maintenance work on your house, you obviously need an assortment of tools. Many people build up a tool chest one item at a time, buying what is needed when it is needed and not before. There is nothing wrong with this approach in principle, but a completely tool-less household clearly invites getting stuck in an emergency. Leaking pipes and conked-out water heaters have a perverse habit of occurring in the middle of the night or on Christmas Day.

If no job seems beyond a handyman's attainments, a fully equipped and stocked workshop with power tools is indeed a blessing. But this would be a costly investment for the person who looks with misgivings even upon a screwdriver and a pair of pliers. Something in between these extremes offers the most practical solution. One should own and keep handy a selection of indispensable implements, even in an apartment house where the super-intendent is supposed to be the jack-of-all-trades but often isn't. A good basic selection can later be extended in any direction as the owner's skills and interests expand to more sophisticated areas.

The first step for a beginner is to compile a list of tools that are absolutely essential. It is ridiculous to call a plumber at ten to fifteen dollars an hour to fix a leaky faucet or unclog a drain when the homeowner can do the same job in minutes—with the proper tools. The following list, accompanied by tips on buying and using tools, should satisfy the needs of all but those expert carpenters and home mechanics who do not need the advice anyway.

The Essential Tools

Claw hammer	Screwdrivers	Pliers
Wrenches	Pipe wrench	Plumber's helper
Hand drill and bits	Chisels	Plane
Clamps and vise	Knife	Saws
Flexible rule	Spirit level	Files and rasp

Even the most amateurish of amateurs, male or female, should always buy hand tools of the best quality. Avoid the cheap tools that are gaudily packaged for Christmas or Father's Day to tempt unsuspecting women as gifts for their husbands. Good tools, like good furniture, last a lifetime. Inferior "bargain" tools will wear out fast—but not fast enough to get them out of your way when there's a job to be done. They can cause unpleasant accidents by slipping or breaking under pressure.

Hammers

Hammers come in numerous specialized shapes and sizes; the all-purpose type is a 16-ounce claw hammer. The bell face, which is the part that hits the nail, is virtually flat, and the opposite end of the head is shaped like

18

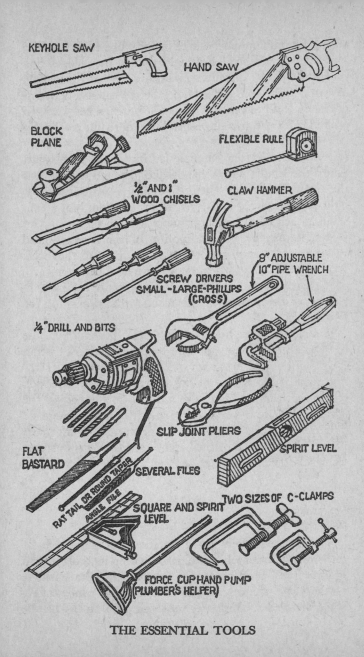

THE ESSENTIAL TOOLS

a claw for pulling nails out of wood. The head fits onto a wooden handle which is held tightly by wedges that spread the wood, but after much use the head may tend to work itself loose. One of the better hammers consists of a one-piece head and metal handle with leather wrapped around it for the grip. It costs a little more but is virtually indestructible.

Workmen judge a hammer by its "heft" or balance. Grasp the handle with a handshake grip and hold it near the end when driving a nail. Use only a wrist action for light taps, the wrist and forearm for medium blows, and shoulder action with a slight wrist movement for heavier blows. Remember it's the motion of the hammer head through an arc—not your muscle—that delivers the force. Accuracy in striking is more important than strength.

An auxiliary tool, the *nailset*, is used to drive a finishing nail below the surface of the wood without marring the finish.

If a nail starts to bend as it is being driven, strike the head at a slight angle opposite to the direction of bend. Or pull it out and try another nail. To extract a nail without marring the surface of the wood, place a wood block under the hammer claw. Press down on the end of the handle to rotate the claw upward with great leverage.

If the head of a wooden hammer starts to work loose, pound the other end of the handle vertically against something solid, such as a concrete floor.

Screwdrivers

Three screwdrivers make up the recommended basic set: small with 3-inch blade; large with 6-inch blade; and Phillips head. For these one might substitute a single ratchet-drive, spiral screwdriver with an assortment of replaceable blades. With this tool you push on the handle to turn the blade, either to drive a screw or the reverse. It may also be set with the driving mechanism locked out. When drilling bits are added to the assortment, the ratchet screwdriver also becomes a miniature hand drill.

Because a screwdriver is so handy an implement, it is only too often misused as a chisel, scraper, punch, or prying tool. Such heavy forces may damage the blade so that it no longer will drive or loosen screws. The tip should be ground straight and square. The flat sides of the blade should taper out to meet the shank, but so gradually that they are nearly parallel at the end.

This careful machining is necessary so that torque (twisting force) is transmitted evenly to both sides of a screw head slot. For the same reason, the proper screwdriver for any given job should just fit the slot, both in width and thickness.

If too narrow for the work, a blade will tend to slip out of the slot, chew up the softer metal of the screwhead, and wear out at the corners. Too wide a blade will gouge out surrounding surfaces when the screw has been driven flush. Too thin a blade will be difficult to turn and may twist or bend under pressure. An assortment of blade sizes should be kept handy, and replaced or repaired if they become rounded or too sharp and lose their squared edges.

A Phillips screwdriver has crossed blades that come to a point, for use with the type of screw that has a crossed-V slot. They're made this way so the screwdriver cannot slip out of the slot. However, the tip is weak and rather easily broken off. The tool should be used with care to avoid excessive pressure. Even with a blunted point, it will still work fairly well on all but the smallest Phillips-type screws.

When using a screwdriver, first bore or drill a pilot hole for the screw with an awl, a hand drill, or by driving in a *center punch* (better than driving in a nail since you don't have to pull it out). The hole should be of smaller diameter than the screw. Gently tap the screw into the hole with a hammer, then apply the screwdriver.

If holding the screw in position causes difficulty, you may want to consider a magnetized screwdriver or one made with little claws that hold the screwhead against the tip.

Pliers

A pliers acts like an extension of the fingers for gripping such objects as nails, rods, wires, etc., with its metal claws. For home repairs a combination, or slip-joint, pliers is universal. The slip-joint permits this pliers to be opened wide at the hinge for gripping objects of large diameter, or narrowed down for smaller work. A good-quality pliers will stay put in either of the slip-joint positions, and its claws will remain parallel for a tight grip on thin materials.

When using pliers as a wrench to turn a bolt, first wrap the bolt in cloth to prevent chewing away the head. For electrical work, pliers should have a special slot for wire cutting.

Wrenches

A wrench is a tool for turning nuts and bolts that comes in two general categories, adjustable and fixed. The jaws of an adjustable wrench may be set for a variety of nut sizes, while a fixed wrench fits only a particular size and usually is purchased in sets.

In home repairs the modern open-end adjustable crescent wrench has largely replaced the standard monkey wrench except for heavy mechanical work. Its crescent-shaped jaws are set at one end of the handle instead of to the side, and at a slight angle for ease in reaching into tight spaces. Two sizes, 10-inch and 6-inch, are recommended for the home workshop.

Fixed wrenches are preferred where exact size of the jaw opening is important for a really firm grip. A set of inexpensive open-end wrenches is a worthwhile investment, since they can be used in places where an adjustable wrench would not fit. Also handy for fixing appliances are the tiny hexagonal or "hex" wrenches that will turn recessed screw heads, such as the set screws on handles and controls. A vice-grip is one of the most useful tools in the wrench-plier family.

A Stillson or pipe wrench for grasping pipes and other round objects has jaws with teeth that bite into the metal. A hinging action produces an exceptionally strong grip. A 12-inch and 18-inch pipe wrench will cover most plumbing jobs a homeowner is apt to tackle.

The proper way to use an adjustable wrench is: (1) Place the jaws around the head of the nut or bolt. (2) Tighten the jaws to the snuggest possible fit. (3) Remove the wrench and tighten the jaws just a trifle more. (4) Replace wrench on the nut and turn. The force should be applied to the back of the handle, that is, so the adjustable jaw turns *into* the jaw opening. (In the opposite direction the adjustable jaw will tend to slip off the nut.)

Saws

A crosscut saw, generally of 24- or 26-inch length with 8-point blade, is the basic tool for all kinds of woodworking. "Points" refer to the number of teeth per inch, from 6 (very coarse) to 11 (very fine).

This saw is designed to cut across the grain of lumber or wood panels, but will also cut with the grain (like a ripsaw) if need be. Handled with a light touch, a crosscut saw may be applied even to rather delicate work.

More elaborate carpentry will call for a *backsaw, keyhole saw*, and *coping saw* or *jigsaw* to cut in curves. Cutting metal requires a *hacksaw*.

A substitute for these specialized saws in most home needs is the handy *all-purpose saw*. Only 6 or 8 inches long, with a narrow, tapered blade and a pistol-grip handle, it can fit into tight corners, cut curves as well as straight lines, and, with its fine-toothed edge, cut metal as well as wood. It is actually better than any of the regular saws for cutting hard plastics, plaster, wallboard, and certain other common materials.

A crosscut saw should be held at an angle of 45 degrees with the board being cut. If using it as a ripsaw (cutting with the grain), increase the angle to 60 degrees. Hold the handle with the index finger pointed along the top of the blade, helping to guide the saw straight. The teeth cut when you push down.

If you intend to cut up logs for firewood, a so-called Swedish *tree saw* is the ticket. This is a metal bow with a large-toothed, replaceable blade. The saw can be used by two people working together or by a single person.

Clamps and Vise

For nearly all kinds of work with adhesives, it is necessary to clamp the glued parts together for a time in order to set the joint for maximum strength. For this purpose wood clamps are made in a variety of sizes and shapes. Other types of clamps or a vise, which is a kind of clamp in a fixed position, may be used either in gluing or to hold work rigidly, such as a blade being sharpened with a file.

For woodworking the handiest clamp is a *hand screw*, which consists of two wooden jaws and two adjustable

24

screws. In clamping, first tighten lightly with both screws, then apply final pressure with the outside screw only. In addition, one or two *C-clamps* with jaw openings from 3 to 6 inches can be used for a wide variety of jobs around the house.

SAW GUIDE C-CLAMPED IN POSITION

Miscellaneous

The *plumber's helper*, more properly a *force cup* or *plunger*, gives first aid in most cases of clogged drains.

For the tool to work properly, have several inches of water in the bottom of the sink, tub, or toilet bowl. Position the rubber cup over the drain opening and hold the handle with both hands. Pressing the handle down suddenly will exert hydraulic pressure (which is why the cup must be under water). Jerking it upward will release the pressure to create a suction.

Repeating the push-pull action rapidly and vigorously ten or a dozen times will help dislodge foreign matter in the drain. The job is done when water drains out of the basin in one quick gurgle.

Hand drill and bits. Since drilling a hole precedes almost any job that requires fasteners, screws, etc., selecting the tool used for this purpose calls for thought. Many homeowners insist that they would not be without a *power drill*, and there is no question it saves a lot of time and effort. However, the same job can be done at a slower pace with much less costly hand tools.

Among these are the traditional *brace and bit*, which consists of a cutting device (the bit) affixed to a handle that turns it; a *hand drill*, which looks something like an eggbeater; and a *push drill*, which works much like a ratchet screwdriver. By replacing the cutting bit with a screwdriver tip, some models of these drills may also be used as a high-torque screwdriver.

Hand drills have one advantage over power drills in being less vulnerable to mistakes. When you drill a hole completely through any material, the other side splinters (if wood) or crumples (if metal). If both sides are visible, as on a door, drilling should be stopped as soon as the point of the bit starts to break through. Finish drilling the hole from the other side. Power drills are apt to plunge all the way through before you can stop them.

Knives and chisels both are implements for working wood to a desired shape after larger tools have done the main cutting and drilling. A good jackknife may be adequate, but a *utility knife* is safer. This consists of a razor-like replaceable blade affixed by screws to a handle. For serious whittlers, a *hunting knife* with its heavy blade can cut wood in strips rather than splinters.

Chisels with one-inch blades and half-inch blades should be sufficient for most home carpentry. Here are some things to know about them:

Hold a chisel in one hand, which applies the pressure, while the other hand guides the blade over the work. For smoother finish, guide the chisel cuts at an angle to the direction of cut. If hammering is necessary, use only a wooden, rubber, or plastic faced hammer, since a steel one may split the handle. Tap lightly only. Or use a *cold chisel*, which is solid steel.

Remove a small amount of wood at a time. For rough cuts, hold the chisel edge with the beveled side down. For delicate finishing cuts, hold the chisel bevel side up.

Files and rasps. Files are used for grinding off rough edges and surfaces of hard materials, whether wood or metal. The object being ground or sharpened must be held rigidly, for example, in a vise. A rasp is a very coarse file used to smooth wood across the grain, as at the end of a board or the top edge of a door. At least one file and one rasp, of medium size and coarseness, should be in every toolbox.

Planes. A carpenter's plane is basically a chisel held at a fixed angle so as to shave off a layer of wood parallel to the surface. A *block plane* is used with one hand, a *bench plane* with two hands. The latter is more accurate for trimming long straight pieces. The smaller block plane has advantages in trimming small areas or in corners and along edges.

Smoother planing will result by holding the blade at a slight angle to the direction of movement. Also be careful not to rock the plane at the ends of the work, which would remove more material at the ends than at the middle.

Measuring instruments. More amateur repair jobs are botched by a quarter of an inch or a slightly off angle than by any other type of error. Measuring a job is absolutely essential, and it can't be done with rulers intended for a classroom or tailor shop. Hence the toolbox should contain at least these items:

(1) *Flexible rule* at least 6 feet long, preferably of metal or plastic that holds itself rigid (unlike a cloth tape

measure). (2) Adjustable *square* that can be slid along the edge of a board to mark off exact right angles where other things are to be attached. (3) A *spirit level*, which by centering an air bubble in a glass full of liquid indicates true vertical and true horizontal lines. In laying out a job, always measure with meticulous accuracy, using a sharp pencil to mark the dimensions of lumber or the center of a hole to be drilled. Use the square and the spirit level to make sure your lines are straight.

Relevant instructions. You don't have to become a draftsman in order to read the diagrams supplied by architects and equipment manufacturers, but it's helpful to understand their secret code. Such drawings are often essential to making a successful repair.

Solid lines indicate what is visible, dotted lines what is not visible or lies behind the visible part. Extension lines are used to indicate dimensions that are easier to read when placed away from the crowded part of a diagram. Dimensions are given in feet ('), inches ("), and fractions (or in equivalent metric units). Thus 3' x 2" x 4" is a 3-foot length of a two-by-four. A small circle indicates a screw; a small circle enclosing a square indicates a bolt.

It will be seen that most symbols in a drawing are easily interpreted by anyone who uses common sense. On the opposite page, for example, are mechanical drawings for a sawhorse and a miter box.

Other Desirable Tools

As we stated at the beginning, our tool list has been boiled down to essentials, but there are many others a handyman can use on occasion. If the occasions are few in number, such expensive tools as an electric hammer for making holes in masonry, cement mixer for small cement jobs, asphalt slicker for driveway repair, floor sander, stapling gun, paint sprayer, etc., probably should be rented when needed rather than purchased. Owning and stocking the following tools and supplies could be considered from the point of view of the kind of work you intend to do:

Pry bar or crate opener	Measuring tape (25- or 50-foot)
Star drill for masonry	Ratchet screwdriver
Locking-type wrench pliers	Needlenose pliers
Hand stapler	Tack puller
Caulking gun	Plumber's drain auger
Glass cutter	Outdoor telescoping ladder
Miter box	Ratchet wrench
Tin snips	Knife grinder
Oilstone sharpener	Soldering iron (electric)
Basin wrench	Pipe cutter

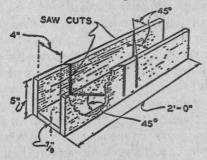

MITER BOX

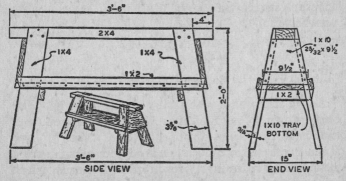

SIDE VIEW   END VIEW

HOW TO MAKE A SAWHORSE

Again we start with a list of materials the mechanic should never be without. Boiling it down to manageable proportions is even more difficult than in the case of tools. The variety of nails, screws, fasteners, and adhesives available today is bewildering. Some are designed for a particular purpose only, like the parts of an automobile, and won't fit anywhere else. The more adventurous type of handyman sometimes wishes he owned a hardware store.

Nevertheless, a few ground rules will simplify the selection of items to be stocked at home: (1) Keep duplicates of items already installed in your home, for example, washers to match the particular size used in your faucets. (2) When buying nails, etc., buy more than needed for the particular job, but not too many—just enough for possible future need as spares. (3) Store the supply of *each* item in a separate, labeled container where you can easily find it. Never trust to memory. Never mix odds and ends of spare parts. Label specialized items for their specialized application, e.g., "chrome screws for refrigerator shelving." (4) Fit the material to the potential job, such as the proper adhesive for asbestos tiles rather than a general-purpose glue.

Here's a starting list:

Nails	Screws	Putty
Fasteners	Washers and packing	Adhesives
Lubricating oil	Tapes	Sandpaper
Fuses	Wire	Scrap wood
Plastic repair kit	Spackling (for plaster)	Cement

Nails

Nails come in many sizes and varieties, ranging from the common nail to highly specialized types, as shown in

NAIL HEADS, DIFFERENT TYPES AVAILABLE

NAIL POINTS, DIFFERENT TYPES AVAILABLE

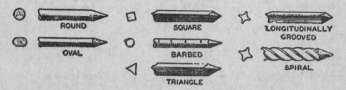

NAIL SHANKS, DIFFERENT TYPES AVAILABLE

the illustrations. The designation of size by the penny system originated anciently in their cost by weight in English pence (d). Today the designation is correlated to length in inches; thus, a 6-penny (6d) nail is 2 inches long.

The common nail is used for rough construction work that requires great holding power. A box nail is similar but thinner, less likely to split the wood of, for example, a box. Finishing nails have a small head that may easily be punched below the surface of wood with a nailset. Small nails, often called brads or wire nails, are for fine work. Roofing nails are for nailing down roof shingles

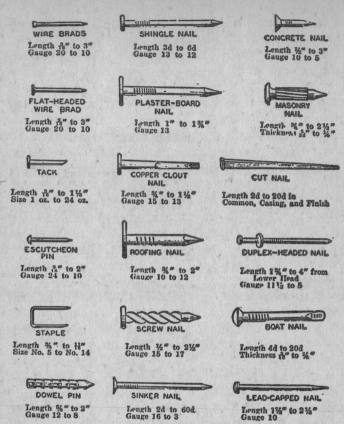

WIRE BRADS
Length 7/8" to 3"
Gauge 20 to 10

SHINGLE NAIL
Length 3d to 6d
Gauge 13 to 12

CONCRETE NAIL
Length 1/2" to 3"
Gauge 10 to 5

FLAT-HEADED WIRE BRAD
Length 7/8" to 3"
Gauge 20 to 10

PLASTER-BOARD NAIL
Length 1" to 1¾"
Gauge 13

MASONRY NAIL
Length ¾" to 2½"
Thickness 3/32" to ¼"

TACK
Length 7/8" to 1½"
Size 1 oz. to 24 oz.

COPPER CLOUT NAIL
Length ¾" to 1½"
Gauge 15 to 13

CUT NAIL
Length 2d to 20d in Common, Casing, and Finish

ESCUTCHEON PIN
Length 3/8" to 2"
Gauge 24 to 10

ROOFING NAIL
Length ¾" to 2"
Gauge 10 to 12

DUPLEX-HEADED NAIL
Length 1¾" to 4" from Lower Head
Gauge 11½ to 5

STAPLE
Length ¾" to 1½"
Size No. 5 to No. 14

SCREW NAIL
Length ½" to 2½"
Gauge 15 to 17

BOAT NAIL
Length 4d to 20d
Thickness 3/32" to ¼"

DOWEL PIN
Length 5/8" to 2"
Gauge 12 to 8

SINKER NAIL
Length 2d to 60d
Gauge 16 to 3

LEAD-CAPPED NAIL
Length 1½" to 2½"
Gauge 10

SPECIAL NAILS, SOME COMMONLY USED TYPES

and should not be driven into thin wood, which they are apt to split.

A threaded or "screw nail" is driven in with a hammer but holds like a wood screw. It is almost impossible to remove, so should not be used on temporary construction. It is ideal, however, for cabinet work and hardwood floors. Varieties in threading are adapted to particular uses as shown.

Special nails—When a job presents special problems of fastening, penetrating a material, sealing against leakage, etc., one will usually find a nail specifically designed for the purpose. Some of these are shown in the illustration.

Concrete and masonry nails are of hardened steel, stiff enough to be driven into concrete or mortar without bending. In roofing work, a lead-capped nail makes a leak-proof joint when driven through metal, since the soft head flattens itself against the surface. On the other hand, the duplex-headed nail has an auxiliary head so that it may be pulled out without injuring a wooden board—useful when constructing a temporary platform, concrete form, etc. The copper clout nail resists corrosion and has a flat end which may be readily clinched (bent after the nail is driven). This is advantageous in building boats or outdoor trellises. The boat nail, with a similar function, also has a decorative head.

In selecting a nail, be sure it is not so large as to split the wood, but within that limitation it should be the largest possible in order to get the greatest holding power. Avoid driving a line of nails along the same streak of grain; stagger them instead. In very dry hardwood it may be wise to drill small pilot holes first. Toenailing—driving nails at an angle—gives a stronger hold than straight nailing, and is the best technique for joining boards at a corner.

Screws

The selection of wood screws for a particular job is made by looking at four characteristics: the length, the head, the shank, and the gauge or thickness. Proper length is determined by the thickness of the pieces to be joined. Theoretically, the shank or smooth part of the screw should be just long enough to reach through the top

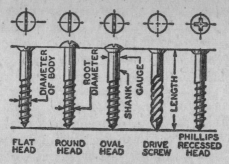

WOOD SCREWS

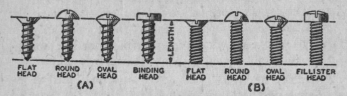

METAL SCREWS USED TO FASTEN
CONSTRUCTION WORK

A, SHEET METAL SCREWS
B, MACHINE SCREWS

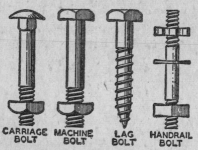

TYPES OF BOLTS

board. The threaded part should bite well into the bottom board, but leave at least an eighth of an inch of wood beyond the end of its point. Pilot holes should be drilled through the two pieces according to the diameters of the shank and the threaded body. Hardware dealers usually have a chart showing the correct sizes.

A flat-headed or oval-headed screw is intended to be countersunk; round-headed screws protrude from the surface. The difference for the most part is decorative; functionally there is no difference. The gauge of a screw is the diameter of the body, measured in the valleys between spiral threadings. As with nails, holding power is proportionate to length and gauge.

Screws used to join pieces of sheet metal resemble wood screws except that they have no shank and there are relatively few turns to the thread. They are handy in some other applications because they can grip thin layers of wood, as in fastening a tie rack to a hollow plywood door.

Machine screws, as the name implies, are used in assembling metal parts. They must exactly fit the threaded holes designed to receive them; attempting to force in a misfit will most likely strip the threads. For this reason, machine screws should be carefully stored and identified with the mechanism that requires them.

Stove bolts are similar to flat- or round-headed machine screws but are supplied with either square or hexagonal nuts that are fastened with a wrench. To tighten the nut it is usually necessary to hold the head with a screwdriver; to keep it tight insert a lock washer under the nut.

Fasteners

Besides nails, screws, and bolts, modern ingenuity with hardware has produced a variety of fasteners for meeting common problems. Hanging something heavier than a picture on a wall presents one such problem. Interior walls are usually hollow and an ordinary nail or wood-screw would simply break through into empty space.

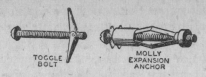

TOGGLE BOLT   MOLLY EXPANSION ANCHOR

FASTENERS

Toggle bolts and anchors solve this by tightening themselves against the inner, hidden side of a hollow wall. First a hole is drilled into which the device is inserted. Turning with a screwdriver opens up expanding wings or ribs to hold flat against the other side of the wall.

A toggle bolt can be used only once, because unscrewing the bolt drops the expansion wings inside the wall. A screw anchor also remains permanently locked in position; however, the tightening bolt may be unscrewed whenever necessary to take down a fixture or replace it with another.

Nylon anchors or plugs are hollow sleeves used to hold an ordinary wood screw tightly in a drilled hole. As the screw is inserted, it splits the back end of the plug so as to wedge it in place.

Expansion-type anchors very similar in principle are used to solve the problem of nailing wooden shelves, cabinets, etc., to a solid masonry wall, or when bolting down an appliance on a masonry floor.

When furring strips are used on a masonry wall, specially hardened steel nails can be driven through the wood into the concrete. However, their grip in the masonry is not strong enough to directly support shelves or mechanical equipment hung on the wall. It is better to drill holes and insert anchors as illustrated. If you do a great deal of this sort of work, special tools may be required. They include a heavyweight hammer (at least 2½ pounds), carbide bits for your drill, and what is called a stud driver.

Small fiber or plastic anchors are adequate for light strains on masonry, such as hanging decorations or fire tools on the fireplace brickwork, fastening shutters on stucco, or putting up mirrors in the basement.

Note—To prevent cracking of plaster when hammering a picture hook into the wall, stick a strip of Scotch tape over the spot where the nail will enter.

Adhesives

Modern chemistry has revolutionized the art of bonding things together so they'll never (well, hardly ever) come apart. At one time the only practical glue was an organic material made from fish or hooves and reliable only on porous materials such as wood and paper. Being water soluble, a glued bond is vulnerable to dampness and heat.

Today's glues for the most part are of synthetic rather than animal origin, more properly called adhesives. The categories include polyvinyl, casein, plastic resin, and resorcinol.

Before tackling any gluing job, read the label on the adhesive product to make sure it suits the materials you are bonding. Follow the manufacturer's directions exactly. For example, a waterproof resorcinol glue can be used on crockery and plastics as well as on wood, and outdoors as well as indoors. *But*—it may be applied *only* when temperatures are 70 degrees Fahrenheit or more, not in an unheated garage or on half-frozen lumber, and the parts must be clamped firmly together for 8 to 10 hours.

Epoxy cements are remarkable materials that harden in a solid mass that is completely waterproof, solvent-proof, and permanent if properly mixed, applied, and cured. An epoxy can be used to fill in and repair cracks

37

in pipes, radiators, or metal gutters, for bonding metal to tile, and, in clear finish, for repairing and permanent bonding of marble, glass, masonry, and china.

Putties

Putties are in the same class as adhesives in the variety of their composition, and in the need for applying the right putty to each job. For example, the putty used for installing windowpanes is not the same as the compound used for sealing the edges of a bathtub. Wood putties or "plastics" are good to have around for filling in holes or gouges in wood.

When purchasing putty, consider carefully the type required and the color. Wood plastics, for example, dry so densely as to resist staining. Hence one must choose the plastic of a color to match the stain of the wood being repaired.

Tapes

Everyone is familiar with the many uses of cellophane tape, especially in paperwork or wrapping packages. This tape is a bit too sticky for most home-repair applications —for instance, it will peel the paint off a plaster wall— but it has relatives that are "musts" in the toolbox.

Masking tape is basically intended for marking off an edge when painting or spraying, but its easy-on, easy-off quality makes it handy for all sorts of odd jobs. It can be used for wrapping small objects such as a set of screws, and labeling them; for holding glued objects together; for temporary sealing of a window or crack; for posting instructions at a work site, and so on.

Electrician's tape has similar adhesive and pliable qualities, but is backed with a black plastic or cloth strip for insulation when wrapped around an electric wire. It is also very strong and difficult to tear, hence useful for tight bindings.

Miscellaneous Items

Washers may mean the rubber or plastic ones that prevent leakage at the seat of a water valve, or metal ones placed under the head of a screw, bolt, or nut to hold it tightly. Since the first kind wear out and the second get lost, it is prudent to keep a small supply of assorted washers on hand.

Packing refers to the malleable materials used to seal a faucet handle or a lubricated bearing. It is subject to wear and to replacement every time such a mechanism is taken apart.

Lubricating oil is the elixir of life for all machines with moving parts. It can also be used to free up rusted screws for removal. A very light "penetrating" oil is especially constituted for the latter purpose. A light "household" machine oil is suitable for most small appliances. Larger machines such as pumps, oil burners, etc., take heavier grades such as SAE 20. Follow manufacturer's specifications.

Keep lubricating oils in closed containers to prevent evaporation and contamination with dirt. If kept in an oil can, stick a cork on the end of the spout.

Sandpaper comes in various degrees of fineness and several types should be kept on hand. Flint paper, garnet paper, and emery cloth use natural mineral grits, but papers of synthetic aluminum oxide and silicon carbide are tougher and wear longer. Sandpaper is an expendable, inexpensive item that should be quickly discarded when it becomes smooth or "loaded" with particles of wood.

To protect the fingers when hand-sanding, wrap the

sandpaper around a block of wood and use the block as a handle.

Blocks and other odds-and-ends of scrap wood are indispensable in many operations involving hammering, prying, or propping up. The illustration on page 25 shows one being used as a sawing guide. Another common use is to prevent hammering damage when driving a nail. Place a wood block over the nail head and hammer the block.

Fuses for the electrical system should be kept in or near the fuse block just as you store spare light bulbs. Unlike a light bulb, however, when a fuse blows it's usually the circuit rather than the fuse itself that is at fault. Replace a fuse *only* with another of the same capacity, generally 15 amps. If the new fuse also blows, a short circuit or other trouble in the circuit is indicated.

A larger fuse would keep the circuit open, but at the risk of overloaded wires and a fire. Remember that a fuse is a protective device; to bypass it for temporary convenience is foolhardy. Mark each fuse with the part of the house or the appliances it protects, so that if trouble occurs, you will know where to look for it.

Wire includes not only electrical wiring but picture wire and other varieties where strength and permanence of attachment are desirable. Wire is worked most handily with a pliers. The gauge (diameter) of wire indicates (1) its strength, (2) its capacity for conducting electric current.

Hand cleaners. Good, honest toil inevitably means good, honest dirt on clothing and hands. Soiled work clothes are no problem, but cleaning grease, stains, etc., off the hands and face could be. Old-fashioned laundry soap and water are good but slow. Modern "waterless" hand cleaners do a superior job. If you use turpentine or similar solvents to remove paint stains from the hands, always wash up afterward to protect the skin.

Safety Rules for Using Tools

Although only the basic hand tools have been discussed in this chapter, common-sense rules of safety apply to using them just as they do for the most powerful of power tools. All tools greatly magnify or concentrate the ordinary force of human muscles. A hammer awkwardly struck, a wobbling saw, a slipping drill bit can be hazardous or even lethal. The following precautions should be committed to heart by every family member utilizing the tool chest and the workshop.

1. Don't use bad tools, whether of poor quality or in poor repair. A sharp cutting tool is much safer than a dull one, because it takes less force and is less likely to slip. Loose handles on hammers and chisels, etc., are invitations to accidents: Don't tolerate them. Keep tools sharp and repair them promptly; if they can't be fixed put them firmly in the trash barrel and buy new ones.

2. Dress for the job. Beware of long hair, dangling sleeves, scarves, neckties, sweaters, and other loose outerwear that can get caught in the machinery. Wear work shoes, not sneakers (ever drop a hammer on your toe or step on a nail?). Snug-fitting work clothes should cover all vulnerable areas of skin; that's why they're called coveralls. Work gloves also are indispensable.

3. Especially when using power tools, wear safety goggles or a face shield to protect the eyes from flying bits of metal, stone, or other hard materials. Also protect the eyes from paint, caustics, or almost any chemical substance you might have to use, in particular when working on something directly overhead.

4. Own a good stepladder. Never stand on anything

shaky to reach the area of work with tools. Good balance is part of the skill of tool usage, and loss of balance at a critical moment can be hazardous in the extreme.

5. Make sure that all parts of a power tool are secure before turning on the power. A loose or wobbling bit, cutter blade, or grinding head have caused many accidents, not to mention those that fly off into space as the machine gathers speed.

6. Keep the workshop clean and uncluttered. Greasy, slippery tool handles, inflammable piles of trash or sawdust, and objects in the way that can trip up the worker are among the hazards of untidiness.

7. Store tools with safety in mind; many a cut finger has resulted from reaching into a box full of sharp implements. Hang them on racks if possible; otherwise wrap the cutting edges in adhesive tape before putting them away.

8. Before turning on a power tool, make sure you have a firm grip on it; and before laying it down, make sure the power is off and all motion has ceased. When changing a blade or a bit, *pull the plug*. Don't take a chance on the power tool starting accidentally, which it can do if something touches the switch or there's a short circuit. Observe all electrical precautions, such as grounding, specified in the manufacturer's instructions; without them severe shocks are possible.

9. Study the safety guards on your power tools, understand how they're supposed to protect you, and keep them in place at all times—even when the tool is not in use. Never make sudden, impulsive movements around a power saw or similar machine.

10. Make sure the work is held securely in place for a power tool operation. Grip small pieces with clamps, support boards being sawed, and support the part being cut off to prevent binding on the blade or a flying piece of scrap lumber.

11. Keep inflammable liquids such as gasoline well away from electric motors that can throw a spark and explode the vapors.

12. Good lighting and good ventilation are essential. Be extremely careful when you use solvents such as carbon tetrachloride, benzine, turpentine, paint remover, or wood alcohol. It is best to use these outdoors, but if that is not possible, at least open windows wide or otherwise provide for good ventilation. Never use these solvents in a tightly closed area, and keep their containers closed except when actually pouring some out for use.

Chapter 3

HEATING SYSTEMS AND HOW THEY WORK

The first of the four Ws of home maintenance stands for Weather.

Although a house may serve many different personal and social purposes, ever since man lived in caves and tents its original and basic function has been to protect the occupants against inhospitable weather. The natural climate of our region, whether cold or hot, wet or dry, windy or baked by sun, is beyond our control. Inside a house we enclose a bit of climate within four walls and a roof which we can control to our own specifications of comfort.

The heating system of a house, with related functions such as ventilation and related structural elements such as insulation, should more properly be called an *indoor comfort system*. This system should be operated and maintained, or corrected if necessary, with comfort as the goal.

Over the years we have encountered many misconceptions about what constitutes true indoor comfort. Disregarding the human element, what gives some homes a pleasant atmosphere while others seem perpetually uncomfortable? Experts say the key to an agreeable physical environment is *the condition of the air* in the home. Regardless of the method of heating, it's the air within the house that conveys warmth, humidity, etc., to the human bodies it surrounds.

Ideally, comfortable air should meet the following conditions: (1) The air must be the right *temperature*—warmed in winter, cooled (or kept cool) in summer. (2) The air must be *clean*—as free as possible of dust, smoke, pollen, and other irritants. (3) The air must be *fresh*. The house design should make adequate provision for ventilation from the outside. (4) The air must *circulate*. Stagnant air settles into layers of warm air above, cool air below—stratification that causes stuffiness. (5) The air must be of the proper *humidity*—neither too dry nor too moist. In centrally heated homes, excessive dryness is the chief problem in cold weather.

When we talk about air temperature in this list, we are concerned with the heating system proper: the furnace, its fuel, and its pipes or ducts. Cleanliness, freshness, circulation, humidity, and cooling of the air may either be built into the heating system—with fans, blowers, filters, a humidifier—or may involve auxiliary equipment. Sometimes a satisfactory result in indoor comfort can be achieved only by rectifying deficiencies in the house structure itself, as by adding storm windows or attic insulation.

Brief descriptions of popular heating systems and their operation follow.

The simplest, most direct, and most popular method of heating a private residence today is by circulating air that has been warmed by a fire. The heart of any warm-air system is an enclosed furnace burning oil, gas, or in some cases coal, and a jacket or bonnet around the furnace with an air space in between, called a heat exchanger or plenum.

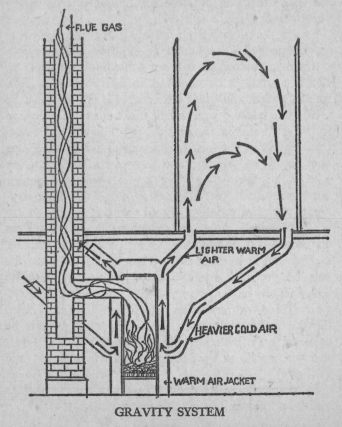

GRAVITY SYSTEM

In small houses one may find a "gravity" system that depends upon circulation of the warmed air by natural convection, unaided. Cool air enters the furnace plenum at the bottom and rises to the top as it is heated. From there it is conveyed upward by ducts to the various rooms of the house.

As the rising warm air enters a room through an outlet or "register," it displaces cool air, which slides down inside a return duct to the furnace plenum, where it is reheated.

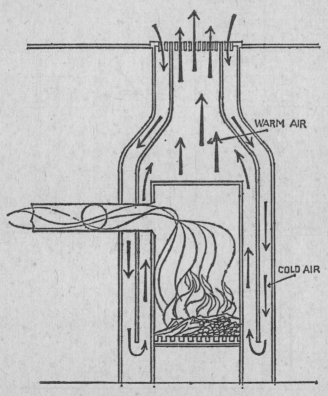

DUCTLESS OR PIPELESS FURNACE

In a "pipeless furnace" arrangement there is only one warm-air outlet, a grating over a hole in the basement ceiling just above the furnace. Cool air returns to the furnace plenum around the perimeter of this grating.

Since the difference in weight between warm air (180°) and cool air (65°) is slight—less than a quarter ounce per cubic foot—the convection currents in a typical gravity system flow slowly. Therefore in any but a very compact house the flow of air needs boosting by a fan, and this is provided in the modern forced-warm-air system.

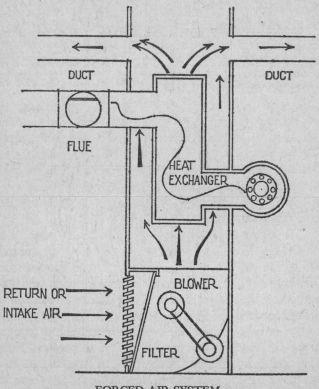

FORCED AIR SYSTEM

Forced Warm Air

The insertion of an electrically operated blower into the return air duct at the base of a warm-air furnace accomplishes several benefits at once.

The fan pulls cool air out of the rooms and drives it through the heat exchanger at the rate of about 1,000 cubic feet per minute, enough for a complete change of air throughout the average house every 15 minutes or so. The moving current of air carries off furnace heat faster than a slow convection current, on the same principle as the cooling-system fan in your car. With forced air a compact furnace and plenum will do the same heating job as a large-gravity one. The air is pulled along with enough force to direct it through a filter, which removes up to 90 percent of floating dust.

Another major improvement that made forced-warm-air heating universally popular was the automatic oil burner and its related controls, including room thermostats. This system combined a furnace that required no stoking, disposal of ashes, or other dusty chores with automatic operation that made it almost instantly responsive. (The workings of automatic controls are discussed in a later section.)

The blower of a forced-warm-air system usually is, or can be, wired for manual as well as automatic control. With the manual switch turned on, the blower runs continuously even when the furnace burner has been turned off by the thermostat. The constant circulation of air reduces stagnation in the house, avoids alternate blasts of hot or cool air from the registers, and reduces temperature differentials from one living area to another. Heating cost is no greater. There may be a saving in fuel, balanced by extra electricity to run the blower—an insignificant cost, if any, relative to the benefits in greater indoor comfort.

Even better in performance is pressurized warm-air heating, a phase of complete comfort climate control. Like an automobile heater, the furnace jacket takes in fresh air from outside and, with the blower running continuously, builds up a slight pressure inside the house. Any air leakage around windows and doors will then be in one direction only—toward the outside—barring the entrance of dust and smog. It is never necessary to open windows. You can clean, humidify, heat, or cool the air at your discretion.

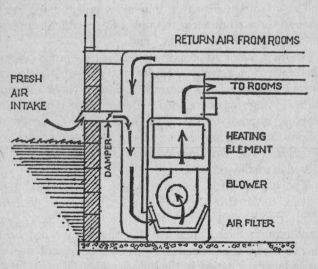

PRESSURIZED SYSTEM

A small outside air duct is piped into the inlet or return duct of the warm-air system. A damper enables you to adjust the amount of air entering from outside to your comfort requirements. All of this air is filtered before being pumped into the house.

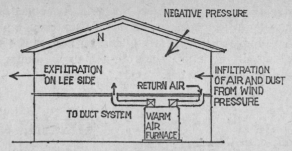

SYSTEM WITHOUT FRESH AIR INTAKE

The pressure differential is negative, from the outside in. On the windy sides of the house air infiltrates carrying atmospheric dust or other contaminants. An equivalent amount of air leaks out through the other two sides less dust and grime left on walls and furnishings.

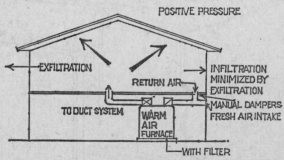

SYSTEM WITH FRESH AIR INTAKE

With fresh air entering through a controlled intake and being pumped to the rooms by the furnace blower, the pressure differential becomes positive, from the inside out. Dust infiltration is eliminated or minimized. and there is more than one complete air change per hour without opening windows.

Hot-Water Heating Systems

In a hot-water heating system, water rather than air is the medium for picking up heat from the furnace, conveying it to the rooms, and dissipating it to the air from radiators.

51

In simplest form, it is gravity-operated. As a boiler filled with water is heated, the warm water rises through pipes to the room radiators. After giving up heat to the surrounding air, the same water returns to the boiler for reheating and another trip upstairs.

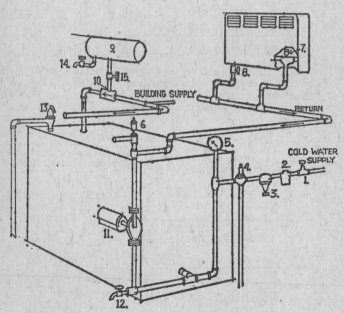

1. STOP COCK
2. STRAINER
3. PRESSURE REDUCING VALVE
4. PRESSURE RELIEF VALVE
5. PRESSURE GAUGE
6. AUTOMATIC AIR VENT
7. AIR VENT ON RADIATOR
8. RADIATOR VALVE
9. AIR CUSHION TANK
10. AIR SEPARATOR
11. CIRCULATION PUMP
12. DRAIN VALVE
13. SAFETY VALVE
14. DRAIN VALVE
15. SHUT-OFF VALVE

HOT WATER BOILER

Insertion of a water pump near the boiler converts this into a modern "forced-hot-water" or hydronic system, with advantages in fast heating action and responsive controls comparable to the forced-warm-air system. However, hot-water heating does not circulate air through the house. Air circulation must be provided by some other means.

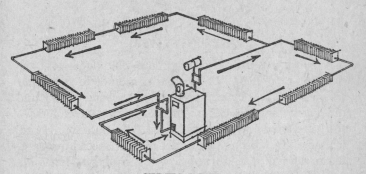

SERIES LOOP

The heating characteristics of a hot-water system depend to a considerable extent upon the piping arrangement. In a "series loop" the radiators in effect are sections of a continuous pipe always filled with water. Hot water from the boiler is piped to the first radiator inlet, leaves at the other end, and continues along a pipe to the next radiator. The water returns to the boiler only after passing through all the radiators in the loop and releasing its heat.

Consequently, none of the radiators may be shut off without shutting down the rest of the loop, and there are no individual valves. Also, the last radiator in a loop will tend to give less heat than the first because it receives somewhat cooled water. This disadvantage is partly overcome by dividing the system into two or more separate loops.

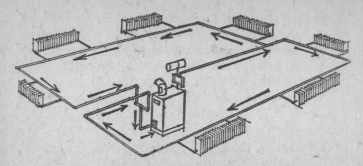

ONE-PIPE SYSTEM

A better system, requiring more plumbing work, is the "one-pipe" loop. The radiators are not in series but are connected by branch pipes to a hot-water main from the boiler. Hot water from the main pipe enters a radiator through a valve-controlled inlet riser and returns to the same main through an outlet pipe. A special fitting at the outlet called a "forced-flow T" creates a Bernouilli (vacuum) effect that sucks used water out of the radiator.

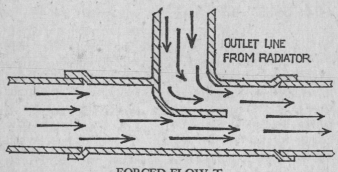

OUTLET LINE FROM RADIATOR

FORCED-FLOW T

Each radiator intake valve may be opened to any desired degree or completely shut off without directly affecting other radiators, and it may be balanced for just the right amount of flow by adjusting the "T."

A remaining disadvantage of the one-pipe system is

that cooled water leaving each radiator and returning to the main pipe mixes there with hot water proceeding to the next room. Hence the more distant radiators will not receive the hottest water and may do a less efficient heating job than those closer to the boiler.

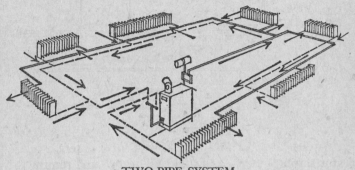

TWO-PIPE SYSTEM

The system is improved, especially in large houses, by installing a second, return-pipe loop that conveys the cooled water from each radiator directly back to the boiler. All radiators in this "two-pipe" system will receive unmixed hot water of approximately the same temperature regardless of their distance along the main pipe line.

Each of the preceding hot-water systems is progressively more costly to install because of added piping, but all of them work on the same basic principle. Important to note here is the fact that the entire system is filled with water. An expansion tank above the boiler or in the attic allows for an increase in the volume of water when heated (about 4 percent increase from 32°F. to 212°F.). If the house is to be left unoccupied in freezing weather, the entire system must be drained.

Steam Heating System

Because of installation cost and other technical problems, steam heat is rarely found in new homes today,

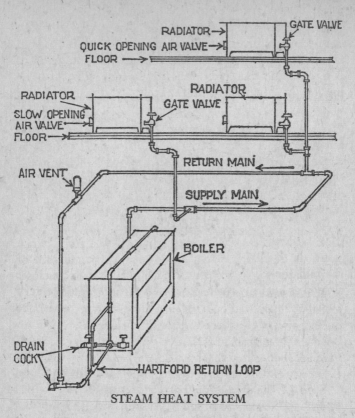

STEAM HEAT SYSTEM

although favored in apartment houses and other large structures for its efficiency. Usually it is a low-pressure system, with the steam at 5 pounds per square inch or less where it leaves the generating boiler. You can quickly distinguish a steam radiator from hot-water heat by its single riser, only one connector pipe instead of two.

What most people call "steam" actually is water mist. You can't see steam; it is an invisible gas, whereas a mist consists of water droplets floating in air. If you watch a teakettle, only the apparently clear space just above the spout contains steam, which immediately condenses into a visible mist as it cools in the air. (Much of the white "smoke" from factory chimneys and auto exhausts on cold days also is condensing water vapor.)

Exactly the same thing happens in a steam radiator. Hot steam piped from a boiler condenses within the radiator into water vapor and finally into water, giving up most of its heat in the process. The condensate trickles out through the same inlet pipe and along the bottom of it back to the boiler. The steam continues flowing in the opposite direction above the trickle. A valve at the intake end of each radiator permits you to turn it on or off without affecting other radiators in the system.

At the end of each radiator opposite to the riser there is an automatic air vent that usually hisses for a while when the radiator is first turned on. This lets air out of the radiator to make room for incoming steam. It closes as soon as hot steam reaches it. The radiator gets hot very quickly (close to 212°F.), and cools rapidly when the steam is shut off.

As a compressed gas (unlike hot water, which is not compressible), steam expands when released from the boiler and travels swiftly to all parts of the piping system, supplying uniform heat virtually without delay. However, a steam radiator must be turned *completely* on or off, not in between. A partially opened inlet valve could trap the returning water condensate until enough builds up to block the entrance of steam.

Keeping the various rooms of a house at a desired temperature with steam heat requires some experimentation with fully opened or closed radiator valves, doors of rooms, etc., until even distribution is achieved.

Electric Heating

Since all types of comfort systems require a direct source of heat inside the house, it is theoretically possible to use an electric furnace for a forced-warm-air, hot-water, or steam-heating system. This, however, is seldom the case; what is meant by electric heat today generally consists of electric space heaters in baseboard units or ceiling panels in each room.

At the heart of each unit is a high-resistance wire or metal strip that, when plugged into an electric circuit, glows red hot and radiates heat to the surroundings. A fan may be added to blow air past the heating element and speed up the delivery of warmth to the room. Each unit is controlled, or controllable, by an individual thermostat; central control for an entire house or zone usually is not feasible with electric heat.

All appliances that heat electrically use a lot of current. Although an all-electric system dispenses with furnace, pipes, ducts, etc., it does require a thoroughly insulated, almost airtight house to avoid wasting the precious heat. Consider that a breakfast toaster may use ten times as much current as the most powerful vacuum cleaner, twenty times as much as a 60-watt light bulb (1,200 watts). You can imagine how many toasters you would need to heat an entire house.

Unless the local utility's kilowatt/hour rate is very low or the climate mild or the quarters occupied only intermittently (as in a motel), central heating by electricity usually is practical only in houses especially designed for it. More commonly, it is installed in bathrooms and other special locations to provide extra heat on short notice.

Radiant Heat

Radiant heat, so-called because it eliminates all visible radiators, usually consists of hot-water pipes embedded in the floor, especially in the concrete floor of a slab-construction house. The system warms the floor and then the house, in response to thermostatic controls like those of other hot-water systems.

Radiant heat has declined in popularity, largely because of the difficulty of repairs. (If a pipe springs a leak, one has to rip up the floor to get at it.) The system also tends to be sluggish in response to changes in temperature, since the entire concrete floor has to be heated up first. This may take an hour or two; then if the weather should turn warm again, the floor will continue to radiate heat no longer wanted.

The time lag in radiant heating can be partly overcome by means of a thermostat on an outside wall that is sensitive to changes in outside temperature, plus thorough insulation of the house. Generally, however, a radiant-heat system that breaks down today will be replaced by a conventional hot-water system rather than repaired.

About the Furnace

Regardless of the fuel it burns, a furnace in principle is not much different from a fireplace. It consists of a metal shell lined with firebrick, with openings at the bottom to admit air for combustion and a flue at the top to permit the escape of smoke, soot, and waste gases up the chimney. These openings are equipped with adjustable dampers to control the flow of air.

Furnaces in old houses may well have been constructed originally for coal. Oil burners were installed inside them beginning about half a century ago. Newer furnaces generally are much smaller, better insulated, and more scientifically proportioned for efficient heat production with fuel economy.

Number 2 fuel oil, the grade commonly used in an oil burner, does not burn in liquid form; you cannot light it with a match. It must be vaporized first. It is therefore the safest of convenient fuels while in storage or traveling through pipes. An oil furnace is electrically operated only in its controls and fans, using a negligible amount of current.

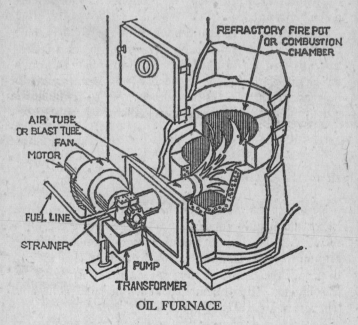

REFRACTORY FIRE POT OR COMBUSTION CHAMBER

AIR TUBE OR BLAST TUBE

FAN

MOTOR

FUEL LINE

STRAINER

PUMP

TRANSFORMER

OIL FURNACE

When the unit receives a signal from your wall thermostat (see page 65), it sends a jet of vaporized oil in a stream of blower-driven air into the firebox. An electric spark then ignites the fuel-and-air mixture. In a warm-air system, the flame heats air in the surrounding heat exchanger jacket. When the temperature in the jacket reaches about 130°F., another thermostatic device triggers the blower, which pushes the heated air up into the rooms. This timing prevents the blower from pumping unheated air through the registers at the start.

When the room reaches the selected temperature, the wall thermostat shuts off the oil burner, but the blower keeps going. It does not stop until the heat exchanger cools down below the starting temperature. In this way, all the heat produced is utilized and drastic ups and downs in room temperature are avoided.

An oil burner that heats water for a hot-water system works the same way, except, of course, that the temperature of water in the boiler rather than of air in the heat exchanger governs the sequence and timing.

When the water is hot enough, a pump starts in order to push it into the room radiators. With steam heat, a valve opens when the proper boiler pressure is attained. On the downside, the water pump stops or the steam valve closes when the wall thermostat rises above its preset temperature.

A safety device consisting either of a special thermostat or an electric eye in the furnace automatically shuts off the oil supply if the flame fails to ignite or if it should go out after starting. To start the burner again you have to push a "reset" button, which calls your attention to any malfunction.

Other controls will shut off the unit temporarily if temperatures or pressures rise too high. The burner starts again when the proper operating range is restored.

Gas Burners

A gas-burning furnace has pretty much the same characteristics as a gas kitchen range. A pilot flame burns constantly, day and night, whether heat is required or not.

A signal from the wall thermostat opens an electrically

operated valve, which, like the knobs on a gas range, allows a jet of gas to escape into the firebox. The pilot flame ignites it. The motion of the gas jet sucks air along with it, and ordinarily needs no blower.

Because of the explosive nature of gas, special precautions are required to prevent its accidental escape. One is a "draft diverter" installed in the smoke pipe to prevent a chimney downdraft from blowing out the pilot flame on a windy night. If the flame should blow out nevertheless, it is turned off automatically by a thermocouple. This device produces a tiny electric current so long as it is heated by the pilot flame; the current holds the gas valve open. If the flame dies out, so does the thermocouple current, closing the valve. At the same time the electrical connection with the wall thermostat is broken so that gas cannot be released from the main jet.

Escaping gas in a furnace ordinarily flows out the chimney without harm. Nevertheless, any odor of leaking gas should be investigated immediately—and not with a lighted match!

Electric Units

The fuel that produces the energy for electric heat is burned at the powerhouse, so all you can see is the cable and wiring system that conveys the resulting current. An electric heater, whether in a central furnace (warm-air, hot-water, or steam system) or in individual room units, functions at quite high temperatures—400°F. or more. Hence the element has to be enclosed in a protective housing.

As in the other furnace systems, a wall thermostat automatically turns the electric heating element on or off to maintain a comfortable room temperature. But because an extreme temperature buildup can be a fire hazard, the element itself usually has a temperature regulator that shuts it off before the danger point is reached. This could happen, for example, if the unit is overworked in a very cold spell or because a warm-air distribution system is temporarily blocked by furniture or a rug.

Like other electrical devices, the heating system is protected against short circuits or other electrical problems. An overload of current in the wires will blow a fuse or trip a circuit breaker. To restore heat to the house one must then inspect the main fuse panel and either replace a fuse or reset a circuit breaker. Of course, if the circuit continues to "blow" it is a sign of trouble somewhere that must be located and repaired.

"Clean Heat"

The concept of "clean heat" arose in coal-burning days; shoveling coal and ashes was indeed a dusty job. In modern times the concept sometimes is misappropriated for promotion of one fuel over another.

In actuality, oil heat is just as clean as gas or electricity. The fuel is delivered to and stored in a sealed tank; you never see fuel oil unless you want to. It is consumed in a sealed combustion chamber without being exposed to the circulating air or water that heats your home. Oil heating therefore cannot spread household dirt.

Deposits or streaks that occasionally form on walls above convectors or radiators and around warm-air vents are caused by the circulation of dirt particles already in the home. The dirt is brought in by way of openings such as doors and windows or on clothes and shoes. Warm air, as it ascends, picks up these particles, and as it sweeps by, deposits some of the dirt on such surfaces as walls, furniture, and drapes.

The smudge marks are further aggravated by improperly designed heating systems. For instance, some water and steam installations have undersized radiators, requiring excessive temperatures to satisfy comfort requirements. Hot, dry air will raise more dust than properly heated and humidified air. Curiously enough, because of high operating temperatures, the worst offender in this respect is the electric baseboard unit—which brings no combustible fuel into the house at all.

Gas is not completely "clean," either, since burning gas gives off water vapor that often contains sulfur trioxide. Under certain conditions this can cause deterioration of the mortar in masonry. The chimney may require a stainless steel lining to counteract the problem.

Warm-air heating generally is cleaner than hot-water or steam because the forced current of air is repeatedly filtered to remove dust as it enters the furnace jacket on each circuit. If the blower is powerful enough, an individual dust filter may also be installed behind the cold-air return register in each room—especially in the basement, family room, or other areas where people are apt to track in a good deal of dirt.

In today's world we are concerned about "clean air" *outside* as well as inside the home. There is little to choose among home heating systems in respect to air pollution. *Any* fuel when burned, including wood and uranium as well as the conventional ones, gives off pollutants of some sort. Many are visible as smoke and soot, others invisible in the form of moisture, chemicals, gases, or heat. However, air pollution from home heating is of minor consequence compared to other sources, such as industrial complexes, electric power plants, and auto exhausts.

Producers of oil and gas are concerned about eliminating sulfur from their fuels. New devices promote more complete combustion in the furnace, which eliminates major pollutants from the effluent. A homeowner can cooperate by keeping his heating system in correct operating condition. Proper measures to this end are discussed in the section on maintenance.

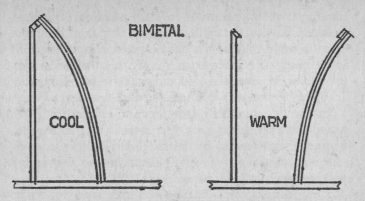

WALL THERMOSTAT

This is how a thermostat works. Bimetallic strip arches in one direction when it cools, making electrical contact that starts the heating unit. When room is warm, it arches the other way and opens the contact, shutting off the heating unit. In thermostats the bimetallic elements are seldom in straight form, may be U-shaped or spiral, like a coil spring, to provide greater span of movement. Sometimes magnets are used to make final contact in quick snap.

Thermostats

Some people look upon the wall thermostat as a kind of manual switch—turn it "up" in a chill and "down" when the house gets too warm. Not so. A thermostat is an *automatic* device. A single setting, usually at about 72°F., should be correct on all days and in all seasons, even midsummer.

The dial of a typical thermostat is first of all a *thermometer* marked off in degrees Fahrenheit, with a pointer that tells you the room temperature at the moment at that location. The thermometer reading doesn't change until the room temperature actually changes. A second pointer, usually red, may be moved around at will.

This second pointer adjusts the triggering point of the *thermostat* to a selected temperature. Behind it is a heat-sensing element. This may consist of a bimetallic strip—two metals with different expansion characteristics riveted or fused together—or of a similar material coiled like a spring. In either case, the strip arches or the spring unwinds when warmed, and the opposite when cooled. Its slight, slow motion is harnessed to an electrical switch.

Let's say the red thermostat pointer is set at 72°F. The thermometer part shows that the room is several degrees warmer than 72°F., so the heater is not running. As the temperature of the room drops, the bimetallic element in the thermostat gradually reaches toward an electrical contact. At exactly 72°F. it will touch the contact and act like a switch, turning on the heating system. Then as the room warms up, the sensing element moves the other way and eventually breaks the contact, shutting off the heater.

The proper temperature setting for a thermostat is determined by personal comfort and by the timing of the heating system. To maintain an average temperature of 72°F. you may find it works best to set the pointer at 70° or 74°F. The timed delay in starting an air blower or water pump after a burner is ignited, and in stopping the same after the furnace is turned off, gives a certain amount of "play" in the thermostat setting.

Having determined the trigger point that keeps the house most comfortable, you will want to leave the thermostat alone most of the time. If it is necessary to change the setting, the pointer should be moved delicately, with finesse, like adjusting a watch. A *single degree* will make a big difference. You then wait a day or so for a thorough "comfort test" before fooling with it any further.

A permanent setting should work all right even on the coldest days. If the house loses heat faster than normally, the thermostat will cool off quickly, too, and keep the heater running until the proper temperature is restored. If not, then something is wrong and may call for corrective steps as described in later chapters. The point is, you do not improve the operation of a thermostat by moving the pointer up and down every few minutes like a Yo-Yo.

It will be seen that the *location* of the thermostat affects its operation. Thermostats are always installed on interior walls, because the relative coolness of an exterior wall will lower the temperature *at the thermostat* even though the rest of the house is warm. For the opposite reason, a thermostat is never installed where the sun will beat on it, or near a radiator, oven, big lamp, or other source of heat. Then the thermostat will be warm when the rest of the house is cold.

In a large house or one with exposure to directional winds it may be necessary to divide the heating system into zones, each with its own thermostat, as shown in the diagram. Electric heating, as noted earlier, generally requires a thermostat for each heating unit, room, or area. Most times, the contractor who installed the heating system of your house will have selected the best available thermostat locations.

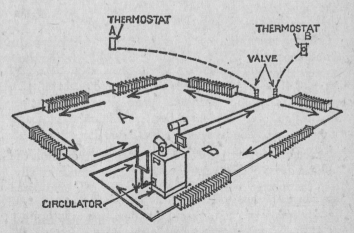

ZONE HEATING SYSTEM

In addition to a wall thermostat, hydronic systems have two other automatic temperature controls called aquastats. They are usually installed in the main hot-water pipe just above the furnace.

The *direct-acting* aquastat, also known as a high-limit control, is normally set at 200°F. If there is any malfunction in the room thermostat, causing the temperature of the boiler water to rise above a safe 200°F., this aquastat will open an electrical circuit to stop the oil burner.

The *reverse-action* or low-limit aquastat is normally set at 120°F., which is the lowest water temperature for adequate radiator heating. When the boiler temperature drops below 120°F. the aquastat stops the circulating water pump, allowing it to rest until the boiler water temperature rises once again to 120°F. or higher.

Aquastats may be adjusted to different temperature settings if necessary, but under ordinary circumstances are never touched.

Humidity Controls

Relative humidity is a percentage of saturation: the amount of water vapor in the air compared to the amount it could carry if saturated. When relative humidity reaches 100 percent (saturation), outdoors it rains and indoors water condenses on glass. Humidity has a direct effect on comfort. We speak of warm, humid days as "muggy" and of cold, humid interiors as "clammy."

The saturation point varies with temperature. Cold air can carry less moisture than warm air. In very cold weather most of the moisture outdoors freezes into snow or frost, leaving the air "crisp"—very dry. As this cold, dry air infiltrates a house through windowsills, door openings, etc., it is heated and expands greatly. Unless water is added to the mass of expanding air, its relative humidity will drop, and it becomes unnaturally dry, with many damaging effects.

Like a blotter, the too-dry air thirstily sops up moisture. When we breathe, it dries the mouth, nose and throat tissues to the point of susceptibility to head colds, sore throats, and sinus difficulties. Dry, chapped skin and brittle hair are other indications of low humidity, along with adverse effects on pianos, furniture, books, art works, rugs, drapes, and upholstery, peeling paint, and shocks from static electricity.

Dry air is uneconomical. The rapid evaporation cools the skin and people tend to turn up the heat to compensate. With proper relative humidity maintained, we feel as warm at 72°F. as we would at 78° with the air too dry. The human body is most comfortable within a range of 20 to 60 percent relative humidity; the lower the outside temperature, the lower the comfort range.

For example, 20 percent humidity might be adequate at 10° below 0, but 60 percent would be better at 70° above. At the latter temperature, it would take 11 pints of water to saturate 10,000 cubic feet of air, or close to 3½ quarts to achieve 60 percent relative humidity. At zero degrees, it would take only two thirds of a pint to saturate 10,000 cubic feet, or only a couple of ounces of water for adequate humidity.

Certain home activities—cooking, laundering, bathing—add humidity to the air by evaporation, but in most cases not nearly enough. Grandmother kept a kettle boiling on the stove; Mother put pans of water on the radiators or filled the bathtub. In modern heating, the forced-warm-air system has a distinct advantage because humidity can be added to the air automatically.

A pan-type humidifier with evaporator plates is standard on most warm-air furnace installations. A pan of water inside the plenum is kept at a constant level by means of a float valve (similar to the one in a toilet tank). The plates evaporate water into the warm air flowing by. The amount of humidity is determined by the number of plates. These have to be cleaned and replaced regularly and performance is not always satisfactory.

Another method simply introduces a dripping pipe into the warm-air plenum. The amount of drip is controlled by a sensitive faucet. The homeowner must adjust the faucet to changing conditions and remember to turn it off at the end of the heating season.

A better device consists of a centrifugal or spray atomizer controlled by a *humidistat*, which automatically reacts to changes in humidity much as a thermostat reacts to temperature. The performance is good, except that when hard water is atomized directly into the furnace plenum it may also atomize lime dust. Carried upstairs, the lime dust coats furniture, rugs, and walls with a gray film.

A vapor-wheel, drum-type water-over-filter controlled by a humidistat yields the best results. Performance is good and the humidifier requires a minimum of maintenance.

Since hot water, steam, and electric heating systems cannot distribute prehumidified air in the house, portable *humidifiers* are recommended. The operating principle is that of passing dry air through a moist filter with the aid of a fan. A console type of humidifier can evaporate up to 12 gallons of water in a 24-hour period.

Fuel Costs

In order to arrive at a meaningful comparison of the costs of heating fuels (oil, gas, liquefied petroleum [LP] gas, electricity) you have to do a little arithmetic. The various units of fuel—gallons, cubic feet, pounds, kilowatt/hours—must be translated into standard units of *heating value*. In this country the standard measuring stick is the *British thermal unit*, abbreviated BTU.

One BTU is the amount of heat or energy required to raise the temperature of one pound of water one degree Fahrenheit. It's about the same as the heat from a lighted wooden match. The metric equivalent of one BTU is 252 calories—the heat energy one would absorb from eating 2½ tablespoons of butter or drinking a couple of stiff Martinis. For convenience, house heating outputs are calculated in a larger unit, the *therm*. One therm equals 100,000 BTU.

Table 3-1: Heat Rating of Fuels

Fuel	Unit of Quantity	Heating Value
Natural gas	100 cubic feet	100,000 BTU = 1 therm
Fuel oil	1 Imperial gallon	168,000 BTU = 1.68 therms
Fuel oil	1 U.S. gallon	140,000 BTU = 1.4 therms
Electricity	1 kilowatt/hour	3,415 BTU = .03415 therm
LP gas	1 bottle (100 pounds)	2,156,000 BTU = 21.56 therms
LP gas	1 U.S. gallon	91,600 BTU = .916 therm

To find the fuel cost per therm, divide the unit price of the fuel by its therm value from the above table. For example, if the price of oil is 22 cents per Imperial gallon, divide 0.22 by 1.68, which means that 22-cent fuel oil costs 13.09 cents per therm.

Making the same calculation for natural gas or electricity takes more work. You first have to find out how much these fuels cost, which is not as simple as it sounds. Unlike oil—priced at so much per gallon, period—gas and electricity usually are priced on a sliding scale. Often the scale starts with a fixed (minimum) charge per month, such as $1.50 for the first 300 cubic feet of gas or less. Here is a typical sliding scale for natural gas:

Table 3-2: Prices of Natural Gas

Amount	Price
First 300 cubic feet ($1.50)	50¢ per 100
Next 900 cubic feet	24¢ " "
" 1,800 " "	22¢ " "
" 6,000 " "	20¢ " "
" 21,000 " "	18¢ " "
" 60,000 " "	16¢ " "
" 210,000 " "	13¢ " "
" 300,000 " "	12¢ " "
" 2,400,000 " "	10¢ " "
" 3,000,000 " "	9¢ " "

On the first of each month the price scale reverts to the beginning, that is, you again pay $1.50 for the first 300 cubic feet and so on down the line. Therefore, the only way to find the actual cost per 100 cubic feet (one therm), is to analyze your gas bill and meter reading month by month. Divide the amount of the bill by the month's difference in meter readings (in hundreds of cubic feet).

From the above table, it is clear that you do not gain the advantage of lower "wholesale" rates unless gas consumption is fairly large. The cost of the first 100,000 cubic feet works out to $166.42, which means an average price of 16.64 cents per 100 feet and the same per therm. At this price gas is a somewhat more costly fuel than oil at 22 cents per gallon.

The monthly sliding scale of prices for electric current is similar, but may vary in practice almost from house to house. In order to qualify for lower rates a home may be required to use electricity for water heating and the kitchen range as well as for space heating. By the therm formula, electricity should cost no more than ½ cent per kilowatt/hour to be competitive with oil at 22 cents. More typical big city rates range between one cent and 2½ cents per kilowatt/hour. At an average of 1.2 cents, the cost of electricity would come to 35.14 cents per therm.

The cost of liquefied petroleum gas also varies widely with the amount consumed. LP gas is usually propane or butane, which may be delivered in 100-pound canisters ("bottles") or pumped by the gallon from a metered truck, like fuel oil. If you use only two bottles a year, the cost might be $13.50 each; if you use more than 50 bottles a year, the cost unit might decrease to $6.50. (A 100-pound bottle equals 23 U.S. gallons at 60°F.) At the wholesale price of $6.50 per 100 pounds, the cost of LP gas comes to 30.15 cents per therm.

Fuel Efficiency

These figures are approximations only, since there is much variation in the efficiency of heating systems. Oil and gas furnaces in good working order generally are rated 80 percent efficient, meaning that an "input" of 100 BTU in fuel produces an "output" of 80 BTU in heated air or water leaving the furnace area. The remaining 20 BTU are dissipated by radiating warmth to the basement and to areas around the chimney as well as in vapors escaping up the flue.

The efficiency of electric heating as a practical matter is impossible to calculate, although the fuel is theoretically rated 100 percent efficient because there is no combustion and no chimney. (Losses through walls, wiring resistance, etc., occur after the current is "delivered" to the house.) You might also have to heat the basement separately at additional cost in current.

A house of average size in a cold-weather area may need about 170,000,000 BTU, or 1,700 therms, to keep it reasonably warm throughout the winter. Taking the efficiency ratings of the four fuels at face value, and adjusting the therm requirements accordingly, we get the following comparison of heating costs:

Table 3-3: Typical Seasonal Costs of Heating

Fuel	Quantity	Cost
Oil @ 22¢ per gal	2,125* therms @ 13.09¢	$278.16
Gas @ 16.64¢ per 100 cu ft	2,125* therms @ 16.64¢	$335.60
Electricity @1.2¢ per kwh	1,700 therms @ 35.14¢	$597.38
LP gas @ $6.50 per 100 lb	2,125* therms @ 30.15¢	$640.69

* 1,700 divided by .80.

Fuel Supply

Besides cost, an important consideration in the choice of a heating fuel is assured supply. Of the fuels analyzed above, only oil and LP gas are stored on the homeowner's premises. If a storm or other interruption of service occurs, an oil tank holds a sufficient reserve to tide the house over all but the most prolonged emergencies.

A general power failure is of course a disaster for all types of automatic equipment, as painfully demonstrated in the East Coast blackout of 1965. However, while the owner of an electrically heated home has no recourse, the owner of an oil- or gas-fired system can protect himself by keeping a small gasoline generator on hand. Its output will not totally replace house current, but will be enough for lights and for operating the automatic heating system controls until the blackout is over.

Even barring such accidents, the user of natural gas and electricity needs assurance that the *local* gas mains and power lines can handle a heavy extra load during extreme cold spells. The chances of inadequate gas or power supply are greatest in areas of recent fast growth. The original lines may have been installed for the relatively modest demands of cooking, lighting, and small appliances. They may not carry enough to feed hundreds of furnaces all going at full blast on a freezing day.

Because of growing shortages of natural gas and electric power, some utilities no longer promote the use of these fuels for home heating.

Low voltage in a power line dims the lights, slows down electric motors, and prevents an electric heating element from attaining an adequate operating temperature. Low gas pressure would reduce the input of BTUs at the furnace. In either case a house could be starved for heat just when most in need.

The modern delivery system for oil eliminates most of these problems, since a home fuel tank holds 200, 250, 500, 1,000 or 1,250 Canadian gallons (depending on the size of the house or apartment building). It is filled regularly with enough oil to last a month or longer. The secret of security is the "degree day."

Degree Days

A degree day is a measure based upon research showing that the average house does not require heating when the outside temperature is 65°F. or higher. When the temperature falls below 65° the amount of heat required will be proportional to the drop. Each degree of difference between the actual temperature and 65° constitutes one degree day. For example: Suppose the highest temperature on a certain day is 40°F. and the lowest is 30°. The "mean temperature" for that day is the average of the extremes, in this case 35° (40 + 30 = 70; 70 ÷ 2 = 35).

Subtracting 35° from 65° gives 30 degree days as the result.

If the mean temperature outside were 50°F., then the difference between 50 and 65 would be only 15 degree days. On that day the house would need only half as much heat (and fuel) as on the 30-degree day.

A fuel dealer derives degree days from the Weather Bureau's daily reports. He then relates this figure to his experience. By checking fuel deliveries to a customer during a test period, he figures out what is called a K-factor. "K" stands for the constant rate at which that customer consumes fuel, measured in degree days per gallon. With this information a fuel oil supplier can predict quite accurately how much oil you will use and when he should refill the tank.

At a large, modern dealership the K-factors, different for each customer, and the degree days are fed into a computer, which automatically schedules fuel deliveries. That is why oil customers no longer have to check their tanks and phone for oil. The oil truck simply arrives on the computed schedule, pumps in a metered supply, and leaves a card stamped with the quantity delivered.

Fuel supply also has some bearing on the price. Natural gas and electricity are provided by public utilities that are, in effect, government-regulated monopolies. The unit-price scale is established by a public service commission. If you don't like the price, you can't shop around for another supplier, because there is none. Fuel oil dealers, in contrast, are in a competitive business. The price can go down as well as up.

Grades of Fuel

Natural gas arrives by pipeline direct from gas wells that are often located thousands of miles away. The heating value of the gas therefore is determined by Nature. While 100,000 BTU per 100 cubic feet is the accepted standard, the heat content may range in fact from 80,000 to 120,000 BTU. In some jurisdictions an adjustment in price is made for variations in BTU content, similar to the "coal adjustment" of earlier days when gas was made by coking coal. (Today in some cities artificial methane gas made from crude oil is being fed into the mains to augment the dwindling natural supply.)

Fuel oil is a distillate—distilled or "cracked" out of the same crude oil that produces gasoline, kerosene, naphtha, and all other petroleum derivatives. It is graded by numbers from 1 to 6, "No. 2 fuel oil" being the grade most generally used in home heating.

Number 1 is a lighter grade, which burns as a liquid in oil stoves and in vaporizing pot and sleeve burners. Number 2 has slightly more BTUs and costs less, but must be forcefully vaporized in pressure or gun burners such as the one in most furnaces. Number 3, the next heavier grade, is seldom used; Number 4, still heavier, is suitable only for large automatic burners.

The next two grades, Number 5 and Number 6, are residual oils—meaning they are components of what is left after the lighter fractions have been distilled away. They must be preheated before they will vaporize; however, they are lower in price per BTU and therefore useful in large installations such as power plants, ships, big factory buildings, etc.

For tips on maintaining or correcting a heating system for maximum comfort and greatest fuel economy, see the next chapter.

Chapter 4

TIPS ON BETTER HEATING

Two more of the four Ws of home maintenance that intimately concern heating are Workmanship and Wear.

Workmanship involves the quality of a house and its equipment. In a new house, that means the workmanship of the builder and contractors, the functional standards they met when they installed the heating, plumbing, wiring, and other basic systems. In an old house one also inherits the labor (or lack of it) put in by previous occupants to maintain the house in good working order and correct any deficiencies.

Since nothing lasts forever, Wear is another normal concern. If a piece of equipment or part of the house structure "goes," the erosion caused by usage and time must be repaired or replaced. Failure to devote attention to routine maintenance constitutes perhaps the chief cause of breakdowns in otherwise excellent heating equipment.

Know How It Works

Peter Sellers, the British film comic, made a career of knocking over hatracks and doing battle with other inanimate objects that refused to work. In an amazing number of cases, balkiness in household equipment is not the fault of the mechanism but of failure to use it properly.

Every year, householders spend a staggering sum for first aid to misunderstood or mistreated appliances of all kinds. Fuel dealers, in particular, have records to prove that one third to one half of all service calls are unnecessary. They politely list these calls under "consumer education." Obviously, if you know how a thing works and what steps to take to prevent mishaps, you'll save yourself discomfort, grief, and expense.

Instruction booklets from equipment manufacturers are too valuable to ignore or mislay. After reading one through (even if it's heavy going), keep it where you can find it—years later, perhaps. In the case of furnace equipment, you might put the instructions, drawings, wiring diagrams, etc., in a large manila envelope tacked to a joist in the furnace area. Always check the instructions before calling for help. (Keep our book handy for reference, too!) Maybe all you have to do in case of interrupted heat is to restart the furnace in a perfectly routine manner. People have been known to call for service when they forgot to turn on the switch.

Oil Burner Maintenance

During an average heating season, a furnace heating unit may operate for about 1,500 hours. This is comparable to driving a car about 75,000 miles a year. Like a car, any furnace mechanism needs an occasional tune-up.

Given this attention once each season, oil burners last for 20 years or more without major parts replacement.

Few homeowners are equipped with either the special skills or the special tools required for tuning and adjusting an oil burner. It is a machine, a sensitive piece of equipment comparable to the carburetor of a car. Only a trained technician can do the job properly. His tune-ups pay for themselves in fuel economy along with trouble-free performance. It makes sense to call for professional routine servicing after the end of each heating season or before the next season begins.

Here are some simple maintenance procedures to follow in between regular tune-ups.

Hot-Water (Hydronic) System. Every four to six weeks, lubricate the burner motor and circulating pump with a few drops of SAE Number 20 oil or its equivalent (similar to nondetergent automobile motor oil). At the same time, fill up the oil opening on the impeller side. This is the piece affixed to the circulating pump, filled with packing to the top. Always turn off both the motor and the pump when lubricating them, to avoid their starting unexpectedly.

Moving parts absolutely require lubrication to function properly, and regular oiling will greatly prolong their life.

Draining. It is unwise to drain a hot-water heating system each summer and refill with fresh water, as some people will suggest. Fresh water contains oxygen, which is corrosive when it comes in contact with the metal of pipes and radiators. Repeated heating and reheating gradually purges oxygen from the water, hence "used" water is better for heating than fresh.

A hydronic system should be drained *only* in an unoccupied house during the winter when there is danger of freezing, or as necessary when pipes are undergoing repair.

Warm-Air System. The main filter installed in a warm-air furnace should be cleaned regularly, at least once each month. This simple yet extremely important procedure is often neglected. As a filter becomes loaded with dirt, it can effectively block entrance of return (cool) air into the furnace jacket for reheating. The frequent result is insufficient heat circulation and a boost in fuel bills by as much as 10 percent.

The filter will be found at the back or side of the furnace where the big return duct joins the plenum. The latter is easily opened and the filter removed for cleaning. Simply shake it out or if this seems insufficient, run a vacuum cleaner over it. Generally you may consider a filter O.K. if you can see light through it when you hold it up to a window or electric bulb.

Some filters of permanent type, such as fiber glass, should be washed in sudsy water, then recoated with an adhesive to trap dirt and contaminants. Others are inexpensive enough to throw away and replace when dirty. It is better to operate a furnace for a short time with no filter at all than to allow a dirty one to block the flow of air.

The blower motor and shaft should receive a few drops of SAE Number 20 oil at the same time the filter is cleaned.

In the various rooms of the house, make certain the warm-air registers are open and completely free of obstruction. Also make sure the grilles permit free flow of return cold air to the furnace. They should not be covered by a carpet, chest, or any other barrier. Occasionally remove each grille and poke a vacuum cleaner hose into the duct to remove accumulated dirt. Look inside the duct to determine if there is any debris stuffed into it.

Lastly, if you have a drum-type humidifier with a pad, it should be cleaned every three to four weeks. A simple rinsing will suffice unless the pad has built up excessive deposits. Soaking overnight in a solution of half vinegar, half water will loosen calcium and lime deposits sufficiently to rinse them off. Spray or evaporative humidifiers should also be checked monthly.

To summarize, *interference* with the flow of air is a main cause of unsatisfactory warm-air heating, and simple as they seem, regular cleaning procedures are a maintenance "must."

Gas Burner Maintenance

A gas-fired hydronic or warm-air system requires the same oiling and cleaning procedures outlined above for oil burning systems. In addition, the following servicing should be done annually:

1. Examine pilot light and burner to make sure holes are not blocked by dirt and lint.
2. Check thermocouple for serviceability.
3. Check heat exchanger for leaks.
4. Confirm valve operation and pilot light cutoff.
5. Test for proper combustion and venting.

Furnace Replacement

The life of a heating system is difficult to measure, since there are so many variables in usage. Assuming proper and regular maintenance, you can expect a warm-air furnace to operate at least 15 years, although many last much longer. Steel boilers usually last for 20 years, and cast-iron boilers have been known to survive for 40 years.

The durability of new furnaces compared to old ones is often called into question. It is true that cast-iron coal furnaces lasted a very long time, some as long as 80 years, but under quite different conditions. Coal firing was more or less continuous throughout the winter. The furnace metal did not contract and expand with repeated cooling and reheating, unlike a modern furnace with its frequent on-and-off periods.

However, continuous heating meant wasting a good deal of coal burned up when heat was not required. The new furnace equipment is responsive even to small changes in temperature. It comes as a package with all controls wired, pumps, blowers, etc., and is easily installed at much lower cost than in the "old days." The units are sized to go through doorways and so can be installed without disassembling and reassembling. One can obtain correct zoning by using two or more furnaces, such as one heating the upper story and a second furnace heating the lower.

When someone asks, with respect to furnaces: "Do they make 'em like they used to?" the answer is: "No, they make 'em better."

Eleven Steps to Fuel Economy

Unlike taxes, mortgage interest, and other costs of owning a home that are beyond your control, heating expenses are not inevitable. If heating costs seem higher than they should be, these eleven recommendations should help reduce fuel consumption substantially.

1. Maintain an efficient heating plant. Observe the maintenance procedures outlined in this chapter, and have the system cleaned and inspected regularly by professional technicians. This function is normally performed

by arrangement with a fuel oil dealer, or in the case of gas, by the service department of the public utility. Improper combustion means wasted fuels, which not only cost money but contribute to neighborhood air pollution.

2. Set the barometric draft regulator to maintain constant draft in the chimney regardless of variable winds and weather conditions. Proper air draft also contributes to better combustion.

3. Place the thermostat in an area where there is free circulation of air, on an inside wall 5 feet above the floor. You will save heat by turning the thermostat down 5 degrees at night, or even more, but never more than 10 degrees. To recover more than 10 degrees for daytime comfort would consume more fuel than any saving you might effect. A two-phase or "day-night" thermostat will reset itself automatically each evening and each morning at designated times.

4. Strip and caulk around all windows and doors. Beware of drafts. The lost heat they represent could account for 15 percent of your heating bill, not to mention discomfort from admitting air that is too dry. You can tell when weather stripping is effective if a light mist appears on the window on extremely cold days.

5. Install storm windows or insulation glass. In many homes, properly installed storm windows can reduce winter heat losses by 50 percent. (They also reduce summer heat infiltration by half.) When the temperature is 70°F. inside and zero outside, a window of average size will lose 900 BTUs per hour to the outer air. A tight storm window will cut the loss to 375 BTUs. (See Chapter 3 for the relationship of BTUs to fuel costs.)

6. If you have a fireplace, close the damper when not in use. An open damper has the same effect as an open window. If your house has a skylight, it may act as a chimney. Place an additional window or insulator under the skylight to prevent the escape of heat.

7. Install overhead and sidewall insulation. Adequate insulation, like storm windows, is one of the smartest investments a homeowner can make for comfort and heating economy. In less than one season, fuel savings will easily cover the installation costs. A typical wood-frame wall 9 feet by 12 feet will lose 1,900 BTUs an hour in zero weather. Two-inch-thick insulation batts in the wall reduce the loss to 750 BTUs. Three-inch batts are recommended for walls and 6-inch for ceilings (see Chapter 7). Check the ground around the perimeter of the foundation after a snowfall. Two or three inches of bare ground is normal, but a foot or more of melt area indicates that the foundation insulation is poor.

8. Seal off and ventilate unused bedrooms and attic. In winter time, heat and moisture tend to rise to the highest point of the house. As a result, you may be unknowingly heating the attic. To minimize heat loss, make sure stairways, doors, windows, and all other openings to the attic are sealed. If you do this, also provide attic ventilation in order to prevent any potential moisture damage.

9. Close drapes at night. Although not as effective as storm windows, double drapes can measurably reduce drafts and heating losses due to ill-fitting windows. If you are in the habit of opening a bedroom window at night, close the bedroom door and the heat register in the room. Otherwise cold air from the bedroom could influence the thermostat, so that even though the bedroom may be cold, other areas of the house could be overheated at high cost in fuel.

10. Circulate the air. Instead of opening windows to admit cold air, use the manual control of a warm-air system to keep the blower fan operating continuously. The constant air circulation will prevent stratification (stuffiness) and maintain an even temperature from floor to ceiling. Also be sure this air is properly humidified.

11. Maintain moderate temperatures. Most people are

comfortable at the recommended temperature of 70° to 72°F. If this does not seem warm enough, the fault may lie in not maintaining proper humidity (see Chapter 3). Of course, some individuals will be happier at 80°, but if economy is the goal, they might be better off leaving the thermostat set at 72° and wearing a sweater or dressing gown. The following table shows the surprising difference in fuel consumption that a few degrees make:

Table 4-1: Fuel Consumption at Different Temperatures

Average annual oil consumption (gals.)	Extra fuel (in gals.) consumed by setting thermostat higher than 70°F.	
	At 76°F	*At 80°F*
800	115	230
1,000	143	285
1,200	170	340
1,400	200	400
1,600	230	460
1,800	258	515
2,000	285	570
3,000	430	860
4,000	570	1,140
5,000	715	1,430

Seasonal Pattern of Heating Costs

Meteorological records and degree-day calculations indicate the following normal distribution of total heating costs throughout the cold weather season:

September	3%	February	18%
October	6%	March	14%
November	10%	April	8%
December	18%	May	5%
January	18%	9-month total	100%

Fuel oil, gas, and electric companies use degree days for long-range forecasts of demand, in order to schedule their refining, shipping, storage, or generating capacity. In some climates they must also take into consideration the wind-chill factor, which the homeowner should understand for proper assessment of his own heating results.

In Montreal, for example, each year averages about 8,000 degree days. The wind-chill factor makes it necessary to boost fuel estimates about 25 percent, to the equivalent of 10,000 degree days. There is also a sharp difference between the central city and the suburbs. The *temperature* may not vary more than a few degrees, but the *heat-holding capacity* of houses in the suburbs is much less than in the city. The difference is the wind.

A cold wind flowing past a house (or a person) removes heat faster than still air. At 0°F., with no wind, the body does not lose heat as rapidly as at 20° in a brisk 18-mph breeze. Under these conditions you would actually feel warmer at 0° than at 20 above.

City houses clustered together or attached in rows receive much less wind-chilling than houses in the country, which for the most part stand exposed on all four sides. The temperature differential between city and suburbs may be as little as one half of one degree in mild weather when there is very little wind. When the temperature drops very low, in the 20s and 30s, this differential may rise to as much as 10 degrees. A windy day magnifies the differential by a surprising amount, as shown on the accompanying chart.

Other factors affecting the city–suburb temperature differential are radiation and smog. When houses stand close together, they radiate less heat from the sidewalls than when standing alone. Carbon dioxide in the urban

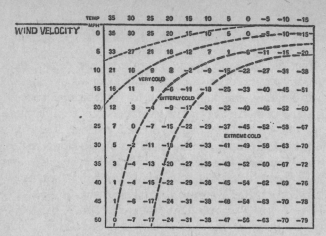

WIND-CHILL FACTOR

To calculate the day's wind-chill factor, start with the temperature. Say it's 30°. Place your finger on the figure 30 at the top of the chart. The wind speeds run down the chart's outer left-hand side. Assume on this particular day the wind is blowing at 20 mph. Run your finger down the column of figures beneath the 30, resting it on the number that lies directly parallel to the 20 at the side of the box. That number should be three, meaning that the wind makes the chill feel like 3° above zero.

atmosphere provides an insulating blanket overhead, reducing radiation from city roofs to an extent equal to approximately one degree on the thermometer.

If you live in a windswept house with a warm-air heating system, you may compensate for the chill factor by raising the temperature of the air flowing through the room registers. Set the *air stat* on the furnace to 240°F. instead of the usual 200°.

Quick Fixes for Common Problems

Over the years in the fuel business we have discovered that certain questions about heating systems are asked again and again. The questions homeowners raise fall into three broad categories: (1) problems which, although puzzling, are minor in nature and easily remedied by the homeowner himself; (2) problems requiring modification by a heating service technician; and (3) those involving extensive repairs or replacement.

All categories are included in this section on quick fixes. Even if you cannot make the repair yourself, it is useful to know what is required and how to deal intelligently with repairmen and contractors.

On-Again, Off-Again Burners

The burner starts, runs for a few minutes, then stops; the warm-air blower does the same, day and night. The usual reason is improper location or settings of the controls.

For the most desirable performance, the fan-limit controls should be located in the furnace plenum where they are most rapidly exposed to temperature changes.

The upper-limit (maximum-air-temperature) control should normally be set at 200°F. The fan control should be set to start the fan at 130° and shut it off at 100°F.

If these settings do not correct the improper cycling of the oil burner and fan, the controls are probably defective and require professional service.

Noisy Water Pumps

Noises from the circulating pump in a hot-water heating system may be corrected by investigating for the following possible deficiencies:

1. The pump may not be properly mounted in the return line of the heating system.

2. The coupling between the pump and the impeller may be loose.

3. The alignment between the pump motor, pump shaft, and impeller shaft may be poor (not perfectly straight).

4. The pump motor and impeller packing may need lubrication.

5. The bearings are loose or worn, requiring replacement.

Cast-Iron Radiators

In old houses it was once considered stylish to paint the cast-iron radiators with shiny aluminum paint. This was a functional error, since the thin aluminum skin thus formed over the cast iron acts as a reflector, that is, bounces the radiator's heat back into the radiator rather than into the room.

Poor heat from an old radiator can be improved about 10 percent by scraping and cleaning the surface, then repainting with an oil- or alkyd-base paint of light color.

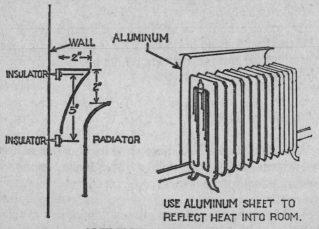

USE ALUMINUM SHEET TO REFLECT HEAT INTO ROOM.

ALUMINUM REFLECTOR

Placing an aluminum reflector *behind* the radiator against an outside wall will also make it more efficient as a heating unit. Use Bakelite insulators between the wall and the aluminum in order to leave a little air space.

Uneven Temperatures

People often find mysterious differences in temperature among rooms or even in different areas of the same room. Some variation is to be expected, but if it exceeds more than a few degrees the cause should be determined and corrected if possible.

There is always loss of heat near a window, since windows do not have the same insulating factor as adjacent wall areas. Ill-fitting windows or those loosened by expansion and contraction can cause enough heat loss for marked discomfort.

Hallways as a rule are warm because they are not in contact with the outside of the building and because warm air tends to stagnate in them. Internal staircases tend to be cooler at the bottom than at the top, especially in a cottage where the upper story may be warmer than the ground floor.

Other heat sources, such as the kitchen range, also produce local variations in temperature. Washing machines, dryers, and even electric lamps can raise the nearby temperature 2 or 3 degrees. Quite often the area immediately above the furnace room will be noticeably warm.

If these differences cause annoyance or discomfort they can be corrected in two principal ways. One is by sealing off the escape routes of lost heat through insulation, caulking, storm windows, etc. In particular, good roof insulation will prevent undue coolness in upper rooms and stairwells. Insulation over the furnace area will prevent a hot spot just above.

The second way is by good circulation of the warmed

air. Avoid putting furniture directly in front of radiators or warm-air outlets. Keep the doors of rooms open most of the time, or whenever they are not needed for privacy. If necessary, use electric fans to circulate the air or allow the blower of a warm-air furnace to run continuously even when the burner is turned off.

Replacing Firebrick

After years of exposure to the heat of an oil or gas fire, the combustion chamber of a furnace begins to deteriorate. When cracks appear, the brick and mortar of which it is composed must be replaced. People sometimes are surprised by the cost of replacement. The reason is the special kind of brickwork required.

Insulated firebrick is made from a fire clay found in only a few places, notably Pennsylvania and Ohio. The creamy color of the brick comes from a small iron content in the clay. The slightest alkalinity (more than 1 percent) makes a clay unusable. The mortar, too, is of special high alumina composition that both bonds the bricks and resists the heat of the fire.

Behind the combustion chamber is a barrier of rock wool for insulation. This is a fibrous material, made from molten rock, that looks like spun glass. The heat rises from the chamber to the surfaces of the surrounding jacket that heat water or air, as the case may be.

A heavy, industrial type of firebrick used in limekilns and similar high-temperature applications is made of magnesitic dolomite. Although they can stand temperatures up to 3,000°F., these bricks are not suitable for home furnaces. The slightest penetration of moisture (which always occurs upon cooling) causes them to fall apart when reheated. They must be kept at high heat at all times. So if someone offers you "bargain" firebrick, beware that it is not industrial dolomite.

Whistling Weather Stripping

A door that appears to be properly weather-stripped may whistle eerily in very cold weather. Hammering it tighter may not help. The cause is shrinkage of wood in the door and door frame if the house is not properly humidified, causing the stripping to warp at an angle that catches the wind and emits sounds like a musical reed.

Take a piece of thin cardboard about 2 inches long and the width of the weather stripping. Place it at the center of the strip. This will flatten out the angle, stop the vibrations, and restore peace and quiet.

Poor Combustion

A furnace that seems to fall short of expectations in cold weather, or one that gives off smoke and soot, may suffer from poor combustion.

In an oil burner, the liquid fuel is changed into a spray of millions of tiny droplets by the action of the nozzle and the pressure of the pump. This spray is initially vaporized and ignited by a spark. After that the heat of the fire itself continues to convert the droplets into a vapor combined with air.

For clean combustion—that is, with a minimum of waste and residue—the combustion chamber must reach the required temperature as rapidly as possible. This avoids smoke. A cracked or crumbling chamber loses heat very rapidly, rendering good combustion impossible. The larger the fire the greater the insulation required of the firebrick.

The second requirement for clean combustion is a good draft of air over the fire, both to vaporize the oil and to carry off the products of combustion through the chimney.

Insufficient draft may be caused by a plugged chimney base, a smoke pipe installed too far into the chimney, too many elbows in the smoke pipe, foreign matter lodged in the chimney, soot accumulation, and other obstructions. These are readily corrected once the cause is found. In some cases, however, the chimney is basically inadequate because of the house design.

Three remedies are available. One is installation of a draft inducer or "booster," basically a fan driving the air currents up the chimney. The second is to raise the height of the chimney, since tall trees or high buildings in the area may cut off normal air flow. Generally speaking, a chimney should be at least 2 feet higher than the highest point of the roof. The third is the addition of an "H" cap to the chimney.

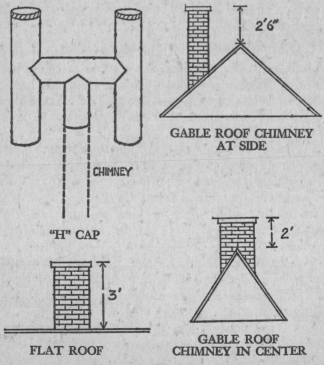

CHIMNEY

"H" CAP

GABLE ROOF CHIMNEY
AT SIDE

2′6″

FLAT ROOF

3′

GABLE ROOF
CHIMNEY IN CENTER

2′

Too Cold at Night

Suppose a house gets quite warm in the afternoon on a sunny day, but at night the temperature falls rapidly. Setting the thermostat higher only results in overheating the house. The problem here is often the sun striking the thermostat at certain hours. Its warm rays cause the thermostat to shut off the oil burner.

This effect is not noticeable so long as the sun shines, contributing its own warmth to the house. But when night falls and the temperature drops, the burner has to run for a considerable time to recover the heat.

Changing the thermostat setting to a higher point doesn't reheat the house any faster, but does make the oil burner run longer—until, in fact, the house becomes *too* warm. The solution is relocation of the thermostat, as explained in Chapter 3.

Noisy Hot-Water Systems

In a hot-water or hydronic heating system, noisy operation may be traced to these correctable deficiencies:

1. *Oil burner.* Parts may be poorly aligned between the

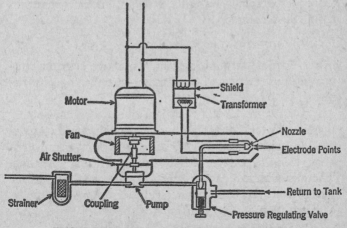

HIGH PRESSURE ATOMIZING BURNER

pump motor and shaft. The oil burner mounting may need to be placed on an insulating pad of rubber cork. Flame roar may be caused by poor combustion, due to incorrect adjustment of air-oil mixture.

2. *Circulating pump*. The pump may be improperly mounted. A coupling may be loose or broken. Lubrication may have been neglected.

3. *Combustion chamber*. The chamber may be too small or too large. Brickwork may have deteriorated to a point of replacement (see the note on firebrick, above).

4. *Pipes*. Creaking and cracking noises in a house with hot-water or steam heat, usually at night, are caused by expansion of pipes from the high temperature of the water or steam. The noise can become excruciating if the expanding pipe scrapes against a nail or some other rigid material in the building. As the pipe cools off and contracts, the noises stop—only to be repeated on the next expansion cycle.

Sometimes a wall has to be opened to get at the source of noise. A simpler remedy is to install flexible rubber couplings on the radiator return pipes. This dampens the vibrations before they enter a room, and at times will muffle them completely.

Noisy Warm-Air System

In a forced-warm-air system, the above remarks concerning oil burner and combustion chamber equally apply. In addition:

5. *Ductwork*. Check the main ducts to establish that the sheet metal is of the proper gauge; thin metal may expand or contract with a loud bang. The ducts may be too small to carry the forced-air stream without vibration. There should be a canvas connector between the furnace plenum and the trunk lines (see illustration) to dampen any vibration and noise being transmitted from the furnace to the ducts.

6. *Circulating fan or blower.* The fan may be poorly installed or improperly mounted. Drive pulleys may be

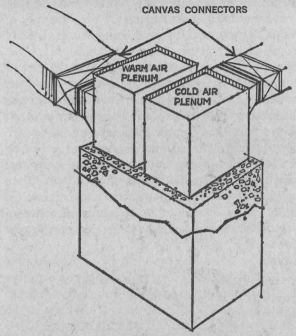

CANVAS CONNECTORS

either too tight or too loose; at correct tension there will be about one inch of play, measured by pressing down on the belt with the thumb when the fan is at rest. Some direct-drive (beltless) blower motors are of inferior design, cheaper at first cost but apt to become noisy and troublesome as they wear.

7. *Chimney.* A blocked or partially obstructed flue may cause chimney noise.

Two-Family House

Endless arguments about heating arise between a tenant occupying the upper story of a two-family house and the landlord, who usually lives downstairs and sets the thermostat to his own ideas of comfort. Even allowing for personal tastes—some people like a house warmer than others—there often is an actual temperature difference of two to five degrees, which would be noticeable. Usually it's the upper story that stays too cool.

Insufficient roof insulation most often is at the root of this situation. For lack of insulation the upper story loses heat rapidly to the sky. But on the same thermostat setting, the lower story remains warm because it is insulated from the roof by the air in the upper apartment.

For best results and maximum harmony, the heating system should be divided into two zones, upper and lower, each with its own thermostat. (See Chapter 3 for a diagram of a zone system.) Short of this, insulation added under the roof should effect a marked improvement—up to 25 percent saving in fuel cost, too.

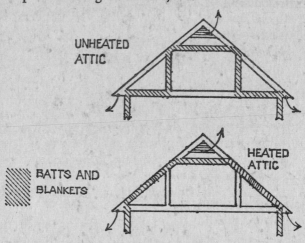

UNHEATED ATTIC

HEATED ATTIC

BATTS AND BLANKETS

ROOF AND ATTIC INSULATION

Noisy Steam Radiators

Loud knocking when a steam radiator is first turned on

is caused by trapped water—the condensate that normally drains out of the inlet pipe and feeds back to the boiler. When hot steam strikes this water, it instantly boils, giving off sounds like the blows of a hammer.

The cause may be simply a partially opened shut-off valve. It should be either fully opened or fully closed. If knocking persists even with correct handling of the valve, check the pitch of the radiator with a carpenter's level. It should be a trifle lower at the inlet valve end, so as to permit condensing water to escape.

Sometimes a house settles, altering or reversing the pitch of the radiator so that some water always remains trapped in it. If this is so, raise the radiator in such a manner as to restore the proper pitch. Pry up the end opposite the inlet valve with a wrecking bar (small crowbar or "jimmy") and insert a piece of wood one quarter of an inch thick under the leg.

Look out for sags and low spots in the horizontal or return mains of the boiler. These can be raised by means of pipe straps to provide better pitch to the drain.

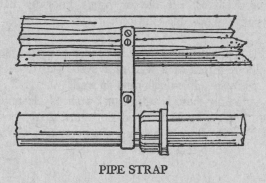

PIPE STRAP

Cold Steam Radiators

If a steam radiator stays cold even with the valve wide open, the air vent at the opposite end may be at fault.

Sometimes just a speck of dirt is enough to hold it closed, thus barring the escape of air in the radiator and blocking the entrance of steam. A gentle tap on the air valve will often be enough to release it.

If the trouble persists, the valve should be replaced. They are inexpensive and easily installed; just make sure the radiator is fully turned off while you replace an air valve.

Some air valves are adjustable. If air escapes slowly, the radiator will heat slowly, whereas if the air escapes swiftly, the radiator heats quickly. Generally the valves nearest the boiler should be adjusted for slow release of air, while those on the more remote radiators should be opened to the maximum. This compensates for distance so that all the radiators will heat up at about the same rate.

Cold Basement Floors

When a basement room is finished for living space, the concrete floor may feel uncomfortably cold, even when covered with asphalt tile or other flooring materials. There are two possible solutions:

1. Place the radiators of a hydronic heating system or the inlet registers of a warm-air system as close to the floor level as possible on an outside wall.

2. Assuming there is sufficient overhead clearance (10 feet or more), build a raised floor one foot above the present level. Run a heating duct or hot-water pipe through this one-foot space.

Damp Finished Basements

Condensation on the walls of a finished basement in cold weather usually must be ascribed to poor building practices. Often the inside wall panels have been applied

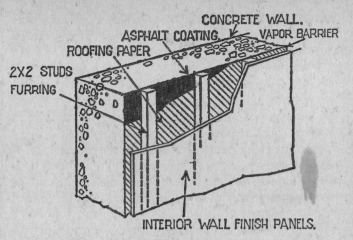

2X2 STUDS FURRING — **ROOFING PAPER** — **ASPHALT COATING** — **CONCRETE WALL.** — **VAPOR BARRIER** — **INTERIOR WALL FINISH PANELS.**

BASEMENT WALL CONSTRUCTION

directly to the masonry. Moisture will condense where the cold wall meets warm interior air.

To correct this, remove the inside paneling. Cover the masonry wall with a waterproofing compound, such as hot tar or roofing asphalt. Then apply vapor-proofed building paper with the moisture barrier facing into the house. Allow it to overlap at the edges about 4 inches.

You are now ready to fasten the furring—2- × 2-inch or 3- × 1-inch studs or strips of wood. The interior panels will be attached to this furring, leaving an air space as insulation between them and the masonry wall. Sealing the overlaps of the building paper around the edges will prevent moisture penetration into the air space.

A damp basement in *warm* weather is a different problem; see Chapter 5.

Pressurized Oil Burners

When heating servicemen recommend a pressurized oil burner, they are often asked why. This device is winning increased favor for its efficiency in heating. If your furnace is due for replacement, the pressurized type can be a major improvement.

A pressurized oil burner uses a 3,450-rpm motor with a specially designed fan in place of the conventional 1,725-rpm motor and fan. It thus injects a better mixture of fuel and air, promotes more complete combustion, and results in using less oil to obtain the same amount of heat.

With special air-turbulence and flame-retaining spinners, a pattern of air is established for uniform and positive flame. A delayed-action valve allows the burner motor to come to full speed before any oil is discharged through the nozzle.

These elements in combination with a furnace of special design assure a very much higher degree of efficiency, reflected not only in lower fuel bills but in greater comfort.

Attic Moisture

Sometimes a homeowner will thoroughly insulate an attic roof, only to find discoloration on the ceiling of the living quarters just as if the roof were leaking. The cause is moisture condensing in the attic, and the cure is better attic ventilation.

In the days of wooden shingles, attic ventilation was an unusual problem because the roof "breathed"—air passed in and out past the interstices formed by uneven surfaces of the wood shingles. If such a roof is covered with asphalt shingles or other modern materials giving a tight seal, it can no longer "breathe." Accumulated warm air in the attic will condense on the cold inside surface of the roof just as it would on a glass of ice water.

This moisture may lead not only to pseudo "leaks" but to fungus growths that rot wood and give off a foul odor.

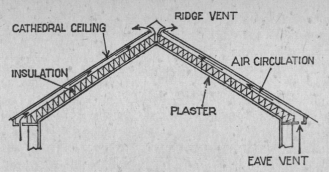

ROOF VENTILATION

The sketch shows proper roof ventilation over a cathedral ceiling, using both eave and ridge vents.

An attic fan, although usually installed to help cool the house in summer, may also be used for better ventilation in winter. See Chapter 5 for details of an attic fan installation.

Bad Odor from Ducts

Especially in a newly constructed house, suspect the presence of mice. They can find a cozy haven in an air duct while it is being installed and remain there after the house is occupied. Their nests and debris have a foul odor that is picked up and circulated by the forced-air system. Have the ducts opened to enable you to rout the intruders.

Checking a Chimney

If the brickwork of a chimney begins to disintegrate internally, the debris will obstruct the furnace draft, and the openings between bricks may cause hot spots on adjacent walls. The latter is a fire hazard that should be corrected at once.

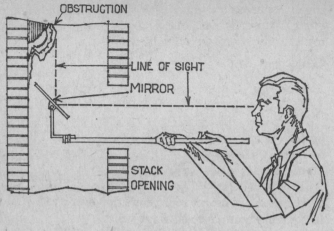

OBSTRUCTION
LINE OF SIGHT
MIRROR
STACK OPENING

CHECKING A CHIMNEY

A deteriorating chimney may also be a health hazard. We know of one case, in a gas-heated home, where the lady of the family constantly felt tired and headachy. Doctors could find neither cause nor cure for her mysterious malady. The mystery was solved when the home-owner noticed water appearing over the fireplace. Investigation disclosed cracks in the mortar of the chimney tile, caused by a reaction with sulfur trioxide vapors from gas consumption. Washed away over the years by rain, the crumbling mortar created openings for poisonous flue gas to escape into the home.

When repairing chimney cracks or restoring mortar joints, always use waterproof mortar.

If the chimney is too narrow to permit physical entry for inspection, it may still be examined from below as shown in the illustration.

Remove the smoke pipe where it enters the chimney from the furnace. Rig up a handle for a mirror that will enable you to extend it into the chimney at a 45-degree angle. Assuming the chimney is straight or only slightly offset (as most of them are), you will be able to see to the top of it for any obstruction or damage.

Humidity for Travelers

People who have learned to humidify the air in their homes and who are uncomfortable without it—because of a sinus condition, skin irritation, or similar problem—often encounter over-dry air in hotel or motel rooms when traveling in winter. Here are some simple remedies:

1. Before retiring, run the hot shower for several minutes with the bathroom door open.
2. Wet some towels, wring them out just enough to prevent dripping, and drape them over the radiator or as near as possible to the source of heat.

In a railroad sleeping compartment, half-fill the washbasin with water. Twist a towel to act as a wick, placing one end in the water, the other draped around a faucet or fixture to hold it out in the air. It will probably have evaporated all of the water by morning.

Furnace Air Entry

Sometimes poor combustion in a furnace is caused by a paucity of air entering from the furnace room. This may be an acute lack if the room is small and thoroughly blocked off from the rest of the house.

One rule of thumb concerns the size of the air opening into the furnace room. It should provide 10 square inches per gallon of oil consumed per hour. To allow a factor of safety in case air flow becomes obstructed in some way, it is customary to double this; e.g., an opening 5 inches by 4 inches (20 square inches) is adequate for a typical single-family home consuming one gallon of oil per hour.

Another formula concerns the size of the furnace room supplying the air. Consumption of one gallon of oil calls for 1,331 cubic feet of air. Again, for practical considerations, it is wise to add 50 percent, so that 2,000 cubic feet of available air per hour is the rule of thumb.

Suppose a house 30 feet by 24 feet has a basement 10 feet high; it encloses 7,200 cubic feet of air. This is quite adequate, since the burner does not run continuously and additional air will infiltrate normally through basement and other openings.

However, if the boiler or furnace room area is much smaller and space very tight, heating engineers would recommend an air intake directly from outside the house. The sketch shows how to plan such an intake for a burner below ground level.

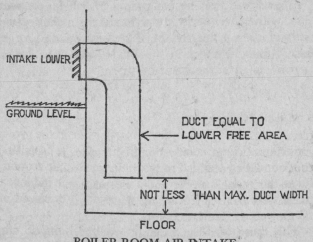

BOILER ROOM AIR INTAKE

106

Oversize Nozzles

On the theory that too much is always better than too little, homeowners have been known to install a larger burner nozzle than specified in their furnaces in order to "get more heat." The result is more heat, all right, but at a cost of burning up fuel as if money were going out of style.

The earlier sketch shows details of the conventional nozzle installed in most oil burners. Its proportions are exactly calculated to fit the size of the house and the demand for heat in BTUs per hour. Replacement by a pressurized burner will save fuel through increased efficiency of heat production. Replacement by a *larger* nozzle can waste as much as 50 percent of the fuel by overheating the furnace.

One common symptom of this condition is heavy smoke pouring from the chimney, the smoke consisting of unburned elements in the oil. The wastage can be summarily stopped just by installing a nozzle of the proper dimensions.

Indoor Fuel Tanks

In new construction today the fuel oil tank is usually placed outside the house, sometimes buried in the ground, sometimes not. Formerly the tank might be installed in the foundation and the rest of the house built around it. Over the years, however, it was found that indoor fuel tanks were subject to rusting, whereas tanks placed outdoors were virtually immune.

The cause of the rusting is condensation of atmospheric moisture inside a tank due to frequent changes in the indoor temperature. Being heavier than oil, the water collects at the bottom of the tank, some of it below the lowest possible level for a draincock. Eventually the corrosive effect can rust out a hole in the tank.

An outdoor tank always remains at the same temperature as the surrounding air or earth. Temperature changes occur slowly and gradually, without the frequent ups and downs of a heated house. Moisture condensation is very slight, and usually carried along with the fuel oil into the furnace rather than settling to the bottom of the tank.

In an old house a basement fuel tank may have been installed without filler-tube connection to the outside. This interferes with delivery, obliging the serviceman to drag his hose down basement steps or through a window. The sketch shows proper installation of an outdoor filler tube. When installing observe local fire codes concern-

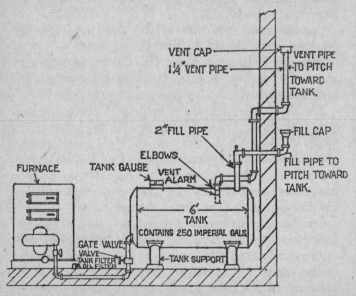

FUEL TANK INSTALLATION

ing the safe and proper distance of the furnace from the fuel tank.

Droopy Plants, Protruding Nails, Electric Shocks

During the winter in some homes, the house plants become droopy, nails protrude or fall out of the walls, and the occupants receive sharp electric shocks every time they touch a doorknob or pick up the phone. All of these are symptoms of lack of humidity.

The plants droop despite frequent watering because dry indoor air increases the evaporating rate from leaves, the soil, and even from the earthenware pot itself.

Wood is normally a holder of moisture and shrinks if the relative humidity of the surrounding air is reduced. For example, a cubic foot of wood in air at 60 percent relative humidity can hold nearly 3½ pints of water. At 10 percent relative humidity the same wood will hold less than one pint. Hence it gives up its moisture to dry air, getting smaller in bulk as a result.

Shrinking of wood during winter dryness opens cracks in the woodwork and causes nails to get loose and work their way out until they protrude enough to fall.

The friction of shoe leather against carpeting generates static electricity that builds up in the body unless grounded. In air of proper humidity, the moisture acts as a ground that leaks away the electricity as fast as it is formed. In dry air the static electricity in your body is not grounded but is discharged only when you touch any metal object, sometimes with surprising force.

One way to avoid shocks is to remember to brush a doorknob (or refrigerator, metal cabinet, etc.) lightly with the hand before actually taking hold of it. This dissipates the electricity without the spark that would occur at the last moment if you reached out in the normal way to grasp the object.

But a better way by far is to add to the heating system some method of keeping humidity in the house at a proper level. See Chapter 3 for methods of controlling humidity in winter.

Dirty Radiators

If a radiator collects enough dirt, lint, or soot on its surfaces it will not give out as much heat as it should, and may cost money in wasted fuel. Give radiators of any type, including electric ones, a good vacuum cleaning from time to time when they are not in use.

Noisy Heating Pipes

Basic causes of a noisy hot-water system, originating in the furnace or circulating pump, should be corrected first as suggested on pages 89 and 95–97. However, if such vibrations cannot be 100 percent eliminated, the pipes will continue to carry the sound upstairs, amplifying it like a pipe organ.

Install small rubber pads between the pipe and each pipe hanger in the basement. These will throttle or dampen any remaining unwelcome noises, and probably avoid the expense and trouble of breaking through plaster to trace the cause.

Basement Too Warm

If a basement that is theoretically unheated—has no radiator or warm-air outlets—nevertheless gets too hot for comfort, it is a sign of wasted heat. Most commonly, the furnace is not insulated and sheds heat into the basement through excessive radiation. Contributing sources might also be lack of insulation on hot-water piping and storage tank.

If the problem is a new one in the house, the owner should suspect a malfunction: The furnace is over-fired or contains excessive soot, or the boiler water is dirty.

In any case, the heat is coming from somewhere and if not wanted in the basement, it should be diverted to more useful areas. Sometimes a basement is especially well insulated and tight, meaning the heat is not "wasted," but accumulated and not "lost." Here are two suggested ways to utilize it:

1. Install additional ductwork to divert the basement's warm air into an unheated garage.

2. Install a tempering tank in the supply line for a water heater. As fresh cold water enters it is stored for a time in this tank, where the surrounding warm basement air will raise its temperature by quite a few degrees. This saves BTUs in heating water for the hot-water faucets. If the fresh water supply is very cold, the fuel saving can be substantial.

Chapter 5

AIR-CONDITIONING—
KEEPING COOL

The term "air-conditioning" literally means anything one might do for the sake of greater comfort to alter the *condition* of air enclosed in a home. Thus it includes heating as well as cooling, humidifying as well as de-humidifying, filtering, ventilation, and air circulation. Today, however, we generally limit this term specifically to describe equipment and methods for *cooling* your home in hot weather.

In our climate there are five practical methods of cooling, listed in upward order of effectiveness and cost: (1) room fans, (2) window fans, (3) attic fans, (4) room airconditioners, and (5) central air-conditioning. In warmer climates two additional methods could be considered: (6) evaporative cooling, i.e., with running water, and (7) the heat pump, which both heats and cools as required by the season.

Room Fans

Room fans do not actually cool the air in a room, but they stir it up. The temperature inside your house could be several degrees cooler than outside in the hot sun, and yet feel oppressively warm and stuffy if the air doesn't move. Air movement increases the evaporation of moisture from the skin, and it is this evaporation (made evident as perspiration) that nature utilizes to cool the body at the skin surfaces. The quicker the drops of sweat disappear from the brow, the cooler you feel.

A good room fan has large blades in proportion to its size, ranging from a small table model to a 7-foot pedestal floor fan that turns at a top speed of about 1,000 revolutions per minute (rpm), sometimes with adjustments for lower speeds as well. It can be set to propel air in one direction only or to oscillate from side to side. Circular floor models send air in all directions through vents in the housing, thus avoiding direct air currents.

Electric fans take relatively little electric current and are economical to operate 24 hours a day. They should be oiled at least once each season, and wiped clean of dust and dirt. Cover with a bag or cloth when storing a fan for the winter.

Window Fans

A window fan exchanges inside air for outside air. You can use it for night cooling, or whenever the temperature inside the home is higher than the temperature outside. A time switch can be installed to turn off the fan automatically at any time desired. When you have cooled your house at night, keep the windows and doors closed next morning or as long as it stays cooler indoors than out.

Fans are rated by the amount of air they move in cubic feet per minute (cfm). Dealers in such equipment often provide engineering advice that takes into consideration the size of the area to be cooled, the air inlets and outlets, the horsepower of the fan motor, and the rpm of the fan blade. To determine the fan size yourself:

1. Calculate the cubic volume of the area to be served (multiply room length × width × ceiling height, omitting closet space). Divide the volume by 1.5 for the minimum cfm requirement. The resulting figure is the cfm that will provide one complete change of air every 1.5 minutes, a minimum based on summer heat in the cities. If your area enjoys cooler summers than the city, divide the cubic footage by 2 (one air change every 2 minutes).

2. Select a fan that has a cfm rating about 20 percent larger than your calculated minimum. For example, if the area equals 15,000 cubic feet less closets, the 1.5 factor gives a fan capacity of 10,000 cfm, but you should select one with a capacity of 12,000 cfm. The additional 2,000 cfm are an allowance to overcome static, friction, and other resistance to the movement of air. The operating costs are small.

Window fans range in size from 20 to 30 inches. The popular 20-inch size will generally provide about 15 to 20 air changes per hour for the average three-bedroom house. It is easy to install requiring no construction work other than mounting in a window.

When cooling with a fan, you should close off any portion of the house you do not wish to cool; otherwise, the fan will not provide the proper number of air changes per unit of time. A window fan has some disadvantages. It may pull dust and pollen into your home, and it may be noisy.

Attic Fans

Next to full-scale air-conditioning, an attic fan offers the most complete cure for homes suffering from oppressive summer heat. Like a window fan, it exchanges inside for outside air, but in the opposite direction: It pumps warm air out through the attic on the same principle as a kitchen exhaust fan. This air is replaced from below through opened windows.

Under the hot summer sun, a roof absorbs great heat.

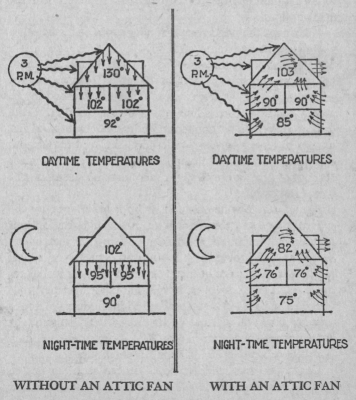

DAYTIME TEMPERATURES   DAYTIME TEMPERATURES

NIGHT-TIME TEMPERATURES   NIGHT-TIME TEMPERATURES

WITHOUT AN ATTIC FAN   WITH AN ATTIC FAN

Since an attic fan requires considerable construction work, the following steps might be tried first:

1. Paint the roof white. Light colors absorb less heat than dark colors. Use only a specially constituted roof paint.

2. Install adequate insulation in the attic.

3. If you have a forced-warm-air furnace, setting the blower switch on manual control (with the burner off) will keep air in circulation and pump cooler air from the basement into the house. If basement is damp, you may require a dehumidifier in the basement to avoid clamminess or odors.

4. Curtain the windows with new types of fabric especially designed to repel sunlight.

Attic temperatures often rise to 25 degrees or more hotter than outside; as high as 130 to 150 degrees is not uncommon on a 90-degree day. This heat, trapped in the attic, penetrates to the living area by radiation from the ceiling as well as by convection currents through ceiling openings. Unless forced ventilation is utilized to dissipate the heat, attic heat built up during the day will radiate throughout the house all night long, making sleep difficult if not impossible.

Attic fan size is determined, as with other fans, by the size of house and the number of air changes desired per minute. For example, a house measuring 40 feet by 50 feet with a 9-foot ceiling has an air capacity of 18,000 cubic feet. A change of air every two minutes would require a fan capacity of at least 9,000 cubic feet per minute. Normally a 1/3-horsepower, 36-inch attic fan properly installed will provide 40 air changes per hour for the average three-bedroom house. A 1/2-horsepower, 42-inch fan would provide 60 air changes per hour.

When you remove attic heat with an attic fan during the day, close the attic off from the rest of the house.

Otherwise the powerful exhaust fan upstairs will pull hot outside air into the house downstairs. Because night air is cooler, the attic may be opened again at night.

ATTIC-FAN INSTALLATION

The cost of attic fans runs from $100 up, plus installation, which in some cases may approach the cost of air-conditioning. If you are skilled at carpentry, following are typical instructions issued by attic-fan manufacturers:

1. Determine correct size of exhaust opening between house and attic. Lay out opening, using square to assure good corners.
2. Cut ceiling plaster with chisel, tilting toward center. Use fine-tooth saw if drywall construction.
3. Cut header sections to match ceiling joists. Nail into position to frame opening.
4. Adjust spring tension of shutter to assure quiet fan operation and optimum air delivery.
5. Place shutter in position, fasten with hardware. Wide edge assures trim fit.
6. Cut 1- × 3-inch strips of wood. Nail to frame formed by joists and header section to form base for fan unit.
7. Wire to junction box on fan. It can easily be wired to a two-speed switch.
8. Lay felt strips on base. Place fan unit squarely on felt for perfect seal. No need to strap down.
9. Fan is then installed without weakened joints in truss roof construction. The air will be exhausted through attic louvers, vents, a dormer, or other normal ventilation openings. Ventilation is considered adequate when you have openings to the outside totaling one square foot of free open area for every 300 square feet of attic space.

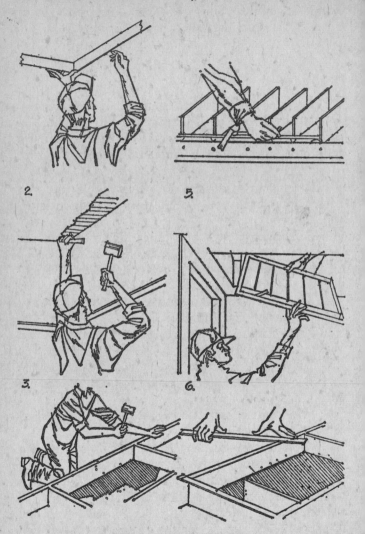

7.

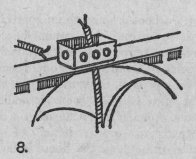

8.

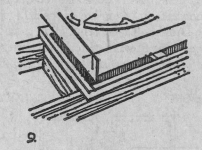

9.

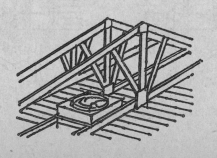

While fans do cool a house to an appreciable degree and cost little to operate, they cannot be compared to air-conditioning in terms of benefits—any more than a wood stove could be compared to modern central heating.

The ideal arrangement, of course, is central air-conditioning of the entire house. A room airconditioner operates on the same principle, but is suitable for cooling only one or two rooms at a time. A battery of room conditioners installed throughout the house is uneconomical, since they are heavy users of electric current. Other sources of energy, including oil and gas, may be used to power central air-conditioning.

A room airconditioner cools by compression. This works by constantly changing a special gas (usually freon) into a liquid and vice versa, all in a closed system whereby none of the flowing material is consumed or lost. Each time the liquid is released from pressure and ex-

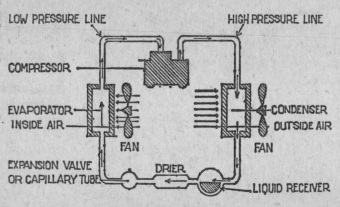

COMPRESSION SYSTEM

pands into a gas, the gas absorbs heat and cools the surrounding area. Here is what happens step by step:

1. A motor-driven compressor "squeezes" the gas, places it under high pressure.

2. The gas passes through a condenser outside the house.

3. A fan blowing outside air through the condenser cools the gas and liquefies it. (Note at this step that even though the outside air may be "hot," the blower makes it hotter. The machine is using a temperature *difference* to transfer BTUs of heat—the principle of a heat pump. Similarly, a refrigerator pours warmed air into the kitchen.)

4. This liquid collects in a receiving chamber from which it is forced into a small tube by the pressure of the gas behind it and then to an air evaporator inside the house.

5. As the liquid enters the evaporator it expands to its gaseous state, absorbing heat in the process and thereby cooling the tubes of the evaporator. A second fan blows over these cool tubes and forces the cooled air into the room. Any moisture in the air condenses on the tubes and is directed outside to evaporate.

6. As the gas in the evaporator absorbs heat from its surroundings, it becomes warm again. It is then sucked through the compressor once more and pumped through the outside condenser where its heat is again dispelled as in steps 1 to 3. The process is continuous.

TIPS ON ROOM AIR-CONDITIONING

Windows and doors of the room or rooms to be cooled should be kept shut. The conditioner recirculates the same air over and over again, freshening it by passing it through a filter on the return cycle. This filtering generally makes it "fresher" than the outside air.

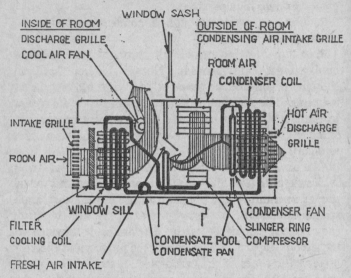

INSIDE OF ROOM
DISCHARGE GRILLE
COOL AIR FAN

WINDOW SASH

OUTSIDE OF ROOM
CONDENSING AIR INTAKE GRILLE

ROOM AIR
CONDENSER COIL

INTAKE GRILLE

HOT AIR
DISCHARGE
GRILLE

ROOM AIR→

WINDOW SILL

FILTER
COOLING COIL

FRESH AIR INTAKE

CONDENSATE POOL
CONDENSATE PAN

CONDENSER FAN
SLINGER RING
COMPRESSOR

AIR MOVEMENT THROUGH WINDOW

Most types have a setting marked VENT or FRESH AIR that opens a valve to admit outside air through the machine. This valve may be opened occasionally if the recirculated air in the room becomes stale or smoky, but should normally be kept closed during a cooling cycle. (With it open you'd in effect be trying to cool all the air in Canada.) Also, air entering the room through the VENT valve does *not* pass through the filter, but brings with it dust and humidity from outdoors.

The machine may also have an EXHAUST setting. This acts like a simple exhaust fan, and should never be used during a cooling cycle. (You would then be consuming electricity to pump cooled air outdoors.)

If one room airconditioner is being used for two or more connected rooms, the second room will get more cooling if an ordinary electric fan is installed in or near the doorway to speed up circulation of the air. This device sometimes will benefit a sleeper who is bothered by the sound of an airconditioner in the same room with him at night.

Most airconditioners come equipped with a thermostat or can be wired to one. Like the thermostat for a heater, it can be set at the most comfortable temperature. The thermostat determines when the compressor cuts in and out, even though the fan runs continuously and keeps the air in motion.

Don't plug in an airconditioner to an ordinary wall outlet in a circuit also serving the lights or other appliances. It should have its own circuit, possibly requiring new wiring of higher capacity than the others in your home.

AIRCONDITIONER MAINTENANCE

An airconditioner like any other piece of equipment requires maintenance in order to deliver its maximum capacity and avoid breakdowns. Following are the routine procedures to follow before calling for a professional serviceman:

1. Pull out the plug from its wall outlet.
2. Turn controls to the OFF position.
3. Remove front grille and clean the filter, at least once each season and preferably more often. If it is the disposable type, replace it.
4. Gently clean the interior of the unit, the fan, motor,

123

compressor, and coils with a vacuum hose and soft brush. You will find that the circulating air deposits a great amount of dust.

5. Check fan blade and belts for wear.

6. Tighten all loose bolts and fittings.

7. Oil the motor in accordance with manufacturer's instructions. As with most electric motors, do not over-lubricate; a few drops will generally suffice.

8. Examine exterior of the machine to see that it is free from insects, leaves, debris, etc., that may block air circulation.

9. If the machine vibrates noisily or thumps while compressing, shut it off at once and call for service.

Although an airconditioner dehumidifies the circulating air, it may not do so adequately during humid, muggy weather. (If the exterior screen drips, this is normal, but if dripping is excessive you may have to find some way to divert the water from the side of the house.) If the cooled air feels clammy, you may want to install a room dehumidifier (see page 132) when operating the air-conditioner.

AIRCONDITIONER CAPACITIES

Airconditioners are rated by heat-removing capacity in British thermal units (BTUs). Where temperatures do not usually exceed 95 degrees, a machine rated at 6,000 BTUs per hour will cool a room with 100 to 230 square feet of floor space. (*Note*—Although *cubic* footage of air must be cooled, manufacturers' charts list *square* footage of room area because it's easier to measure and ceiling heights are more or less standard in most houses. If you have a cathedral ceiling, you may have to allow more than room-rated BTU capacity.)

Where temperatures exceed 95 degrees, a capacity of 6,900 BTUs will be required to cool the same 100- to

230-square-foot area on the hottest days. Approximately one kilowatt hour of electricity is required to remove each 6,500 BTUs with an electrical airconditioner. This is the same amount of current consumed by ten 100-watt light bulbs each hour.

Some airconditioners, especially older ones, are rated in "tons." One ton is the amount of heat required to melt a ton of ice, equal to 288,000 BTUs per 24 hours, or 12,000 BTUs per hour. Thus, in the jargon of the trade, a "half-ton" or 6,000-BTU airconditioner is the standard size for a single room. It's quite important to fit an airconditioner to its job. Too small a unit will not do the job of cooling. Too large an airconditioner does not dehumidify properly because it cools a room too quickly and then shuts off, not allowing time for efficient dehumidification.

Central Air-Conditioning

The benefits of central air-conditioning—the deluxe way to cool a home—are so great that the majority of new homes built today either include it or at least provide for future installation. In some areas, real estate people predict a day not far off when homes without air-conditioning will be hard to sell.

Central air-conditioning permits you to maintain thermostatically controlled comfort all year round. High summer temperature is usually accompanied by high humidity. As much as 90 quarts of water can be wrung from the air within a home by a system rated at 34,000 BTU. Air-conditioning ends mildew, sticking doors, and other dampness problems caused by high indoor humidity. And it's good for the health.

Good temperature control helps maintain good dispositions. Doctors often prescribe air-conditioning for heart patients and people with limited physical reserves. During very hot weather the heart has to work harder to remove body heat; custom climate control is said to reduce heart strain and blood pressure. The filtered air also protects people from allergenic dust and other airborne irritants, bringing relief to sufferers from asthma, hay fever, skin eruptions, and other serious problems.

Doors and windows stay closed, shutting out dust and insects. Traffic and neighborhood noise are kept outside, too. Up to 390 pounds of contaminating dirt fall on every square mile every day in the city and suburbs. It has been estimated that as much as 250 pounds of this dirt is arrested *before* entering an air-conditioned home, thereby reducing housework. Cleaning, redecorating, and repainting are kept to a minimum.

These benefits highlight the essential difference between central air-conditioning and any other type of cooling system, such as attic fans. You can "dial the weather"—maintain exact temperature and humidity control in the home, completely independent of outside conditions.

AIR-CONDITIONING INSTALLATION

A central air-conditioning system can be separate from a heating system with its own ducts, but if you have a forced-warm-air system, the air-conditioning can be integrated with it. This is a much less complex and less expensive installation. The compressor and condenser may be located outside the home and the evaporator coil located in the plenum of the warm-air furnace. All the long duct runs in the basement should be insulated.

Cooling requires a greater amount of air flow than heating. Hence the installation in a warm-air system may require a larger blower fan and motor. It may be advisable, if not absolutely necessary, to enlarge the distribution ducts or relocate some of them. Larger ducts decrease the velocity of the cooled air and reduce the noise of air-conditioning.

For greatest uniformity in room comfort conditions, cold-air-supply grilles should be high in the walls or in the ceiling, whereas hot-air-supply grilles should be near or in the floor. If economy dictates the use of a single grille for both heating and cooling, the near floor location is preferred.

Noise is reduced when airconditioner mechanisms are located as remotely as possible from living and sleeping rooms. The illustrations show attic and crawl-space plans

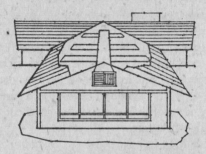

Attic flush-mounted installation system carries the conditioned air to the areas to be cooled. The ducts should be insulated in the attic.

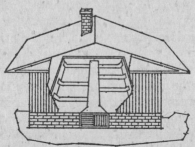

This crawl-space installation carries the conditioned air to the areas to be cooled, through insulated ductwork between the floor and the basement.

127

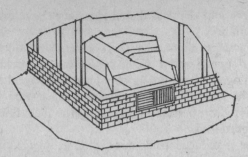

This is an airconditioner than can be installed to operate with a forced-warm-air heating system.

for a separate system, and a basement plan for an "add on" to the warm-air heating system. The mounting in each case is flush with the wall. Even more desirable is to mount the compressor and condenser on a concrete slab completely outside the house under a weatherproof housing. Then only the evaporative coil and the filter—the least noisy parts—need be mounted in the duct system.

A typical central airconditioner rated at 34,000 BTUs that can be added to a forced-air furnace may cost about $600 before installation. A new house with a built-in conditioner may cost about $600 more than one without air-conditioning, so the duct system comes "free."

Cooling by Absorption

The previous remarks assume an airconditioner that is electrically operated, with the same operating cost characteristics as room airconditioners, in proportion to BTU capacity. Another method is available using fuel oil or gas as the source of energy, a "magic flame" that cools as well as heats. Called absorption cooling, it works in a similar manner to gas-burning refrigerators and is completely noiseless.

The cooling cycle starts at the generator, a sealed chamber containing water and a chemical absorbent in solution. The system is under a partial vacuum—less than atmospheric pressure—so the solution boils at a lower temperature than it would in the open. A flame under this generator boils the solution and pushes it upward much like water rising in a coffee percolator. It enters a separator where baffles separate the water from the absorbent chemical.

The chemical now flows back to the absorber where it is cooled by the surrounding air. Meanwhile the water rises as a vapor to the top of the system, where it is condensed back into liquid and flows downward to the cooling coils. Here, because of the partial vacuum, the water flashes into a vapor comparable to an icy-cold fog. It chills the tubes in the cooling coil, and a fan blowing across this coil provides cool air for the house.

Having absorbed the heat from the cooled air, the water continues downward to rejoin the absorbent chemical and repeat the cycle. Since there are no moving parts, there is no noise other than the quiet whir of a fan and little to wear out. Like the compressor system, it efficiently utilizes *differences* in temperature to extract heat from air, but by means of quiet chemical action rather than thumping mechanical pump action.

The absorption system may be air cooled or water cooled. If enough water is readily available, water-cooling is more economical. A water-cooled fuel airconditioner requires about 13 cubic feet of gas or 1/10 gallon of oil (plus a small amount of electricity) to remove each 6,500 BTUs of heat. An air-cooled one requires 21 cubic feet of gas (0.16 gallon of oil) for the same cooling effect.

A water-cooled condenser of any type requires large quantities of water to disperse the heat—about 75 to 150 gallons per hour for each 12,000 BTUs. The water can be diverted to an outdoor cooling tower and reused; however, such a tower is noisy and should be located well away from the house or neighbors. The fuel saving thus may be offset by the costs of water supply and disposal.

Other Types of Cooling

The *water-evaporation* method of cooling is suitable only in hot, very dry climates, since it adds humidity to the air rather than subtracting from it. The first automobile airconditioners, developed in the southwestern United States, were of this type.

Air drawn into the car by its motion or boosted by a fan passes through a chamber containing excelsior or similar material soaked in water. Water evaporating from the excelsior cools the air driven into the car. The water evaporates quickly into the cooled air and must be frequently replaced; it would take 5 to 10 gallons per hour to cool an average-size house.

A *heat pump* may be compared to a refrigerator that works backward or forward. If you put your hand above an air-cooled refrigerator (as most of them are) in the kitchen you will feel warm air rising. This is the heat being extracted from food and in freezing the ice cubes. Inside the refrigerator, of course, the air will feel cold. A heat pump is a similar device that may be set up to pump either the warm air or the cold air into a room, as desired.

In summer, the pump takes heat from the house air and forces it outdoors, like an ordinary airconditioner. In winter, the process is reversed and the pump extracts heat from the outside air and puts it into the house. Even with very low temperatures, air contains a certain amount of heat; this makes the operation of the heat pump possible.

Naturally, the lower the outside temperature, the more the pump must work to provide heat to warm the house.

For this reason, when heat pumps are used in very cold climates, they are usually hooked up with a resistance-type electric heater to provide additional heat when required.

At this time, heat pumps are most effective in warmer areas where the outside temperature seldom drops to a very low reading; but every year these units become more efficient and are thus able to operate in colder climates. The beauty of the heat pump, besides the fact that it uses Nature's heat, is that it doesn't need expensive flues or wiring, and it is both noiseless and clean.

One sometimes finds heat pumps in motel rooms in Florida. The cooling capacity usually is satisfactory, but an auxiliary heater may be needed to handle part of the cold-weather load. The cost of operation so far is prohibitively high in cold climates. Heat pumps await a breakthrough in technology to become generally practical.

Another heating/cooling system of the future, existing already in a few large buildings, is *all-energy* or *total energy* production at home. In this system a diesel engine or turbine burning conventional household fuel oil is hooked up to a generator that produces all the electricity for household needs, including air-cooling. The heat simultaneously generated by the engine, instead of being wasted as in an automobile or truck, is harnessed to supply house heat in winter and continuous hot water for domestic use.

The home thus becomes completely self-sustaining, independent of electric or gas utility connections and able to function despite power failures, low pipeline pressures, storms, or other calamities. Theoretically the system utilizes practically 100 percent of the BTUs in the fuel oil consumed, at large savings in total energy cost.

A comparable example is a typical automobile heater using hot water—waste heat—from the engine cooling system, at no cost in gasoline. Like a car also, a home may be energized even in the most isolated locations. The effect on rural real estate values could be sensational. At present, however, designs for a compact, home-size all-energy unit have not progressed beyond the drawing boards.

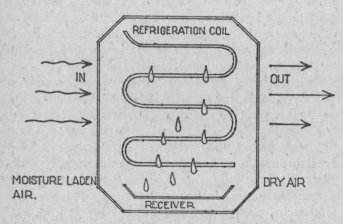

DEHUMIDIFIER OPERATION

Air Dehumidifiers

In connection with home heating (Chapter 3), a principal concern was to maintain a proper level of relative humidity in the heated air. During a warm, humid summer, a homeowner's concern is just the opposite: how to *remove* humidity from the moisture-bearing outdoor air lest it cause both discomfort and dampness damage inside the house.

One common result of summer humidity is an excessively damp basement. Areas below ground and below frost level tend to maintain a constant temperature, around 60 degrees, winter and summer. Air entering a basement at 80 degrees or higher will deposit surprising amounts of water as condensation on the cool walls, floor, pipes, equipment, and any furniture the room may contain. The resulting dampness is often bad enough to cause plaster to fall from a finished ceiling, to render a radio unplayable, or to turn clean bedsheets into a clams' nest.

A number of steps may be taken to combat this:

1. Keep cellar windows closed except on driest days.
2. Install an exhaust fan in one of the cellar windows.
3. Install an ordinary electric fan in the basement to keep the air stirred up so as to retain water vapor rather than condense it. If the basement adjoins a crawl space with the normal side vents, the fan may be directed toward the crawl space so as to exhaust moist basement air through these vents.
4. Manually turn on the blower of a warm-air furnace so as to pump basement air through the upstairs ducts. This will work best only on very dry days, since at other times the basement air may be clammy and perhaps moldy in odor.
5. Install an electric dehumidifier.

In principle a dehumidifier is still another version of a refrigerator. A motor-driven fan circulates the moisture-filled air over a refrigerated coil. Moisture condenses on this coil and collects in a receiving pan under the machine. Dry air then is discharged into the room. The only catch is that the collected water must be disposed of promptly or it will evaporate back into the air.

Therefore the best location for the dehumidifier is adjacent to a drain where the water is allowed to trickle out. If a basement has no floor drain, the dehumidifier may have to be suspended from the ceiling joists on a platform and the water condensate directed into a laundry tub, or into a hose poked through a slightly opened cellar window. Otherwise the owner must remember to empty the receiving pan at regular intervals, carrying it upstairs if necessary—much like emptying the drip pan under an old-fashioned icebox.

A dehumidifier may also be desirable in living quarters, either in the absence of air-conditioning or because room airconditioners do only a partial job of dehumidification. Take advantage of crisp, dry, breezy, summer days to thoroughly ventilate the house by opening windows and doors.

Electronic Air Cleaners

An electronic air cleaner adds another refinement to home comfort by removing particulate matter floating in the circulated air. A portable unit may be used with any type of heating system; or an integrated unit may be installed into a warm-air system. The electric power consumption is about 10 watts per 1,000 cfm plus 40 watts required to energize the rectifier tube which converts alternating house current (AC) to direct current (DC). Total consumption comes to about 1.5 kwh per day.

The voltages necessary to precipitate dust particles are usually obtained by means of an electronic high-voltage direct-current power pack operating from a 110–120 volt, 60-cycle, single-phase AC outlet. In a typical case, a potential of 12,000 volts may be built up to create an ionizing field, and some 6,000 volts between the plates where the precipitation of dust occurs.

These voltages, which are capable of giving a person a momentary shock like that of an automobile spark plug, necessitate some safety measures. A typical arrangement makes the equipment inoperative when any door affording access to high-voltage parts is opened. The precipitator will resume operating only after all doors are closed.

Air cleaners remove pollutants from the air and to a

large extent solve the dust problem in a home. They are very effective if used in conjunction with central air-conditioning as you would then be able to keep your home under positive pressure (from outside in). People with allergic conditions find them indispensable if the home is near a factory or other dust-producing source.

Chapter 6

WATER AND PLUMBING

The most vital of our four Ws of home maintenance unquestionably is Water. Man can live without the comforts of central heating or electricity or even a roof over his head, but he cannot survive three days without water. H_2O, a remarkable gift of nature, both nourishes us and disposes of wastes. No wonder, then, that the plumbing of a house engages the constant concern of its owner and that plumbers make very good pay.

A home plumbing system actually is comprised of three systems for cold water, hot water, and drainage. The first two systems consist of connected piping kept constantly full of water under pressure.

This pressure, originating either as a head of water in the municipal mains or from the lifting power of a pump, enables water in the pipes to push uphill against the force of gravity. It assures you of a ready flow whenever you open a faucet, but it also means instant loss of water, loss of pressure, or even a flood should any fixture or pipe spring an accidental leak.

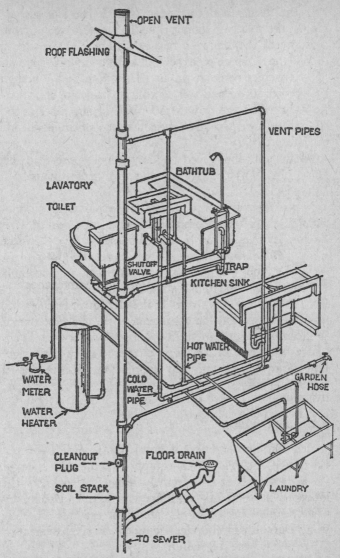

OPEN VENT

ROOF FLASHING

VENT PIPES

LAVATORY

TOILET

BATHTUB

SHUTOFF VALVE

TRAP

KITCHEN SINK

WATER METER

WATER HEATER

COLD WATER PIPE

HOT WATER PIPE

GARDEN HOSE

CLEANOUT PLUG

FLOOR DRAIN

SOIL STACK

LAUNDRY

TO SEWER

HOUSE PLUMBING SYSTEM (INCLUDING WATER
SUPPLY AND WASTE DISPOSAL)

In the third plumbing system, the drainage or sewage piping, the water no longer is under pressure except from gravity and the tendency of water to seek its own level. Hence the drainage pipes seldom leak to any great extent. Most troubles come from an obstruction in the system that causes water and soil to collect, back up, and overflow, or when the downward pitch of the pipes is too slight to carry drainage to the sewer or septic tank outside the house.

Really you don't need to know much more than this about plumbing in order to cope with typical household emergencies.

Major repairs to any of the three plumbing systems should be left to a licensed plumber. A good deal of what he does is governed by building codes that have the force of law. But minor plumbing repairs are well within the skills of anyone who can use a screwdriver and a wrench. It is hardly sensible to pay a plumber the minimum charge for a service call, say 10 to 15 dollars, for installing a 10-cent washer in a dripping faucet. Even if a pipe bursts, you can often stave off heavy damage by knowing in advance what to do. Yet it is our experience that many householders neglect a few simple facts at the risk of serious difficulties.

Know Your Valves

Every utility entering a house from outside—water, electricity, fuel oil, gas—is equipped with a main shut-off valve or switch. It is extremely important to know the locations of *all* of these entrance valves. In an emergency situation they can be interrelated. For example, flooding water can short-circuit electric motors in the basement.

List and tag the following:

1. Main water entrance valve, usually near the water

meter in the basement or utility room, sometimes buried outside under a metal cover in the ground.

2. Main cold water valve, usually at the front of the building.

3. Main hot water valve, usually near the top of the hot-water tank or below it on the feed line.

4. Main electrical switch, usually in or near the fuse box under a fastened cover; it may be a large circuit breaker.

5. Main gas valve, usually at the top left side of the gas meter.

6. Main oil-line valve, usually on the outlet pipe of the fuel tank, or where that pipe enters the oil burner, or in both places.

Every adult in the house should know where to find main valves in a hurry and how to use them. When a sudden emergency threatens a flood, a quick turn of one or more valve handles will shut off everything until you can locate the cause of trouble or until the plumber arrives. Trying blindly to find these valves can cause great confusion at a bad time.

Besides the main valves, locate all branch valves throughout the house. There should be separate hot- and cold-water valves for each sink, tub, washing machine, or other fixture that uses water. Tag or label these in such a way that the correct valve governing flow to a fixture can be located quickly. Besides water valves, you may have individual gas valves, steam valves, hot-water-heating valves, and of course the individual fuses or circuit breakers for the electrical system.

Till the Plumber Arrives

Armed with the above information, here is what to do in various types of emergency situations:

Burst cold-water pipe. Close main shut-off valve. If you encounter difficulty because the valve is old, broken, or rusted from disuse, call the city waterworks or private water company immediately. At your request they will come quickly to shut off the water outside—quickly, because they are fearful of burst pipes, too.

Frozen pipe. If exposed or accessible, thaw with hot compresses, an electrical heating pad, or large-wattage bulb. If pipes are concealed, it is best to thaw by electricity. Open a faucet and start thawing from that point. Check for the cause of the freeze-up and take measures to prevent a recurrence. It may be necessary to insulate the pipe, or change its location, or to introduce heat into the area around it.

Burst hot-water tank, pipes, or heater. Shut off the hot-water valve. If the leak continues, shut off the cold-water valve as well.

Blocked sinks and drains. Do not use drain cleaner when a sink is completely blocked. This probably would not happen at all if the drains were regularly cleared when slow drainage first occurred. See page 154 for methods of unblocking drains.

Blocked water closet. Do not flush the toilet, as it almost certainly will overflow. If necessary to use it before arrival of the plumber, flush with a pail of water, but stop pouring before the water gets too high in the bowl.

Overflowing toilet tank. Stop the flow of incoming water by raising the float rod (the one with a floating ball at the end of it). Keep it in raised position by placing a wrench or piece of wood under the rod and across the top of the open tank; or tie it to an overhead fixture. If this is not effective, raise or remove the rubber-ball valve at the bottom of the tank and let the water drain into the bowl until the plumber arrives.

Gas leak. Shut off the valve at the top left side of the gas meter. This is done by aligning the upper and lower handles of the divided gas valve on the supply line. Do not use a flame to look for a gas leak. Ventilate the area thoroughly until help arrives.

Burst fuel tank. A rare but distressing problem, this could happen to a very old *indoor* tank that has rusted along the bottom because of accumulated water condensation. Drive a wooden peg or wedge into the leak with a hammer. Turn off the oil burner and shut the oil supply valve. Ventilate the area thoroughly to void any vapors, and do not use a flame. Call your fuel dealer, who will drain the tank and spread a sandlike mixture to absorb spilled oil and reduce the odor.

Heat for Hot Water

The supply of hot water for faucets can get its heat from the same source as the rest of the house, such as a "sidearm" from the main oil burner, or from a separate heating system. When the same furnace heats water for both radiators and faucets, the plumbing lines are entirely separate; no radiator water reaches the faucets. Separate hot-water heaters may be fired by oil, gas, electricity, or bottled LP gas.

Having the unique advantage of being completely portable, bottled gas is typical of mobile homes, trailers, and country homes. Otherwise it is less convenient and more costly than other fuels for water heating, so is rather rare in urban or suburban dwellings. More commonly it is used there for cooking, either because natural-gas mains do not reach the area or as a hedge against frequent power failures.

Recovery Rates

Besides the cost of fuel, the principal concern with hot-water heaters is the *recovery rate*. "Not enough hot water" is so frequent a complaint in large families as to become a cliché. The average usage of hot water by the average family is about 20 gallons per person per day, or the sum of the following activities:

Table 6-1: Family Uses of Hot Water

Activity	Amount
Hand washing	12–15 gals.
Shaving	3½ gals.
Hair washing	5 gals.
Showers	10–15 gals.
Tub baths	10–15 gals.
Preparing food	6 gals.
Rinsing dishes	3–5 gals.
Automatic dishwasher	7–9 gals. per load
Automatic clothes washer	15–30 gals. per load

From the above estimates it is not hard to understand why a 30-gallon hot-water tank may run suddenly cool if sister Susie decides to take a shower exactly when Mother is doing the family wash. The obvious solution might appear to be a larger tank and water heater, but this can involve a contradiction.

When not being used at the faucets—which means during most of each 24-hour day—the hot water in a tank gradually cools. The fuel already consumed to heat this water goes partly to waste, and a large tankful of hot water loses more BTUs by cooling in storage than a smaller tankful. Therefore the ideal or at least most economical combination is the *smallest* feasible tank with the *fastest* possible replacement of the hot water as it is dispensed.

Fuels differ markedly in the rate of hot water recovery. The differences involve not only the BTU content of a fuel but *how fast* its BTUs can be delivered for heating the water. The rates of delivery of gas and electricity are limited, respectively, by pressure in the gas main (or LPG tank) and kilowattage in the power line. Fuel oil, however, can be speeded up to fire a water heater at the rate of one gallon per hour, equivalent to 128,000 BTUs. To raise the temperature of an Imperial gallon of water 100°F. requires 1,000 BTUs.*

Table 6-2: 30-Gallon Water Heater Recovery Rates

Type	Rate
Electric	8 gals. per hour
Gas	30 gals. per hour
Fuel oil	120 gals. per hour

Because of recovery rates and other variable factors in water heater performance, the average fuel requirements and costs of hot water are difficult to estimate. Family habits vary too, though it may be impolite to observe that some people are fussier than others. The following approximations are based on hot water usage of 20 Imperial gallons per person per day, or 100 gallons for a family of five, requiring 100,000 BTUs per day. Electricity is rated at 100 percent efficiency, fuel oil and gas at 80 percent efficiency.

Table 6-3: Fuel Needs for Hot Water
(100 gallons per day raised 100°F. in temperature)

Fuel	Units per Day	@	Unit Cost	Cost per Day	Cost per Month
Electricity	24.4 kwh	@	1.2¢	29.2¢	$8.76
LP gas	1.04 therms	@	30.15¢	31.2¢	9.36
Natural gas	1.04 therms	@	16.64¢	17.3¢	5.19
Fuel oil	0.75 gals.	@	22¢	16.5¢	4.95

* For a U.S. gallon, the equivalent is 830 BTUs.

Fresh water from most natural sources in this country is more or less hard, meaning that it contains minerals such as calcium and magnesium. These form scaly precipitates on the insides of pipes and tanks. Underground water generally has a higher mineral content than surface water from rivers or reservoirs; if your water mixes with soap to form a curd or ring on the bathtub, it is definitely hard. That's why detergents have largely replaced soap for heavy-duty washing. Detergents (technically "syndets") are a synthetic product of petroleum, less affected by hard water than soap made from animal or vegetable fats and oils.

In a hot-water heater the mineral deposits from hard water eventually cause trouble. Over a period of time they build up in the tank, to a point where they may significantly reduce the amount of water the tank can contain. Mineral clogging of pipes can cut the hot-water supply to a trickle.

The stony encrustrations also impede transfer of heat to the water, wasting fuel. In an electric heater, where the element is immersed, deposits can render it virtually useless. If the process has gone too far, you will need a plumber and quite possibly replacement of the heater.

Hardness deposits are most troublesome in hot-water lines because heat accelerates the chemical process of precipitating minerals, as in a steam iron. Since there is no practical way to "boil off" these deposits, the best preventive is to install a water softener in the hot-water lines.

The softening equipment uses common salt (sodium chloride) as the catalyst to remove hardness minerals. If sodium in drinking water should be undesirable for reasons of health, it is a simple matter to bypass the water conditioner with a cold-water line. Softened water containing sodium would then feed only (1) the hot-water heater, and (2) cold-water outlets for bathing and laundering facilities. Untreated cold water would (3) run to kitchen fixtures and to outdoor faucets for the garden hose.

Rusty Water

Red water (or green or blue) flowing from hot-water taps and staining porcelain comes from metallic elements suspended in the water. While present all the time, they are not noticeable until there has been a heavy accumulation. Redness comes from iron, blue-green from copper or brass, and may indicate oxidation (rusting) of these metals in a tank or pipe.

True "red water" comes from the presence of harmless iron-forming bacteria. You see their handiwork when an unused valve is turned on for the first time, dislodging the accumulated iron oxides from low spots in the line. You can take the following preventive measures to avoid discolored hot water:

1. Drain about a gallon from the tank at least once every 30 days, by opening the drain cock at the bottom of the boiler.

2. If discoloration has already occurred, drain and flush the entire tank every 30 days until the condition improves.

3. Put a water conditioner into the hot-water intake line, as recommended above for removing hardness minerals. Water-softening equipment can be set up to remove iron as well.

Chemical inhibitors in a hot-water tank are not recommended for domestic use because of danger to the hands and other parts of the body.

Using Too Much Fuel

When a water heater appears to be functioning properly and yet fuel bills run uncommonly high, excessive heat loss is indicated. An uninsulated boiler loses heat to the air around it. People often notice an abrupt change when a boiler is moved from one location to another, for instance out of a warm furnace room into a cool garage.

To prevent heat losses the boiler should be well insulated. You may purchase a prefabricated jacket made of cellular, porous material such as cork, rock wool, or fiber glass that completely covers the tank around the sides and on top. Alternatively, the tank may be wrapped in several windings of flexible asbestos sheets and covered with muslin.

If properly installed, the insulation should never be hot to the touch; in fact, no warmer than room temperature. This relative coolness shows the heat is being retained inside the boiler.

Insulating the hot-water-delivery pipes, especially long ones, will also help reduce heat loss. Use porous sheathing clamped around the pipes or cover with insulating tape.

Cold Water Too Warm

If you have to let a tap run a long time before the water gets drinkably cold, it is probably being warmed in the pipes through unwanted heat transfer. This is a frequent complaint in apartment houses, where cold water may travel a long way through the heated interior or where the cold- and hot-water pipes run close together. Insulation of the pipes, both cold and hot, should help. On cold-water pipes, insulating tape also prevents condensation and dripping.

When cold and hot water emerge from the same mixing spout, as in bathroom and kitchen fixtures, there may be some infiltration of hot water into the cold-water line because of worn-out valves. Hot-water faucet washers and packing usually wear out first. Repair the valves as described later in this chapter.

Gurgling Noises

Gurgling or rumbling noises in a hot-water tank or a sudden surge of boiling water when a tap is first turned on are ominous signs calling for the services of a plumber. They indicate restricted water circulation for one or more of the following causes:

1. Worn-out ceramic lining in the tank, creating "hot spots" where the water boils.
2. Corroded riser pipe from the tank to the fixture.
3. Corroded feeder pipe to the tank, restricting circulation.
4. Mineral deposits from hard water as described above.
5. Excessively high pilot flame in a gas burner, which heats the water when burner is turned off.

Other Plumbing Noises

A *chattering* sound when a faucet is turned on indicates a worn washer or a loosening of the internal parts. (See Leaking Faucets, page 152.)

Hammering in pipes, usually called water hammer, is produced by sudden stoppage of water flow when a faucet

147

is turned off. The rushing water "bounces" back from the closed valve, vibrating inside the pipe until its momentum is dissipated. Water hammer constantly repeated can rupture a pipe, especially at elbows and joints.

Water hammer is corrected by installing antihammer air chambers to absorb the shock. The simplest kind consists of a vertical, two-foot length of pipe, tightly capped at the upper end and cut into the water line just before it enters a fixture. Air enclosed in this pipe compresses from the rebound of the water, absorbing the shock and damping the vibration. Always install one just ahead of an automatic clothes washer, with its quick-closing valves.

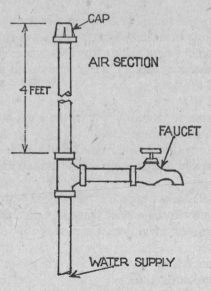

WATER HAMMER

If a hammering water line already has this feature (and every professional plumbing job would include an air chamber at a high point in the system or at a low point alongside the water meter), the air pipe may have filled gradually with water. It must be uncapped, drained, and recapped—a process called "bleeding."

Vibration noises similar to but not necessarily as violent as water hammer may occur if a pipe is not rigidly supported along its entire length, especially wherever the pipe makes a sharp turn. The water hits this turn like a sports car skidding around a bend. Install extra braces or straps on both sides of each elbow or tee. Also look for sagging pipes or supporting brackets that have worked loose.

Leaking Toilet Tanks

Water dripping from a toilet tank will sometimes form a pool on the bathroom floor, leading to many an unnecessary plumber call. Most often the tank is quite intact; there is no crack or leak in it for water to escape. The source of the drip is condensation or "sweating" on the *outside* of the tank because the water it contains is much colder than the room air.

First make sure you do not have a "simmering" or "singing" toilet. If water is draining slowly but constantly into the bowl, the incoming cold water never has a chance to warm up to room temperature. Fixing *that* leak (see below) will usually solve the sweating problem.

If not, you can install a tempering valve that admits a little warm water with the cold water when the toilet bowl is refilled. Another approach is a product called electrotape, which is applied by an adhesive backing to the exterior surface of the tank and plugged into an electric outlet. It acts like an electric heating pad to warm the tank and stop the sweating.

Still another method is to insulate the *inside* of the tank to prevent the outside from getting too cold. Insulating jackets or liners that fit most toilet tanks are available from plumbing-supply dealers.

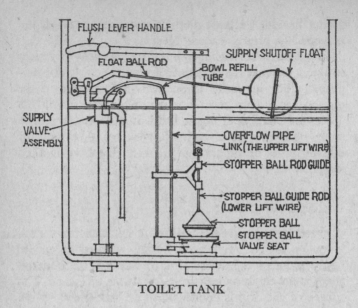

FLUSH LEVER HANDLE

FLOAT BALL ROD

SUPPLY SHUTOFF FLOAT

BOWL REFILL TUBE

SUPPLY VALVE ASSEMBLY

OVERFLOW PIPE

LINK (THE UPPER LIFT WIRE)

STOPPER BALL ROD GUIDE

STOPPER BALL GUIDE ROD (LOWER LIFT WIRE)

STOPPER BALL

STOPPER BALL VALVE SEAT

TOILET TANK

Toilet Tank Repairs

A simmering toilet not only constitutes a nuisance but can waste a fantastic amount of water. Although the mechanism may look complicated when you first uncover the toilet tank, it is quite simple in principle and usually not difficult to repair.

The key parts requiring attention are the flush valve, float ball, and the intake valve operated by the float (see illustration). If the entire mechanism is badly corroded, possibly because of a corrosive water supply, one may replace the usual copper parts with plastic parts. Often the plunger may stick or bind because of corrosion and dirt that can be freed up without replacing any parts.

Here is how the water closet works: When the handle is depressed, the trip arm raises a lift wire through the guide, lifting the flush valve off its seat at the bottom of the tank and allowing the water to empty rapidly into the bowl. As the water level drops in the tank, the float ball drops with it, opening the intake valve to admit fresh water into the tank. Simultaneously, the flush valve drops back into its seat, closing off the further escape of water.

Water continues to rise in the tank until the float ball reaches a certain level and shuts the intake valve. Before this happens a small tube has been refilling the bowl with water through the overflow pipe. The action is so timed as to trap water in the waste pipe and keep sewer gases from entering from below. The overflow pipe also has the emergency function of draining excess water into the bowl before it overflows.

To check out a nonfunctioning or leaking toilet, remove the cover and take the following steps in the order given:

1. Jiggle the handle. This action may seat a sticking plunger. Watch the action to detect the point of sticking. Straightening the relevant parts and cleaning off the rust and mineral deposits may be all that is required.

2. Lift the float ball gently to avoid breaking the float arm. If this stops the flowing water and the noise, the peak water level is too low. Bend the arm slightly downward so that the float ball will rise to the cutoff position at a lower water level.

3. Unscrew the float ball which may be taking in water. If so, replace with a new one.

4. Prop up the float arm to stop the intake of water, or shut the cutoff valve if one is provided under the tank. Raise the flush valve and unscrew it from the lift wire. Usually made of rubber, this ball may get soft or out of shape and fail to seat properly. Install a new one.

5. Look for mineral deposits on the flush valve seat and scrape it clean with steel wool.

6. If the flush valve is now watertight and the float ball rises as far as it can, but water still runs into the overflow pipe, the intake valve is leaking. Sometimes this can be repaired by installing a new washer, as in a faucet, but sometimes not. Better call a plumber to replace the entire float-valve assembly.

SIZE OF LEAK	CU. FT. PER DAY
. . . . . STEADY DROP	3
● 1/64	6
● 1/32	23
● 1/16	93
⬤ 1/8	400

Leaking Faucets

.If a faucet drips when closed or vibrates with a singing or fluttering noise when opened, the trouble is usually the washer at the lower end of the spindle. If the faucet leaks around the spindle or handle when opened, new packing is needed.

Before tackling either job, shut off the nearest intake valve. Place a cloth on any handy surface to receive the parts. As each is removed, place the part on the cloth in a line so you will remember the proper order when reassembling.

To replace a washer:

1. Disassemble the faucet—the handle, packing nut, packing, and spindle—in that order. If these parts are

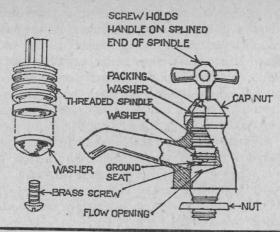

SCREW HOLDS HANDLE ON SPLINED END OF SPINDLE

PACKING WASHER

THREADED SPINDLE

WASHER

CAP NUT

WASHER

GROUND SEAT

BRASS SCREW

FLOW OPENING

NUT

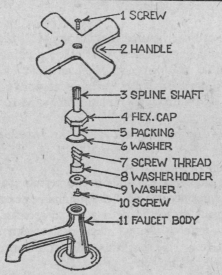

1 SCREW
2 HANDLE
3 SPLINE SHAFT
4 HEX. CAP
5 PACKING
6 WASHER
7 SCREW THREAD
8 WASHER HOLDER
9 WASHER
10 SCREW
11 FAUCET BODY

enclosed by a decorative housing, first wrap the housing with cloth to protect the finish and unscrew with a wrench. You may have to set the handle back on the spindle and use it to unscrew the spindle.

2. Remove the screw and worn washer from the spindle. Scrape all the worn washer parts from the cup and install a new washer of the proper size.

Note—If you don't have the right washer, you may be able to use the old one temporarily by turning it upside down. The worn side will be grooved, the unworn side smooth. Or you can cut a homemade one out of leather (cold water) or rubber (hot water).

3. Examine the seat on the faucet body. If it is nicked or rough, it requires refacing with a special tool. When using a refacing tool, be sure to hold it vertically.

4. Reassemble the faucet. Handles of mixing faucets (cold and hot with a common spout) should be set in matched positions.

To replace the packing:

1. Remove the handle, packing nut, and old packing.

2. Install a new packing washer. If a packing washer is not available, you can make the equivalent by wrapping stranded graphite-asbestos wicking around the spindle, or by using a putty-like graphite compound sold in hardware stores.

3. Turn the packing nut down tight against the new packing.

After prolonged use and several repairs, some valves will no longer provide tight shutoff and must be replaced. In this event, it would be a good idea to upgrade the quality. A number of new faucet designs aimed at easier operation, longer washer life, and better flow characteristics are on the market.

Clogged Drains

Clearing a clogged or sluggish drain is no great problem if the obstruction occurs close to the point of water entry. It becomes progressively more serious farther along the drainage system, for example in the main soil pipe leading to the sewer.

The first step, often overlooked, is to peer down into the drain with a flashlight to see if some object has dropped into it. With a bent-wire coat hanger you may be able to snare the object and lift it out. Many a lost kitchen paring knife or child's toothbrush has been recovered in this way.

Small obstructions caused by entangled hair and lint may often be forced down or drawn up with the ordinary rubber force cup or "plumber's helper." Its use is described on page 25.

Two bits of preventive medicine can help.

1. Combine a little family discipline with propaganda to keep indissoluble materials out of the drains. Grease should never be poured into the sink, while coffee grounds can settle at the bottom of the trap like sand. Toilets should not be used to dispose of fibrous materials like cloth, hard paper, cotton swabs, or filter cigarette ends. Place a waste basket in the bathroom for trash and hair combings.

2. Give drains a mild treatment with either drain cleaner or washing soda every week or so. Grease and soap clinging to a pipe may sometimes be removed simply by flushing with boiling water.

Drain cleaners. The basic ingredient of a drain cleaner is usually lye (sodium hydroxide), often mixed with aluminum shavings that are sometimes zinc coated. When water is added to the mixture, a violent gas-forming reaction and production of heat loosen the grease and soap so they can be flushed away. At the same time the caustic frees the hair or lint that may be clinging to the grease.

If you use lye, put one tablespoonful in the drain (after removing the sieve or basket) and flush with one cup of *cold* water. Allow to remain five minutes and flush with more water. *Use cold water only with lye.* Do not use a chemical cleaner in a pipe that is completely stopped up, because it must be brought into direct contact with the stoppage to be effective.

With washing soda, pour three tablespoonsful into the drain basket and run very hot water slowly through the drain until the granules are completely dissolved.

To open a badly clogged drain, remove all the water possible from the inlet of the drain, then slowly dissolve one 13-ounce can of lye in two quarts of cold water. Use only a pyrex, enamel, or stainless-steel container for this —never aluminum. Stir with a stick, plastic, or stainless-steel spoon, then pour the solution (which will be heated up and agitated by the lye) carefully and slowly into the drain. After ten minutes, flush thoroughly with cold water. *Wear work gloves and protective glasses when working with lye.*

Handle any caustic with extreme care; follow directions on the container. If lye spills on the hands or clothing, wash with cold water immediately. If any gets into the eyes, flush with cold water and call a doctor. Thoroughly wash and rinse all utensils used with a drain cleaner before putting them away or using them for any other purpose.

Cleaning a Sink Trap

A sink trap is a U-shaped section of pipe under a fixture that traps a small amount of water so that (1) sewer odors will not rise through the drain, and (2) dirt and sediment will be kept immersed and prevented from settling. At times it is necessary to clean out accumulations in this trap that stop or slow the drainage.

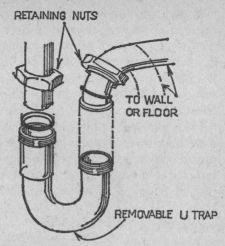

RETAINING NUTS

TO WALL OR FLOOR

REMOVABLE U TRAP

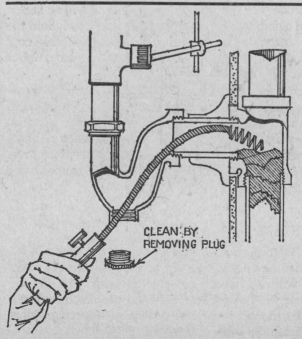

CLEAN BY REMOVING PLUG

Most traps have a screw-in plug at the lower point of the "U." Place a pail beneath it and unscrew the cap nut with a wrench. Remember that since the screw is upside down, you must turn with a clockwise motion to loosen it (equivalent to counterclockwise if looking up at it from the floor). If the nut is difficult to turn, apply penetrating oil.

Corrosion may cause the plug to stick fast in the opening. Unscrew the bottom nut a turn or two, then lightly tap it with a hammer. After removing the plug, reach into the trap with a screw auger ("snake") if you have one, or with any instrument that will break up the ac-

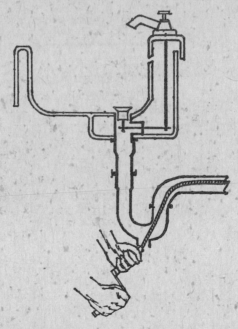

cumulations. Be especially careful to protect the hands and face if you have recently poured a caustic cleaner into this drain. Flush a little hot water down the drain

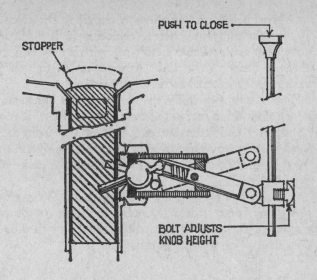

PUSH TO CLOSE

STOPPER

BOLT ADJUSTS
KNOB HEIGHT

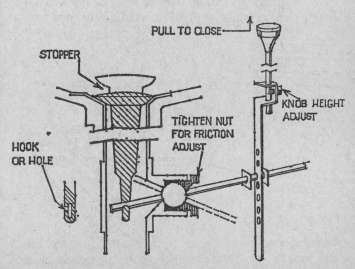

PULL TO CLOSE

STOPPER

KNOB HEIGHT
ADJUST

TIGHTEN NUT
FOR FRICTION
ADJUST

HOOK
OR HOLE

TWO POPULAR STYLES OF BUILT-IN BATHROOM
SINK STOPPERS

and through the opened plug to complete the cleanup.

Clean the plug itself before replacing it. If it is badly worn, you are probably better off with a new one than taking a chance on a leak. Attempting to tighten the cap nut too much could strip the threads.

Floor drains. Generally the clogging in a basement or garage floor drain consists of sand, dirt, and lint. Remove the strainer and ladle out as much of the sediment as possible. You may have to chip away a little of the concrete around the strainer to free it. Flush the drain with clean water.

If pressure is needed, try a garden hose. Wrap cloths around the hose where it enters the drain to prevent backflow. You may have to stand on the cloth plug to keep it in place (wear your rubbers!).

Closet Augers

If you have recurring trouble with a blocked toilet bowl, a closet auger or "snake" would be a good invest-

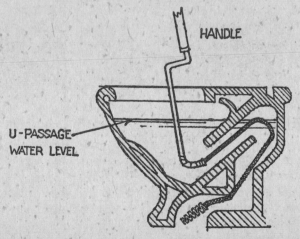

CLOSET AUGER

ment. The tool is so designed that when you rotate a crank handle at one end, a spring-loaded, snakelike wire worms its way through the "U" passage as far as the drain pipe. This "U" passage is restricted and most objects are stopped at the head of the restriction, blocking the passage of flush water.

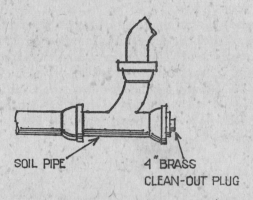

SOIL PIPE   4" BRASS
        CLEAN-OUT PLUG

The auger may also be poked through the clean-out opening of a soil pipe that has become clogged. This opening usually is covered with a four-inch brass plug, which may be removed in the same manner as the plug under a trap (see above). Before replacing the plug, put some water-pump grease around the thread, which will make it easier to open next time.

Septic Tanks

Assuming soil conditions to be suitable, which is determined by a percolation test, a septic tank is a satisfactory way to dispose of sewage in the absence of a municipal sewage system. Problems arise only when the system is overloaded, either by excessive use of water in the household or by neglect of routine maintenance.

A septic tank is simply a watertight tank of masonry

or steel in which sewage solids are allowed time to decompose by bacterial action. The insoluble portions settle to the bottom, while a liquid effluent leaves near the top of the tank to be absorbed by the soil. The absorption is accomplished through a drainage field consisting of large clay pipe beneath the soil laid out with open spaces between the sections.

A septic tank system should be inspected annually and cleaned when about one third of the tank is filled with the combination of sludge at the bottom and scum at the top. This is done by professionals known as "honey dippers" who pump out the tank, leaving a small amount of sludge as "seed" to start the bacterial action anew. On the average, pumping out is required at two- to four-year intervals.

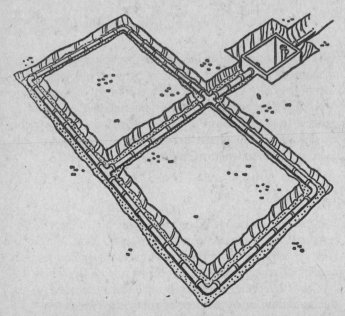

Closed or continuous tile system arrangement for level ground.

Eventually the drainage field may become clogged, in which case the pipes must be dug up and relaid in a new location. Clogging occurs when the soil no longer can absorb the effluent. Soils typically become glutted when a rural area grows urbanized and heavily populated. Since septic tanks do not "purify" sewage—merely condition it for easier absorption—this saturation leads to unsanitary conditions calling for construction of a sewer system.

Grease is the enemy of septic tanks, since it slows the bacterial action. Kitchen grease should be saved in a can and disposed of as garbage rather than poured down a household drain. Another enemy is too much water, as from a home laundry, dishwasher, or garbage disposer. Following are minimum septic tank capacities if you have such equipment; without them the capacity may be safely reduced about one-third.

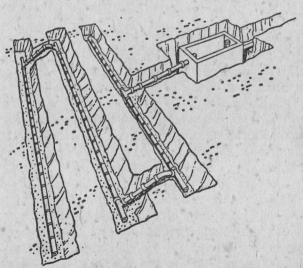

Serial distribution system arrangement for sloping ground.

DRAINAGE FIELD

Table 6-4: Septic Tank Minimum Capacity

No. of persons	No. of bedrooms	Tank capacity
Up to 4	1 or 2	750 gals.
6	3	900 gals.
8	4	1,050 gals.
10	5	1,250 gals.
Each add'l.	—	125 gals.
—	Each add'l.	250 gals.

Septic tank life may be extended by the same precautions that avoid clogged drains—no trash or other insoluble matter, and regular use of drain cleaners to combat grease. Caustics do not impede septic tank action in any way if used in moderate amounts. Trouble usually is signaled by a gurgling in waste pipes or toilet bowl after release into them of a substantial amount of water.

Garden Hose Trickles

While many causes of low water pressure from a garden hose are possible, the commonest is what is called electrolytic action. In an old house the original plumbing may have consisted of galvanized iron pipes that deteriorated and were replaced by copper piping. The garden hose connection may have been left as is to save expense. Thus you would have an iron pipe joined to a copper pipe. These two metals immersed in water react chemically like the metal terminals in a battery. The resulting electrolysis accelerates corrosion.

The best solution is to replace the iron pipe with a copper or plastic one. If this involves tearing out a wall, an alternative is to insert a dialectric fitting between the copper and iron which retards the corrosive effect.

Poor-Tasting Water

In many locations where water comes from a lake or a well, a seasonal phenomenon occurs in the spring and sometimes also in the fall, giving the water a more or less unpleasant odor and taste. It comes from decaying vegetation or from silt stirred up by changing the level of a lake. Usually such contamination is harmless, but to make sure you should collect a sample of the water for testing by the Provincial authorities. The service is free.

The simplest way to improve the taste and smell of otherwise pure water is to install a modern water filter in the kitchen. It requires no extra plumbing. Simply take off the aerator on the faucet and screw on an adapter that comes with the filtering appliance. Whenever you want fresh, clear, springlike water for drinking or cooking, making tea or coffee, etc., a short hose connects the faucet adapter to the filtering machine. At the press of a button, the water may be made to bypass the filter if desired in volume for dishwashing and other household tasks.

How to Purify Water

In certain situations—such as a flood, earthquake, ruptured water main, or when camping—the normal supply of water may become contaminated and unsafe to drink. Terrible diseases ranging from infectious hepatitis to dysentery and typhoid fever can be spread by polluted water. Here are ways to purify it:

1. Strain the water through a clean cloth into a container to remove sediment and floating debris.

2. Boil the water vigorously for at least three minutes.

3. Allow the water to cool. It is now safe to drink.

4. To improve the taste, add a pinch of salt to each quart of water, or aerate it by pouring back and forth from one clean glass into another.

If boiling is not possible, water may be purified with a number of chemicals found in most households or easily obtainable. First, strain the suspected water as in Step 1 above. Then:

2. Add two drops of sodium hypochlorite laundry bleach containing 5 to 6 percent available chlorine (Clorox, Purex, Rose-X, or other brands; consult the label), to each quart of clear water. Make it four drops if water is cloudy. If the amount of available chlorine is not stated on the label, add 10 drops to the clear and 20 drops to the cloudy water.

3. Mix thoroughly by stirring or shaking in a container.

4. Let stand for 30 minutes. The water is safe if a slight chlorine odor is detectable. If not, repeat the dosage and let stand for another 15 minutes.

Instead of chlorine you may use tincture of iodine, two percent, from a first-aid kit or the medicine chest. Add five drops to each quart of clear water or 10 drops to each quart of cloudy water, stir and let stand for 30 minutes.

Chlorine and iodine tablets for purifying water, convenient to carry anywhere, are sold in drugstores and outdoor outfitters. Follow directions on the label.

Chapter 7

AIDS TO A COZY HOME

The two Ws of home maintenance that stand for Workmanship and Wear account for a myriad small jobs—and some large ones—that crop up every day. The Workmanship category may be either negative or positive: errors of omission or commission in the structure of the house; or on the positive side, improvements the present owner would like to make. Wear and its partner Tear, however, are as inevitable as time and tide. Nothing lasts forever.

This chapter presents a miscellany of structural details from basement to attic having to do with comfort, items that often need fixing or could be improved, with tips on what to do or order done for a cozier, more livable home.

Insulation

In our chapters on heating and cooling we refer frequently to insulation as the cure for many problems in those areas. Insulation of roof and walls has the function of keeping heat inside during the winter and outside during the summer. Like the insulation on individual fixtures or pipes, it drastically reduces waste of fuel or power and saves money. It should properly be installed when the house is built—and few houses today are built without it—but in old houses the insulation may have lost efficiency or even be absent. You can detect ineffective roof insulation, for example, when the snow melts off quickly in winter while in summer the attic gets insufferably hot.

Installing insulation without professional help is not difficult in the floor of an unfinished attic, under an attic roof, or under floors reachable from a basement or crawl space. With a bit more sophisticated carpentry, you can add insulation to a wall.

Insulating Materials

Nature provides the finest insulation free of charge: the air. Insulating materials actually are traps for air, on the same order as an animal's fur or a woolen coat. Tiny pockets formed by the fibers or grains of these materials hold air, and thermal effectiveness depends upon how well they do it.

Rock-solid substances are not good thermal insulators; a thick stone wall may be one of the worst. A stiff, board-like material could have fair to good insulating properties if it is internally structured like a honeycomb or sponge; styrofoam is an example. For practical purposes, inexpensive granular or fibrous materials are the choice when covering large areas.

Loose fill consists of mineral wool, vermiculite, or similar stuff worked into loose flakes and sold in large bags. You can insulate the floor of an unfinished attic simply by pouring the fill on the subfloor between the rafters. Wood flooring may be nailed over it later if the attic is to be occupied, but this is not essential for good thermal results.

Many times the built-in insulation of a house wall will consist of loose fill sprayed into the wall from outside—the cheapest way for a builder to do it. The particles of fill tend to settle over the years, losing thermal efficiency as they become compacted by their own weight. Spraying new insulation into the wall would be costly; usually the wall has to be reinsulated in some other way.

Flexible insulation known as *blanket* or *batts* is packaged for easy attachment to a wall or overhead. The blanket comes in a long continuous roll; batts are four to eight feet long and from one to six inches thick. The standard widths are such as to fit between studs 16 inches apart or 24 inches apart. Blanket or batt insulation for a roof should be from three to six inches thick, the latter being recommended with air-conditioning. (It takes more insulation to keep heat out than in, which seems logical in view of the heat potential of the sun as compared to a furnace.) Two-inch thickness is sufficient for a wall.

Flexible insulation should be installed with a vapor barrier facing the inside, heated part of the house. Some batts come with a vapor barrier of asphalt-impregnated paper or reflective foil already attached on one side. The paper wrapping of a batt or blanket extends beyond the width of the enclosed insulation so that it may be readily stapled into place. (Stapling guns may be rented from building supply dealers.)

The *reflective foil* referred to above can act both as vapor barrier and as insulator; it "bounces" the heat back where it came from. Foil is more effective for keeping out the summer heat than as winter insulation, although it may be the best all-around answer in particular cases. Insulating aluminum foil comes in layers that open accordion-fashion to leave air spaces in between; the more layers the better the thermal properties.

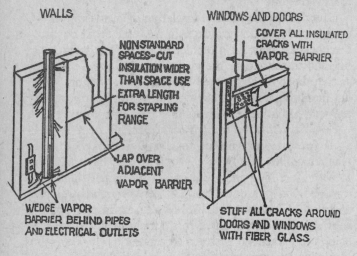

WALLS

NON STANDARD SPACES - CUT INSULATION WIDER THAN SPACE USE EXTRA LENGTH FOR STAPLING RANGE

LAP OVER ADJACENT VAPOR BARRIER

WEDGE VAPOR BARRIER BEHIND PIPES AND ELECTRICAL OUTLETS

WINDOWS AND DOORS

COVER ALL INSULATED CRACKS WITH VAPOR BARRIER

STUFF ALL CRACKS AROUND DOORS AND WINDOWS WITH FIBER GLASS

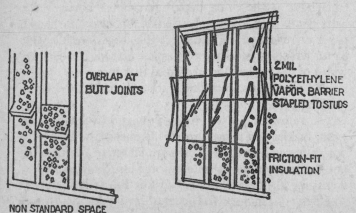

OVERLAP AT BUTT JOINTS

NON STANDARD SPACE

2 MIL POLYETHYLENE VAPOR BARRIER STAPLED TO STUDS

FRICTION-FIT INSULATION

WALLS WITH FRICTION-FIT INSULATION

Spraying loose fill inside an old wall in which the existing insulation has settled not only is costly but most contractors will not guarantee the work. Adding an insulation layer outside the wall may also be costly if it

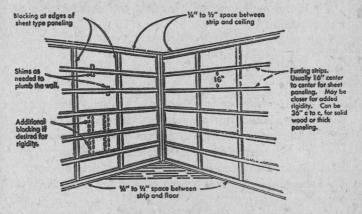

FURRING STRIPS

calls for virtual reconstruction of the siding to maintain good appearance. Assuming that sacrifice of four inches of interior space can be tolerated, the better way is to add new insulation on the inside, as follows:

1. Place 2- × 3-inch studs against the existing wall, either 16 or 24 inches apart, and purchase either 15- or 23-inch thermal resistance batts, 2 inches thick.

2. With a stapling gun, staple the batts to the studs by their paper flanges with the staples no more than 6 inches apart. The vapor barrier side should face the interior of the house, and the flanges should overlap on each stud.

3. Cover the insulation with gypsum board from ⅓-to 1-inch thick. This material has fair insulating properties itself, and comes in decorative finishes similar to wood paneling.

4. The completed job may be covered with plywood, paneling, wallpaper, paint, or any other type of finish desired.

The same technique will insulate the underside of a roof or a floor.

Fireplaces

A fireplace not only enhances the beauty and cozy feeling of a home, but provides an alternative source of heat in the event of a power failure or other incapacitation of the normal system. Fireplace problems in an amazing number of cases are due to faulty design—amazing because the essentials are simple and the faults readily curable.

The accompanying diagrams show the features of a properly constructed fireplace. (See Glossary for a table of measurements.) Most complaints center on smokiness, which may arise from any of these causes:

1. Poor technique in building a fire. Make sure the fire is far enough back to heat the rear wall, which increases the draft and helps to suck smoke and sparks out of (instead of into) the room.

2. Fireplace opening too large for the flue. The flue cross section should be not less than one-twelfth the area of the fireplace opening. To determine whether the proportions are correct, hold a piece of sheet metal or dampened cardboard across the top of a smoking fireplace and gradually lower it, thus making the opening smaller

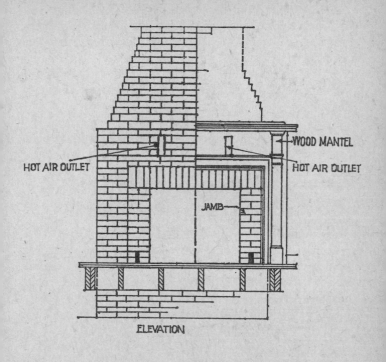

HOT AIR OUTLET

WOOD MANTEL

HOT AIR OUTLET

JAMB

ELEVATION

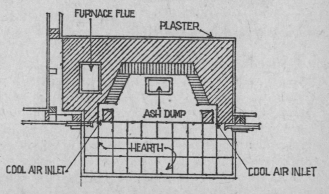

FURNACE FLUE

PLASTER

ASH DUMP

HEARTH

COOL AIR INLET

COOL AIR INLET

DETAILS OF A TYPICAL FIREPLACE

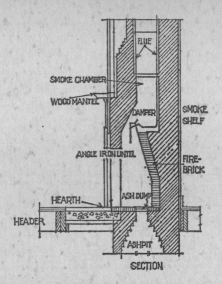

FLUE

SMOKE CHAMBER

WOOD MANTEL

DAMPER

SMOKE SHELF

ANGLE IRON LINTEL

FIRE-BRICK

ASH DUMP

HEARTH

HEADER

ASHPIT

SECTION

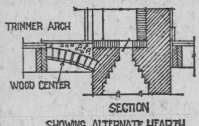

TRIMMER ARCH

WOOD CENTER

SECTION

SHOWING ALTERNATE HEARTH

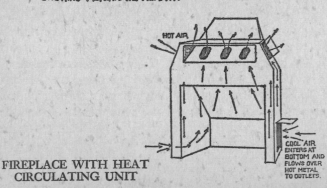

HOT AIR

COOL AIR ENTERS AT BOTTOM AND FLOWS OVER HOT METAL TO OUTLETS.

FIREPLACE WITH HEAT CIRCULATING UNIT

and smaller, until smoke ceases to enter the room. Mark this level with chalk.

Since enlargement of the flue is practically impossible, the answer is to reduce the size of the fireplace opening as you have just measured it. This can be done by raising the hearth, by bringing in the sides with masonry or brick, or by lowering the top with either masonry or a hood.

3. Damper set in place too low. Moving it up is a major operation; instead, lower the top of the fireplace opening and attach a long chain to the damper. You can also get a damper that reaches up about six inches higher than normal, especially designed to cure this common complaint.

4. Too tight a house to supply air to the fire. Efficient weatherstripping, etc., may be sealing off the entry of oxygen. Open a window two or three inches when burning a fire.

5. Warm-air furnace draws away from the fireplace. Here, too, simply open a window.

6. Side-by-side flues may be leaking. To explain this, note that while your fireplace may utilize the same *chimney* as the furnace or a second fireplace, the chimney contains a separate *flue* for each. (Using one flue for both is against fire regulations and building codes.) If leaks occur through uncemented joints between the linings, you will get downdrafts and smoke leaks. Fill all such cracks with waterproof mortar.

7. Chimney too short for proper draft. Raise the chimney with a metal or terra-cotta extension on the cap.

8. Nearby trees or tall buildings or a steep roof line cause wind eddies to blow down the chimney. Extend the flue lining upward with a cement bevel or tile cap, or divert wind currents from the chimney opening with baffles or a venthouse.

VENTHOUSE

9. Structural defects, such as an off-center flue, sharp angle in flue passage, projection of pipes into the flue, or illegal double use of a single flue are among the other possible causes of smokiness. You will need professional help.

10. Sooty chimney. Wood, especially green wood, never is completely consumed by burning and produces quantities of soot. This may collect in the smoke shelf and around the damper so as to cut off part of the draft even when the damper is fully open. Remove as much soot as you can by reaching up into the flue. Also check for fallen bits of brick or mortar, which will call for chimney repair.

A chimney requires periodic cleaning—every year or two, depending on how much the fireplace is used. In cold weather, especially if green wood is burned, creosote forms in the chimney from the acid vapors and water. When creosote ignites, it creates a hot fire. It is difficult to remove, usually must be chipped off with a hoe.

Note: In case creosote or soot cause a chimney fire,

176

throw a large amount of salt on the fire in the fireplace. It blazes up with a hot yellow flame that burns up soot. Then put out the fire on the hearth and hold a wet rug or blanket over the opening to shut off the air. Hopefully this will extinguish or at least check the chimney fire—but while you're doing it, have someone call the fire department.

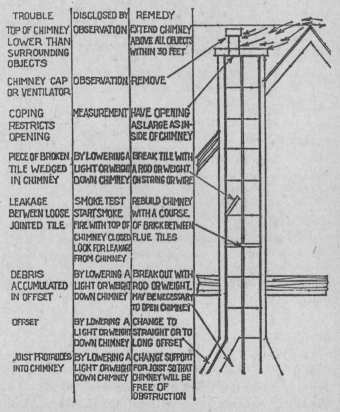

TROUBLE	DISCLOSED BY	REMEDY
TOP OF CHIMNEY LOWER THAN SURROUNDING OBJECTS	OBSERVATION	EXTEND CHIMNEY ABOVE ALL OBJECTS WITHIN 30 FEET
CHIMNEY CAP OR VENTILATOR	OBSERVATION	REMOVE
COPING RESTRICTS OPENING	MEASUREMENT	HAVE OPENING AS LARGE AS INSIDE OF CHIMNEY
PIECE OF BROKEN TILE WEDGED IN CHIMNEY	BY LOWERING A LIGHT OR WEIGHT DOWN CHIMNEY	BREAK TILE WITH A ROD OR WEIGHT ON STRING OR WIRE
LEAKAGE BETWEEN LOOSE JOINTED TILE	SMOKE TEST STARTS SMOKE FIRE WITH TOP OF CHIMNEY CLOSED LOOK FOR LEAKAGE FROM CHIMNEY	REBUILD CHIMNEY WITH A COURSE OF BRICK BETWEEN FLUE TILES
DEBRIS ACCUMULATED IN OFFSET	BY LOWERING A LIGHT OR WEIGHT DOWN CHIMNEY	BREAK OUT WITH ROD OR WEIGHT. MAY BE NECESSARY TO OPEN CHIMNEY
OFFSET	BY LOWERING A LIGHT OR WEIGHT DOWN CHIMNEY	CHANGE TO STRAIGHT OR TO LONG OFFSET
JOIST PROTRUDES INTO CHIMNEY	BY LOWERING A LIGHT OR WEIGHT DOWN CHIMNEY	CHANGE SUPPORT FOR JOIST SO THAT CHIMNEY WILL BE FREE OF OBSTRUCTION

COMMON CHIMNEY TROUBLES—HOW TO DETECT AND REMEDY THEM

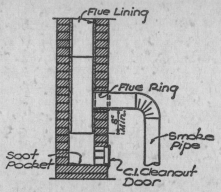

**SOOT POCKET AND CLEANOUT FOR A
CHIMNEY FLUE**

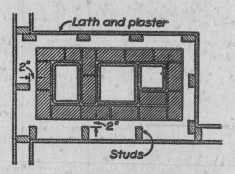

**CHIMNEY PLAN SHOWING PROPER ARRANGEMENT
OF THREE FLUES**

How to Light a Fire

Smoky or ill-burning fireplaces often are simply the result of a city man's lack of experience in igniting wood. Assuming the chimney is all right and the fireplace has a good draft, the following hints may help in avoiding such irritations and to enjoy a crackling hearth.

178

1. Open the damper fully before starting a fire. Forgetting to do so accounts for many a smoked-out family.

2. Don't use green wood; the best firewood is old and seasoned. Green wood, containing up to 40 percent water, will smoke the instant you touch a flame to it. However, if green firewood is available for the asking and you want to take advantage of the money saving, you can speed up the seasoning by stacking a few logs at a time close to the fireplace where the heat will dry them out.

3. Arrange your fire properly. The logs should be of the correct length to lie on the andirons, and preferably no longer. First crumple up some paper toward the back of the fireplace, and on this toss the kindling wood. You don't have to be too neat about it, so long as you use enough kindling and include a handful of small dry twigs or splinters that will catch fire quickly.

4. On this "trash pile" place your largest log on the andiron at the back, a somewhat smaller one in front, and a still smaller one on top of the other two. (*Note:* A single log will not burn. You need at least two so as to trap the rising heat of the kindling between them. For a fast fire three logs are the practical minimum.)

Logs of slightly irregular or knotty shape are best, since they automatically leave an air space between them when laid side by side. If logs are very smooth, move them a bit apart or at a slight angle to one another to provide openings for the draft.

5. Touch a match to the paper at several points, and draw the fire screen. Then find something else to do for a few minutes. When you return, your fire should be burning brightly.

6. Later, when the fire burns low, turn the logs around with a poker or tongs. This will expose unburned, now very dry, portions of the wood to the hot coals under-

neath and quickly revive the blaze. Or add a fresh log on top.

7. If the fire burns too fast, turn the damper to the half-open position. Never shut it completely, however, so long as there is any glow or heat from the remains of a fire.

Water in Basement

A "wet" basement should be distinguished from a "damp" basement. Dampness generally is caused by condensation of moisture in the air inside the house, and may be seasonal. Winter dampness occurs when the basement is warmer than the foundation walls. Summer condensation results from the entry of warm, humid outside air into a cool basement. These problems are generally curable by good humidity control and ventilation, as discussed in our chapters on heating and cooling.

A wet basement is something else again. Here actual liquid water penetrates the basement from outside, in one of two ways. *Leakage* is a flow of water coming in through joints and cracks or other defects in the walls and floors. *Seepage* is a capillary action by which water creeps slowly through weak spots in masonry or concrete. It can even creep upward through a solid concrete slab, which is why such construction should include a vapor barrier underneath the slab.

The cure for these is (1) drainage, to prevent excess water accumulation in the ground outside the foundation walls, and (2) waterproofing.

Draining a Flood

First let us consider the emergency situation of a real flood. It can happen even to a normally dry basement in a year when heavy snows are followed by a quick spring thaw, or after a prolonged period of torrential rains that saturate the soil. The water pours in to a depth of several inches or even several feet.

If the basement has a floor drain, the flood water will eventually flow out through it, but if the drain leads only to water-saturated soil, this may take a long time. To avoid heavy damage to basement contents and to restore the space to usefulness, you will probably want to drain it quickly.

Hopefully you can get the fire department to send a pumper—if they're not overwhelmed with calls at such a time—but their large-size equipment might still leave several inches of water on the floor. If you have or can get the use of a gasoline pump, set it up outside the house with a hose on the outlet to direct the water downgrade. Use a garden hose for the inlet with its open end immersed in the flood. You may need something to hold it down. Pump out as much water as possible and mop up the rest.

On sloping land you can rig up a siphon to remove water without the aid of a pump. You will need long hoses in order to get a substantial difference in grade: that is, the outlet (downhill) end of the hose must be at least a few feet lower than the basement floor. Siphoning will lift water by atmospheric pressure from the basement floor to window level. At that point gravity takes over and the water runs downhill.

To set up the siphon, fill a garden hose with water from the tap and close its nozzle without closing the tap. Carry the closed nozzle end as far downhill as it will go. Carefully remove the other end from the tap, trying not to spill water out of the hose. Close the tap. Note that the hose must be *completely full of water* to start the siphoning action. Shut this end with a clamp. Immerse the clamped end in the flood water, with something to hold it submerged. Remove the clamp.

If you now open the nozzle of the hose at the down-hill end, and you have enough difference in grade, the water should run out and continue to run so long as the intake end remains submerged. Don't let anyone step on the hose or run over it with a vehicle while it is siphoning. That will break the vacuum and oblige you to repeat the whole procedure.

On ground that is too level for direct siphoning, you can use the same principle partway. Place a large empty garbage can on a crate or stairway near a basement window so that the can is higher than ground level. Enlist the family to dip water from the floor with pails or old kitchen pans and pour it into the garbage can. Then use the garden hose as above to siphon the water out of the can to the outside. Do not let it completely empty the can; start refilling while the hose end is still submerged. Exposing an open hose to the atmosphere will break the siphon.

Drainage

Seepage of water is less dramatic than a direct leak, made evident by spreading damp spots where the basement floor meets the foundation wall, especially at corners. Since seepage closely resembles dampness due to condensation, make a test to decide which it is.

Stick a small mirror or piece of glass on a damp spot overnight, using a wad of chewing gum to hold it. Next morning, if the glass is fogged the cause is condensation. If the glass is clear though the wall remains damp, the problem is seepage.

Walk around outside the house looking for clues to inadequate drainage. The slope of the ground surface should always be away from the foundation, never toward it. If dripping water has cut a trough alongside the house, the roof gutter and drainspout system are defective or clogged, and overflow in each heavy rain.

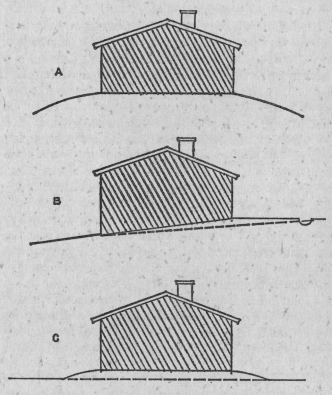

SELECTION OF A BUILDING SITE

A. Elevated site provides good surface drainage away from the house in all directions.

B. Drainage can be routed around a sidehill-located house (note drainage ditch on uphill side).

C. On a flat site, the ground around the house must be built up to drain water away from the basement walls.

First improve the grading if you can; piling an inch or two of dirt against the foundation or planting it with thick sod will help. On a steep slope it may be necessary to dig a rain gutter—a shallow ditch lined with tiles—on the uphill side to divert water around the house, as campers do when pitching a tent.

Next check the roof gutters and downspouts. The gutters should be protected by wire screening from falling leaves, etc., or repeatedly cleaned of such debris. Each downspout should empty on a stone or concrete splash pan or on pavement, and if this is not sufficient to carry water well away from the house, into a dry well.

A dry well is simply a large hole in the ground filled with stones and covered with planks or a cement slab to hold a layer of sod above it. Another way is to fill the hole with a hollow square of concrete blocks. Both schemes are designed to keep out topsoil while the drainage water percolates deeper into the ground.

If gutters and drainspouts are functioning properly, yet seepage into the basement persists, one may suspect the dry wells are "loaded"—cluttered with decaying vegetation. They must then be dug out and reconstructed.

When a house has been built in exceptionally damp soil—not infrequent on filled lands, reclaimed swamps, etc.—the house will need a drainage system specifically for its foundation. This consists of a line of four- or six-inch perforated clay, plastic, or fiber pipes, laid end to

DRAINAGE
(See opposite page)

(1) Vertical downspouts collect water from gutters on the roof which can be discharged into drainage pipes.

(2) Slope pipes a ½ inch downward per foot and run into a storm sewer or dry well. This helps prevent water from flowing back into basement.

(3) A dry well may be constructed of concrete blocks in the form of a hollow square (as illustrated) to keep out top soil.

184

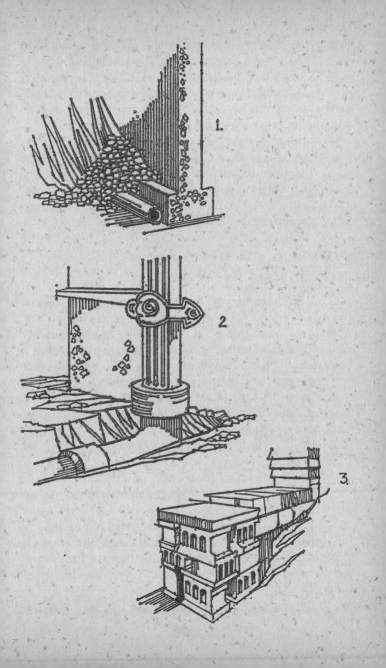

end at the bottom of a trench dug down parallel to the foundation footings. The trench is then covered over.

If such pipes slope downward one-half inch per foot, and drain into a storm sewer or dry well, they will effectively prevent water from flowing toward the basement and building up enough hydraulic pressure to penetrate it.

The old-time farmer's antidote to wet soil takes a little longer to "manufacture." Plant a weeping willow in the yard. This tree thrives on underground water, soaks up huge quantities with its widespread root system, and evaporates it into the air. However in time the roots may grow and penetrate the drainage system.

Waterproofing

The best time to waterproof a basement is, of course, when the house is being built. If the job is done later, the foundation must be exposed down to the footings, and scrubbed clean to remove all dirt and sand.

A heavy coat of asphalt, mastic, or hot tar is then troweled over the outside surface, forming a waterproof membrane. This membrane should be reinforced with a coat of glass fabric in vulnerable areas such as corners and bends. For best results, two layers of membrane should be applied, with a layer of heavy roofing felt in between.

When the foundation consists of concrete block, a double coat of Portland cement plaster must be applied before the asphalt primer.

Waterproofing may also be accomplished from the inside by the use of certain special materials (ordinary cement paints will not be effective). One is a heavy-duty powdered cement which is mixed with water and applied liberally with a heavy brush.

The wall must be clean and porous for this treatment.

An old surface of oil or latex paint will have to be removed. A finish is porous enough for the cement paint if a little water splashed over the wall doesn't run right off but soaks in. All holes and cracks should be patched with quick-setting cement after chipping out loose material with a chisel.

A handier—but more expensive—waterproofing material consists of an epoxy resin in two parts that are mixed just before using. With epoxy, the wall needs no special preparation other than cleaning out and patching the cracks. Applying the epoxy just along the joint where walls meet the floor, rather than over the entire surface, may often be sufficient to halt the seepage. Two coats are required.

Sticking Doors

Moisture will cause wood to swell, and if it swells where a door fits into its frame, the door will stick or bind. The obvious cure might seem to be planing down the edges of the door to make it fit, but in fact this drastic measure should be a last resort. Once the door is planed down, it can never be restored to its original dimensions. When the wood dries, a planed door may be too loose, leaving gaps around the edges for drafts and sounds.

In most cases the sticking door—even if caused by swelling or by settling of the door frame—can be cured by adjusting or, if necessary, repairing the hinges. Even a small amount of play in a loose hinge will be magnified by the length of the door, permitting the door to hang obliquely enough to run against a corner. Here is the best procedure for dealing with the problem.

1. Try each of the hinge screws with a screwdriver. Tighten any that are loose. If a screw won't tighten be-

cause the hole has been gouged out, remove the screw and hammer a wooden plug into the hole. Or fill the hole with matchsticks dipped in glue. Then reinsert and tighten the screw.

2. If hinges are tight but the door still sticks, find the exact place where the rubbing occurs. Close the door and insert a sheet of thin cardboard along the edge, sliding it around until it binds. That point will usually be near one of the outside corners, top or bottom.

3. *Bottom corner sticks.* Open door wide and prop it up with a book or piece of wood. Remove the lower hinge. Cut a piece of cardboard to the right size and slip it behind the hinge as a shim before screwing the hinge back into place. This will push the lower part of the door a fraction of an inch forward, raising the bottom to keep it from rubbing.

4. *Top corner sticks.* Shim out the upper hinge rather than the lower.

5. *Door resists closing.* Cut cardboard shims only half the width of the hinges and insert them under the back half of the hinge leaf, near the pin. This will tilt the hinges a trifle so that the door swings all the way around into the latch.

6. Now check the operation of the door. It may be necessary to shim with two thicknesses of cardboard instead of one, or to add a half-shim to a whole one, or to shim both hinges until a successful combination is found.

7. If adjusting the hinges doesn't solve the problem, or if a door rubs along its entire length or width, then the door must be removed, planed down to proper size, and reset. To remove a door, prop it in a partly open position, then drive the hinge pins upward with a hammer and screwdriver.

Note: If the sticking or rubbing is not caused by the

door itself but by a rug or carpeting, you can install a special type of hinge that lifts the door as it opens.

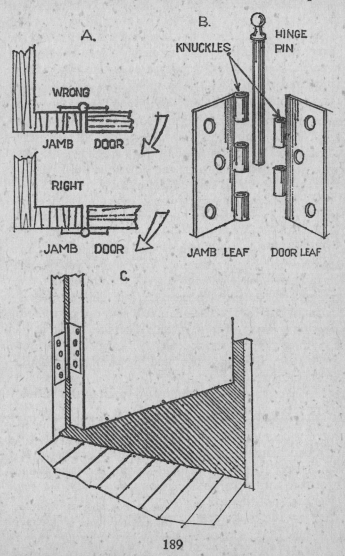

A.

WRONG

JAMB   DOOR

RIGHT

JAMB   DOOR

B.

KNUCKLES

HINGE PIN

JAMB LEAF   DOOR LEAF

C.

This provides clearance for the rug without altering the proper set of the (closed) door in its frame.

Sticking Windows

Dampness affects the wood of windows just as it does doors. If a window appears to be stuck because of swelling, check the stop molding first. This is the wooden strip that holds the window in its groove. Open the window sash wide, prying it past the sticking point if necessary. Put a wooden block against the stop molding and tap it with a hammer. Do this up and down the full length of the molding on both sides of the window.

Also lubricate the vertical tracks with any of the compounds sold for this purpose, or by rubbing them with a paraffin candle.

Hardened paint will cause windows to stick, often as the aftermath of redecorating. To free the window, first run a razor blade along the edge of the stop molding, to preserve a clean edge for the paint job. This may be sufficient; if not, force a flat edged tool such as a putty knife into the aperture. Tap it in with a hammer while at the same time twisting the tool slightly to pry the two surfaces apart. Do this all around the window until the sash comes free.

If you must pry the window open from the bottom, work from the outside if possible to preserve the interior trim. The head of a hatchet or axe is stronger for this purpose than a putty knife. Tap it gently into the crack at several points in succession, lifting the hatchet by the handle a little at a time until the sash can be raised.

Finally, chisel away the paint along the stop molding where it grips the window. Smooth it with sandpaper.

Broken Sash Cords

Double-hung windows generally are made today with spring-loaded counterbalances that are less vulnerable to breaking than the older type with sash cords and weights. In an old house broken sash cords are a common problem because the ropes deteriorate over the years. Replacing them is a much simpler job than might at first appear. About all you need is a large screwdriver.

1. Carefully pry off the stop molding, avoiding damage so that the piece can be used again.

2. Lift out the sash, holding the unbroken cord tightly. Remove the cord from the sash and clip a clothespin just above the knot (or push a nail through the knot) to prevent the cord being pulled into the weight pocket.

3. Remove the access panel cover to expose the sash weights on the inside. You may have to locate this panel under layers of paint by tapping with a hammer to reveal the outlines. The cover generally is held in place with one or two screws.

4. Fish out the lost sash weight. Remove the old cord and cut a new one to the same length. Preferably, replace the cord with metal sash chain, which should last a lifetime. Secure the opposite end with a knot (in cord) or a nail (in chain) to keep it from slipping through the pulley at the top.

5. Pull the cord or chain through the access opening and attach the weight. Replace the weight in the pocket and then the cover.

6. Get the sash in a position where you can easily release the cords and replace the knotted ends.

7. Replace the window in its track and check its operation before replacing the stop molding.

8. At the same time replace the sash cord that is *not* broken, since it is probably stretched or frayed and about due to cause trouble.

9. Lubricate the pulleys with graphite dust, which comes in a tube that can be pressed to blow the dust into place.

Replacing Windowpanes

Windows may become loose as well as too tight, causing the glass panes to rattle and shake in a brisk breeze or whenever a big truck rumbles by. The cause generally is the drying and shrinking of the putty, especially in a house with inadequate humidity control. Replacing the putty involves some of the same procedure as replacing a broken windowpane, which is described in steps as follows:

1. Wear heavy work gloves. Pull the broken pieces straight out in the plane of the window; not at right angles to it, although you may have to rock a piece gently back and forth to free it from the hardened putty. Have a container ready to receive the broken pieces with the least possible handling.

2. Scrape out all of the old putty with a chisel. You may have to tap the chisel with a hammer, taking care not to gouge or chip the wood of the frame.

3. With a pliers pull out all glazier's points, which are triangular bits of metal used to hold the glass in place. If the frame is metal, pry out the spring clips or glazing strips with a screwdriver.

4. Clean out the grooves with a brush. Then paint them with boiled linseed oil or a coat of thinned house paint. This primer helps keep the glazing compound from drying out and assures a better bond.

5. Have a pane of glass cut to size, about one-eighth inch smaller in each dimension than the actual size of the opening. This provides clearance for easier installation and for expansion or irregularities in the frame.

6. Apply a thin layer of putty or glazing compound to the grooves. Known as a "bed," it prevents leakage around the edges of the glass.

7. Press the glass into the prepared bed. Drive glazier's points into the frame on all four sides. Two on each side will suffice for a small pane, three or four for larger glass. They are driven in with a hammer and a special tool that comes with a package of points, or else pushed in with the side of a screwdriver. Whether points, spring clips, or glazing strips are used, they must be anchored firmly to hold the glass in place. (Putty doesn't hold the glass, merely seals it weathertight.)

8. Putty is made with linseed oil; glazing compound is an improvement made with nondrying oils. In either case, roll the material into long strips about the thickness of a pencil. Lay a strip in the groove along the edge of the glass, and press into position with a putty knife. Give it a bevel edge, high enough to match the level of the molding on the interior side.

9. Cut off excess putty to leave a straight edge. Smudges on the glass can be removed with turpentine after the putty dries, a day or two later. Then paint the putty, allowing about one-sixteenth inch of paint to flow onto the glass, assuring a good seal. Excess paint can be scraped off later with a razor blade.

Sagging Floors

When windows stick and doors jam shut despite all efforts to free them up, and if plaster keeps cracking no matter how frequently patched, a sagging floor may be

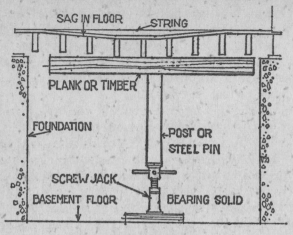

SAGGING FLOOR

suspected. The condition frequently results from major alterations that change the weight distribution of the house, and sometimes from the placing of heavy furniture or equipment, such as a piano.

Check the basement girders with a carpenter's level and a long straightedge. Check the floor above in the same way, or simply put down two or three children's marbles and see if they all roll in the same direction. In the basement look for signs of cracking or rotting especially at points where beams meet or rest on support posts and the foundation.

A sagging beam can be jacked up with a telescopic post that works on the same principle as an automobile jack. These are available in many sizes, are easily installed and not costly. The most important thing to know about them is that installation may be easy but must also be done with patience and precision.

First position the base of the post at the desired point and extend the telescoping section until the top just fits tightly against the sagging girder—but *without* any lifting pressure. Check the post with a carpenter's level to be sure it is standing straight. Affix the top plate to the overhead beam so it will not slip, then turn up the screw until just enough pressure is applied to hold the post secure. Then let it alone for at least 24 hours.

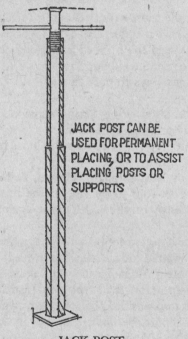

JACK POST

Next day check the plumb of the jack post again. If it's straight, give the screw one-half turn—*no more*. The post must be jacked up very slowly and cautiously, no more than half a turn *per week*. It may take months to correct the sag in your floor. If you try to hurry the job, serious damage could result—to the beam, to plaster, to the basement floor, to plumbing and gas lines. Take it easy!

Squeaky Floors

When a floor squeaks every time someone steps on a certain spot, the cause may be sagging (see page 195) or, more likely, that a single board has worked loose. The trouble may be in the finished hardwood floor (the upper layer), or in the subflooring where it rests on the joists. Here are ways to cure this.

1. Locate the squeak by having someone walk on the floor while you listen from below.
2. Drive a thin wedge between the loose board and the joist that supports it.
3. If the floorboard bulges upward, nail a supporting block of two-by-four to the side of the joist, after forcing the top edge of the block tight against the floorboards.
4. Bridging (the pieces between joists that cross in an X) may be omitted, or not nailed into place, or working loose. Carpenters often install bridging in a new house but conveniently forget to nail it in place. Before nailing a bridge into position, hammer it upward as high as possible to support the floor. You may need a combination of bridging and wedges.
5. If you cannot get at the floor from below, as in a finished basement, first try squirting a powdered lubricant into cracks between the boards. The lubricant is dry, stainless, and obtainable in most hardware stores.
6. Working from above, nail the loose board into a joist. (Locate a joist by tapping with a hammer; the spaces between joists will sound hollow.) Use three-inch

finishing nails driven in at an angle forming a "V." Finish with a nailset to avoid damaging the floor.

Replacing a Lock

In these security-conscious times, replacing a front-door or back-door lock—or any that guard ingress to the house—is not a do-it-yourself job. It should be left to a professional locksmith. Locks on interior doors can be installed by the homeowner, or doorknobs replaced either because they don't work or for decorative reasons.

New locks come with installment kits and detailed instructions, with a cardboard template for positioning the lock on the door. Often the trickiest part is to remove the *old* lock when the hardware holding it in place is concealed.

Begin with the inside knob. Look for a set screw, loosen it, and either slide the knob off the spindle or unscrew it. Also unscrew and remove the decorative plate (escutcheon), which may be a separate piece or permanently attached to the knob.

If there is no set screw, look for a small catch on the shank of the knob; press it down to release the knob. Sometimes the catch will be visible through a small hole only if you turn the knob to the right position. Press this down with a nail. The escutcheon plate also might be held by a tiny catch, or it may have a slot for prying it off with a screwdriver.

With the knob and outside trim removed, a mounting plate may be revealed as well as the latch mechanism itself. These are held by visible screws that are removed so the plates may be pried off.

If there is nothing wrong with the lock except that it sticks, try lubricating it with powdered graphite blown in through the keyhole, spread on the latch bolt, or spread on the key. If this is not sufficient, remove the entire assembly and wash in gasoline. Apply a very small film of cup grease over the working parts before replacing. Do not overgrease; often it is grease accumulating and becoming clogged with dirt that causes the sticking.

Window Shades

If a window shade won't roll up when you want it to, chances are the spring needs winding. Pull the shade down all the way; remove it from the window; wind it up by hand; and replace. This winds up the spring and increases the tension. Simply be careful when reinserting the roller in its brackets not to jog the flat pin at one end so that it unwinds by itself.

If the shade snaps up too fast, do just the opposite. Raise the shade as far as it will go; unroll about halfway down by hand; and replace.

The lazy man's way: To tighten a shade, poke the cord over the top of the roller, down in back of it, and over again two or three times. To unwind the shade, poke the cord around the roller from back to front.

The mechanism of a window shade can get dirt-clogged or bent, correctable with cleaning and a pair of pliers. But since this usually does not happen until the fabric is worn or faded anyway, and since they are inexpensive, the simplest repair is to install new shades.

Squeaking Stairs

Stair squeaks, like floor squeaks, usually are caused by a loose tread scraping against the top of the riser or one of the stringers that support it. Have someone stand on

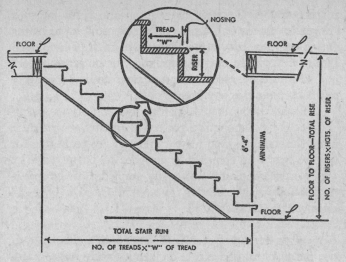

ANGLE OF STAIRS AND TOTAL STAIR RUN

the offending tread to hold it down, then drive two finishing nails at a V-angle into the riser (vertical board) or stringer (side board). But first check the riser to see if it has been kicked loose from the tread immediately below it; nail it tight from underneath.

Wedging may be used instead of nailing, by driving a thin wooden wedge coated with glue into each loose joint until it is snug.

Cracks in Plaster

When cracks appear in the plaster of walls or ceiling, the homeowner begins to worry that his house is "settling." Of course it is "settling," since there is no such thing as an absolutely solid plot of ground or a structure utterly free of strains and stresses or shrinkage. But there is no cause for alarm. The house is not going to fall down.

Since cracks in plaster are a symptom of fundamental unevenness in the house structure, they do tend to persist and to reappear even after being patched or painted over. Hence if they are not too unsightly or bothersome, the homeowner is wise to ignore the cracks until he intends to repaint the room in any event.

The material used for repairing hairline plaster cracks is spackling compound, a plaster-like material that dries more slowly than true plaster and remains malleable for several hours. It comes in a powder to be mixed with water or as a paste to be directly applied. For the spackling job you will need a putty knife and a beer-can opener. Proceed as follows.

1. With the can opener or the corner of a chisel, scrape out the crack to widen it and clean it of any loose, crumbling material.

2. Undercut the crack, making it narrower at the surface than it is underneath, with an overhang on both sides. Without this step, the bond between your patch and the wall may be too weak to hold it in place. After undercutting remove dust and scraps of plaster with a brush.

3. Pick up some spackling compound on the putty knife and apply it at an oblique angle across the crack, holding the knife almost flat against the wall. Make a second stroke in the opposite direction and continue crisscrossing to press the compound into the crack and leave a smooth finish. Apply a second coat if necessary.

4. If a crack or hole is more than about one-quarter inch wide when cleaned out, you will need plaster for patching rather than the spackling compound. Clean out the opening and brush with clean water. Fill the opening with plaster about halfway. Allow this layer to dry, then apply a second coat. Finish off the job with a surface of spackling compound.

5. If your probing removes crumbling plaster right down to the underlying lath (wood, woven metal, or gypsum board), you will need several layers of patching plaster. Wet down each hardened layer before applying the next. For a wide opening, a plasterer's trowel will do a better job than the putty knife. Bear down hard on the rear edge of the trowel as it rubs across the surface. For the first foundation layer, if the opening is large enough, you can use a piece of plaster board cut to size and nailed to the lath.

6. When a hole goes clear through the wall, revealing no lath underneath (for example, behind a light fixture after it is removed), you can supply backing for the plaster patch in one of two ways. Assuming the hole exposes one or more studs, nail plasterboard to the studs. If not, and you do not wish to enlarge the hole excessively, stuff the opening with tightly wadded sheets of newspaper until the paper grips the back edge of the wall. Apply the first layer of plaster on top of this paper.

7. Do not try to hurry the job by filling a deep hole with a single thick layer of plaster. Such a layer will shrink as it dries, and often crack or even fall out. Also, do not hesitate to remove all areas of weak old plaster, even if you have to chip away quite a bit of it before reaching solid ground.

Chapter 8

ELECTRICAL REPAIRS

Unless a homeowner has special knowledge of electricity
and its mysterious ways, he is well advised to leave major
electrical work to a licensed electrician. He should not
attempt to rewire a house, install additional circuits, or
repair complicated appliances. Even if he avoids an electric shock while doing the work, he might leave an improperly wired or poorly repaired circuit that could be
dangerous later on. At the same time, there are many repairs not much more difficult than replacing a light bulb
and completely safe if precautions are taken.

The instantaneous energy we call electricity has never
been completely understood, not even by Professor Ein-
stein. As a practical matter, however, it obeys fairly
simple rules, something like water under pressure in a
pipe.

The current flows through a wire and will flow into

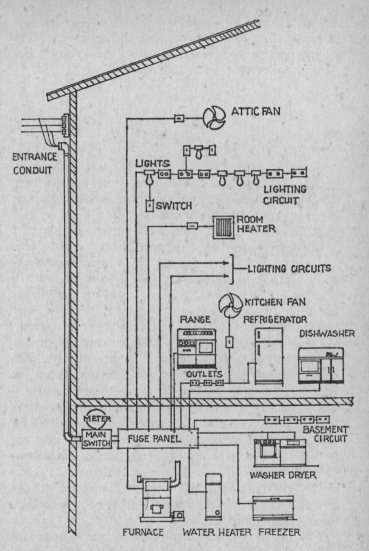

HOUSE WIRING SYSTEM

any other conductive material that touches the wire, such as metals or water. Materials that do not conduct electricity, notably rubber and the air, are used to insulate the wire—prevent it from escaping.

Electric Circuits

Electricity will flow only through a complete circuit. In a typical electric cord one wire carries current to an appliance, where its energy is dissipated in light, heat, or motive power. This "hot" wire is colored black or red. A second wire colored white is the return, or "ground." It is connected to a water pipe or metal structure of the house in contact with the earth, which completes the circuit back to the powerhouse.

In a three-wire cord, the black or red one is again the hot wire and the other two are grounds, whatever their color. The extra ground wire contributes to greater safety in the handling of power tools and other appliances.

Normally the current flow in a ground wire (also called return or negative) is harmless, since its energy has been dissipated. It is analogous to the return flow of a hot-water heating system, where cooled water goes back to the furnace after it has given up its heat. But if a ground wire or other conductor should contact the hot wire through frayed or cracked insulation or in the presence of water, then the flow of current would "short-circuit" the appliance. Current would flow directly to the ground and if you became part of the circuit by contact, directly through your body.

This, briefly, is the basic reason for extremely careful handling of all electrical work, and for the modern three-wire system.

30 AMPERES MAY BE ONLY 120 VOLT	60 AMPERES 120 AND 240 VOLT	100 AMPERES 120 AND 240 VOLT
A 30 AMP. FUSE TYPE MAIN SWITCH	A 60 AMP. FUSE TYPE COMBINATION MAIN SWITCH AND BRANCH CIRCUIT PANEL	COMBINATION MAIN BREAKER AND BRANCH CIRCUIT PANELS
A 30 AMP. COMBINATION MAIN BREAKER AND BRANCH CIRCUIT PANEL	A 60 AMP. COMBINATION MAIN BREAKER AND BRANCH CIRCUIT PANEL	150- AND 200-AMPERE PANELS ARE LARGER BUT SIMILAR IN APPEARANCE TO 100 AMPERE PANEL (PANELS OF THESE CAPACITIES VARY IN APPEARANCE. THE EXACT RATING IS SHOWN ON THE LABEL.)
TOTAL SUPPLY: 3,600 WATTS	14,500 WATTS	24,000 WATTS

FUSE BOX

Amps, Volts, and Watts

The load, or amount of current, that a wire carries is measured in amperes, or "amps" for short. An appliance will "draw" a stated number of amps, which means that the wire will attempt to carry as much current as required by all the lights, etc., connected to it.

An overloaded wire develops heat. The heating coil of an electric heater is essentially a deliberately overloaded wire that is said to have "high resistance." A fuse is a soft wire inserted in the circuit that will melt and break the circuit if overloaded.

The force behind the current, comparable to pressure in a water pipe, is measured in volts. The voltage in a circuit accounts for the wallop of an electric shock and for sparking. Power is measured in watts, equal to volts times amperes. An appliance using two amps of electricity delivered at 110 volts will consume 220 watts. A kilowatt/hour, the unit of cost, equals 1,000 watts per hour; hence your 220-watt appliance would consume 0.22 kwh if you operated it for one hour.

House current today nearly always is 60-cycle AC—meaning alternating current that flows in one direction, then the other, 60 times each second. Direct current (DC) flows in one direction only and is generally found in low-voltage applications such as a flashlight or battery-operated radio. When an appliance requires DC from house current, such as a television set or a radio, it is converted from AC by means of a transformer or rectifier tube.

Table 8-1a: Wattages of Appliances

Appliance	Wattage
Automatic toaster	1,100 watts
Broiler-rotisserie	1,320–1,650 watts
Coffeemaker	Up to 1,100 watts
Deep-fat fryer	1,350 watts
Waffle iron	Up to 1,100 watts
Electric skillet	1,100 watts
Mixer	100 watts

Radio	100 watts
Television	300 watts
Ventilating fan	100 watts
Electric roaster	1,650 watts
Refrigerator*	150 watts
Automatic hand iron	1,000 watts
Ironer	1,650 watts
Floor lamp	150–300 watts
Table lamp	50–150 watts
Vacuum cleaner	125 watts
Fluorescent lights (each tube)	15–40 watts
Portable heater	1,000 watts
Portable electric fan	100 watts
Electric blanket	200 watts

The following appliances normally are connected to individual circuits rather than to general-purpose wall outlets.

Table 8-1b: Wattages of Appliances

Appliance	Wattage
Electric range	8,000–16,000 watts
Electric oven	4,000 watts
Electric water heater	2,000–4,500 watts
Oil burner mechanism	800 watts
Dishwasher	1,000 watts
Waste-disposer	500 watts
Automatic washer	700 watts
Electric clothes dryer	4,500–9,000 watts
Home freezer	350 watts
Water pump	700 watts
Built-in room heater	1,000–1,500 watts
Room airconditioner (¾ ton)	1,200 watts

* Each time a refrigerator starts, it takes several times this wattage for an instant.

Safety in Grounding

Besides completing each circuit, the house grounding system has the important function of providing a safe path for lightning charges that may strike the outdoor power lines. All metal outlet boxes and cable conduits, as well as the return wire, are connected to the common house ground. However, a wall switch may not be grounded unless the installation also includes a convenience outlet.

The three-wire system became advisable, and nowadays is usually required by building codes, with the growth of power tools and other portable appliances. Suppose a short circuit developed in such a tool while you were using it, creating contact between the hot wire and the metal frame of the tool. With the two-wire system, you would instantly become the "ground," attracting the shorted current through your body. So the third wire

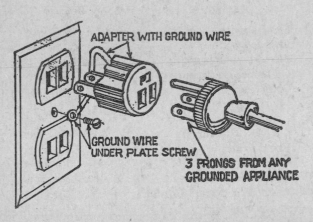

ADAPTING WALL OUTLET TO THREE WIRES

connects the frame of the tool directly to the ground in the house wiring system at the wall outlet. The only damage then in case of a short would be a blown fuse.

In order to plug a three-pronged cord into a standard outlet that accepts only two prongs, you will need an adapter. It has the usual two prongs, plus a short length of wire (often colored green) with a clip on the end of it. After loosening the screw that holds the outlet box in place, insert the clip under the head and retighten the screw. This completes the ground connection for which the third prong and wire are intended.

Caution: Always disconnect an appliance from the power source before attempting even the simplest repair. If working on a wall fixture, unscrew the fuse or open the circuit breaker in its circuit. The danger lies in accidental grounding through the body, and of course the action of electricity comes too fast to duck.

Never remove the back cover of a television set *even if unplugged*, since certain of its components build up a high voltage independent of the house current.

Fuses and Circuit Breakers

When a fuse blows, the cause may be either overloading the circuit (too many lights and appliances plugged in), or a short circuit that overloads the wires when current flows directly to the ground. Frequent fuse-blowing in the absence of a short circuit generally indicates inadequate wiring.

Do not try to correct an overloaded circuit with a larger fuse. Circuits serving lights and wall outlets usually are designed to carry 15 or 20 amperes. Major equipment is best supplied with separate circuits. While the need is self-evident in the high wattage of electric ranges and other heat devices, it also applies to motors that momentarily draw heavy current when they start. These would include the furnace, airconditioner, and refrigerator.

If more circuits are added, the supply of current entering the house may have to be increased. Thus, a 60-amp main switch can accommodate only four 15-amp circuits with their fuses. Putting a larger fuse in each circuit would only cause the wiring to overheat and destroy the insulation, an invitation to fire.

In order to trace the cause of a blown fuse (or a tripped circuit breaker, which has the same electrical effect), first disconnect all lamps and appliances served by that circuit. In Chapters 2 and 6 we recommended posting a list at the fuse box showing which outlets each circuit served; now you can see why.

After turning off all the lights, etc., insert a new fuse. If the new fuse immediately blows, the trouble is a short in the house wiring, not in any particular appliance or fixture.

If the new fuse holds, plug in the appliances and turn on lights in the suspected area one at a time. Wait a minute or two before turning each one off. The trouble will be in the fixture that causes the fuse to blow.

If you can plug in all the appliances without mishap, but after a couple of minutes the fuse blows anyway, the circuit probably is intact but overloaded. One or more of the outlets must be left unused, or shifted to another circuit with a smaller total wattage load.

If all the lights in the house go out at one time, first check to see if the whole neighborhood is without power. Should that be the case, unplug all appliances to protect them when the power surges back on again. If the blackout is confined to your house only, it usually indicates that one of your main cartridge fuses has blown. Changing this is preferably left to an electrician, since it may be a sign of major problems beyond the homeowner's scope.

A circuit breaker is a switch with built-in controls that open it automatically when the line is overloaded. To reset it you merely flip the switch back to the closed or ON position. Of course, if it pops open again you must suspect the same problems as with a blown main fuse.

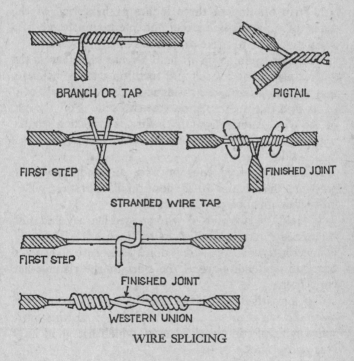

BRANCH OR TAP   PIGTAIL

FIRST STEP   FINISHED JOINT

STRANDED WIRE TAP

FIRST STEP

FINISHED JOINT

WESTERN UNION

WIRE SPLICING

Splicing a Wire

Whenever in the course of a repair it is necessary to remove a wire, the general rule is to observe the way it was attached and put it back the same way. But if a wire must be cut and then attached to another wire, splicing the two ends should be done with electrical efficiency in mind.

Assuming that the wire will not be subject to strain, as inside an outlet or junction box, the "pigtail" splice is a simple but secure electrical contact:

1. Strip off one to three inches of insulation of the wires to be joined. Be careful not to cut any strands of a twisted wire or to make deep nicks in a solid wire.

One way to do this is to hold a razor blade across the wire while rolling it back and forth on a table, making a shallow cut around the insulation. Use fingernails or a pliers to break the insulation free and slide it off the end of the wire. Another way is to slit the insulation lengthwise with a razor blade or pocket knife and peel it like a banana skin.

2. Rub the bared ends of wire on sandpaper or in emery cloth to remove oxidation and discoloration, which interfere with good electrical contact.

3. Hold the two ends of wire crossed like a V and push them into a plastic connector or "wire nut." Twist the connector tight and the job is done. Make sure no exposed bare wire extends beyond the skirt of the thimble-like connector.

4. Alternatively, in the absence of a plastic connector, twist the wires together with a pliers. Wrap the entire splice with plastic electrical tape, which has good insulating properties.

When repairing an appliance or lamp cord that may have to endure some pulling on it, a double-twist or "Western Union" splice is better than the simple pigtail. Each end is separately twisted around the other wire as illustrated, and the whole wrapped in electrical tape. To avoid a wide bulge in the cord and a possible short circuit, cut the two wires at points about four inches apart so the splices will not overlap.

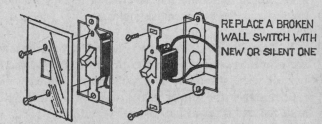

REPLACE A BROKEN WALL SWITCH WITH NEW OR SILENT ONE

1 TWO SCREWS REMOVE COVER   2 TWO SCREWS REMOVE SWITCH

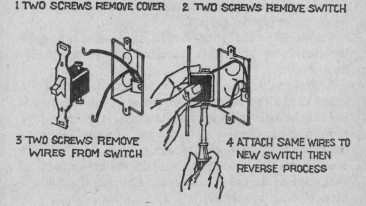

3 TWO SCREWS REMOVE WIRES FROM SWITCH

4 ATTACH SAME WIRES TO NEW SWITCH THEN REVERSE PROCESS

REPAIRING A SWITCH

Repairing a Switch

The "W" of Workmanship figures importantly in trouble with switches, for the reason that builders tend to install the cheapest kind available. The difference in cost could loom large to a builder installing hundreds of switches, but is trivial to a homeowner installing only one or two. If you pull out a defective switch costing about 50 cents at retail, you are certainly better off installing a heavy-duty replacement costing $1.50, which will last a lifetime.

Generally it doesn't pay to attempt repair of a household switch. Replacement is simpler.

1. *Very important*—turn off the power by unscrewing the proper fuse or flipping the circuit breaker at the fuse box; or to be absolutely sure, pull the main house switch.

2. Remove the cover plate, unscrewing and setting aside the two screws that hold it.

3. Remove the two screws that hold the switch in place on the outlet box behind it.

4. Pull the entire switch free of the recess. Loosen the terminal screws at top and bottom of the switch, and unhook the wires.

5. Attach the *same* two wires to the appropriate terminals of the new switch. Be careful to connect the black wire to the dark or brass-colored terminal, the white wire to the light or silver-colored terminal. (This avoids crossing up the house grounding system.)

6. Attach the switch to its box with the two screws.

7. Replace the cover plate or install a new one (which may come with the switch).

Note that you are not limited to switches of the same type as the one replaced if you want an improvement in operation as well as in durability. Among those available today are mercury silent switches, tap-action button switches, time-delay switches (they stay on for a few minutes after being turned off so you can find your way), and dimmer switches that control the brightness of the lights.

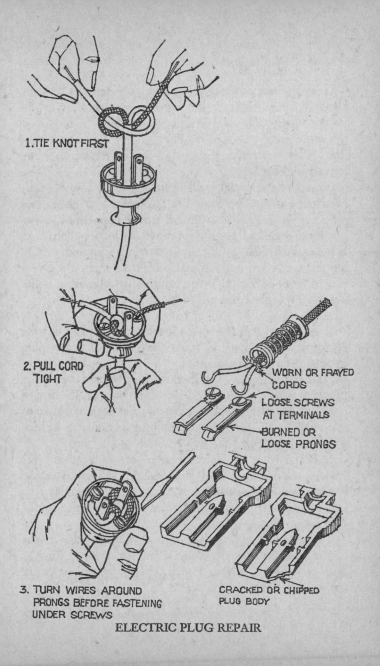

1. TIE KNOT FIRST

2. PULL CORD TIGHT

WORN OR FRAYED CORDS

LOOSE SCREWS AT TERMINALS

BURNED OR LOOSE PRONGS

3. TURN WIRES AROUND PRONGS BEFORE FASTENING UNDER SCREWS

CRACKED OR CHIPPED PLUG BODY

ELECTRIC PLUG REPAIR

If an appliance of any kind suddenly fails to operate, the first thing to look for is some interruption in the power supply. Check the outlet; a fuse may be blown or the outlet may be defective. Try plugging the appliance into another outlet, or test the outlet with a lamp that you know should light.

Assuming the outlet is all right, the most likely source of trouble is the appliance cord, especially at either end where it plugs into the wall and into the appliance. Starting at the wall end, see if the prongs of the plug are loose, bent, or corroded, or if the wires can be jiggled around inside. A cracked or badly beaten up plug should be replaced, since a defective one causes sparking and is a fire hazard. To replace this plug:

1. Examine the plug to see if it can be taken apart for removal of the cord. A round bakelite or rubber plug generally has a cover that slips off over the prongs, revealing the terminals underneath. A gripper-type plastic plug has a hinged panel on the side that can be flipped open with finger pressure, releasing the cord wires from its grip. A solid molded plastic plug cannot be opened and must be cut off.

2. If the wires of the cord have been cut, prepare the ends as previously described in Splicing a Wire. Removing the insulation is not necessary if the replacement plug is the gripper type; its pointed jaws penetrate the insulation to the wire underneath.

3. Connect the prepared cord to a new plug of the round type by tying an Underwriters' knot on the inside. This relieves strain on the cord when it is yanked out of the wall or someone trips over it.

4. Wrap the bare wires around the terminal screws in a clockwise direction, so that tightening the screws will also tighten the wires. Reassemble the plug, including its cover.

Note: To avoid damaging an electric cord in use, always hold the plug itself—not the cord—when pulling it out. If this is hard to do, file down the smooth sides of a round plug to give the hand a better grip. It is dangerous to pry off a tight plug from a live outlet with a screwdriver; if a plug must be pried off, first loosen the fuse that deactivates the circuit.

Sometimes careless painters cover the holes of a wall outlet. When the paint dries, chip it off with a chisel or screwdriver and light taps of a hammer. To avoid accidental electrical contact or paint chips inside the outlet, use a corner of the chisel and tap it downward, upward, or sidewise—never directly into the outlet. If necessary, remove the outlet cover and chip out the paint from the inner side.

Cords for electric skillets, irons, and other appliances often have a flat plug that slips over long prongs inside the appliance. This design is intended to make a more secure connection at a critical point and is not supposed to get too hot to handle. A spring guard protects the cord from abuse when the appliance is disconnected.

This plug consists of two halves screwed together that readily come apart for replacement. The cord wires are attached to terminal screws exactly as at the outlet end. Before putting the two halves of the plug together after repair, make sure the spring guard is properly fitted into the slot provided for it.

If the plugs and cords are all right but the appliance still doesn't work, the next most likely sources of trouble are the switch and/or the contacts of its built-in thermostatic device. Also high on the list is a broken, burned-out, or loose heating element. In most cases such repairs should be left to a manufacturer's service center or representative.

Doorbells

An expert on salesmanship has estimated that 50 percent of the doorbells in this country are out of order at any one time. That's why door-to-door salesmen are taught not only to ring the bell but to knock on the door.

In older houses, the doorbell may be activated by dry cells. Often nothing more is necessary than replacing the dead batteries. But if the bell still doesn't ring, the most frequent sources of trouble are a faulty push button or a loose connection.

Whether it is battery- or power-operated, you can safely remove the push button by loosening the mounting screws. Check the terminal screws in back for tightness.

Next, try bypassing the push button with a screwdriver or bit of wire bridging the terminal screws. (The voltage is low, and shocks are unlikely.) If this short circuit rings the bell, replace the push button.

A power-operated bell or chime gets its low voltage current from a transformer—usually mounted near the main fuse box of the house. Check the fuse that controls this transformer. If it appears that the transformer is at fault, call a serviceman. We would not recommend dabbling with it, since it must carry live 110-volt house current while being checked for proper function.

Other causes of doorbell failure are dirty or pitted contact points in a buzzer, which may be corrected by rubbing with fine sandpaper, or stickiness in the rods that move up and down to operate chimes. Clean them of accumulated dust.

Also check any visible wiring that leads to the doorbell. Sometimes it has been led through a door or window frame that pinches it and frays the insulation. Moisture on the wire might short out the bell.

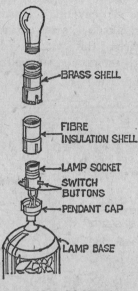

LAMP SOCKET

Repairing a Lamp

A lamp using incandescent light bulbs (the usual kind) generally receives current from a wall outlet via a plug, a connecting cord, a switch, and a lamp socket (which may also contain the switch). See earlier sections of this chapter for replacing a plug or cord. First, however, simply pry the prongs slightly apart for a firmer grip inside the outlet (do not bend prongs toward each other). Repair or replace the plug if this doesn't work.

When a lamp socket gives trouble, the source usually is the switch rather than the socket itself. Both parts are rarely worth repairing, since they are inexpensive to replace. The commonest type consists of a brass shell in three parts with a built-in switch. A wire feeds through the lamp base to a cap covering the terminal screws of the switch. When a bulb is screwed into the socket it touches the live wire of this switch; the brass shell completes the circuit to the ground-wire terminal.

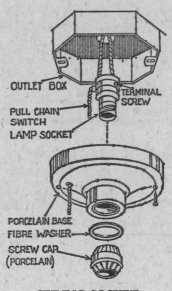

CEILING SOCKET

To replace a lamp socket of this type:

1. Pull the plug from the wall outlet. Take off the lampshade and unscrew the light bulb.

2. Find the word PRESS engraved on the brass shell of

the socket near the bottom cap. Press your thumb hard at this point while grasping the cap, which should then snap free of the shell.

3. A cardboard liner fits around the switch. Remove this liner and check for loose or broken connections at the terminals. Repair these and reassemble the socket.

4. If the lamp still doesn't light, discard the socket and replace with a new one. Try to preserve the original cap from damage, since it probably can be fitted to the new socket and spare you a rather exasperating repair.

5. Before replacing a socket cap, study the construction of the lamp itself. The cap usually is screwed onto the end of a narrow pipe that comes through the entire lamp. Unscrewing it may loosen a number of parts that must be kept track of and replaced in the proper order. Hold the lamp horizontally so as not to lose any nuts and bolts in its innards.

If the cord is frayed or broken, it must be replaced. Here is how to rewire a lamp:

1. Disassemble the lamp socket and disconnect the old wires from the terminals.

2. Tie a string on the end of the old cord before pulling it out through the lamp from the bottom.

3. Tie the string to the new wire and pull it back through the lamp.

4. Connect the wires of the new cord to the terminals of the original socket, and reassemble.

Extension Cord Safety

Whenever a lamp or appliance is hooked up by way of a flexible cord to a wall outlet, people sometimes forget that the cord instantly becomes part of the house electrical system. The same precautions must be observed as if you were rewiring the hidden part of the system within the walls. In some ways an extension cord is even more vulnerable than built-in wiring, because it is exposed to handling and wear and may not be grounded.

An extension cord must be adequate for the power load it will carry. For example, an ordinary No. 18 gauge wire, suitable for lamps or an electric shaver, should not be hooked up to a 1,100-watt electric heater. This cord is rated for no more than 7 amps, whereas the heater draws 10 amps (1,100 divided by 110, the house voltage). A heavy-duty Number 14 cord is needed. The lighter cord would heat up and eventually disintegrate.

The length of a cord also affects its adequacy. A Number 18 wire is fully efficient—will convey a full 7 amperes —for only about 25 feet. Beyond that distance at least 16-gauge wire should be used; otherwise lights won't burn bright enough or an electric fan will run too slow. Here are the safe and sane rules for extension cords.

1. Fit the cord to the appliance and the distance, as just explained. The amperage of each appliance should be listed on the name plate; if not, divide the listed wattage by 110, the household voltage, giving a result in amperes.

2. Never dangle a cord over a metal object that could serve as a ground, such as plumbing pipes, radiators, or metal sills. As the insulation dries out by exposure to heat or rubbing, it may crack and cause a short circuit.

3. Never use an extension cord to hook up outlets in addition to the permanent wall outlets. Again, damage to insulation could easily occur, inviting shorts, shocks, and fire. For this purpose use rigid wiring receptacles affixed to the baseboard. These "surface extensions" contain heavy-duty cables and insulation, and properly safeguarded switches or outlet fixtures.

4. Never run a flexible cord under a rug, under or over a door, or through a window. Abrasion will most likely damage the insulation.

5. Do not plug an extension cord for an appliance into an adapter screwed into a lamp socket, which typically is not designed to carry a heavier load than a 100- to 150-watt bulb.

6. Inspect all electrical cords regularly. Promptly replace any that seem to be deteriorating. Cords are inexpensive, fires are not.

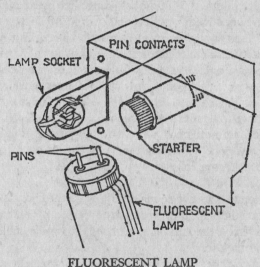

FLUORESCENT LAMP

Fluorescent Lamps

Because fluorescent bulbs work on a totally different principle than traditional incandescent bulbs, their foibles still are somewhat of a mystery to many homeowners.

The glow of a fluorescent lamp does not come from a white-hot filament, but from a phosphor coating on the inside of the glass tube (like a television picture tube).

The tube is filled with mercury vapor, which is heated by small filaments at one end of the tube. The heated vapor causes the phosphors to glow. This is why, with many fluorescent lights, there is a momentary delay while the mercury vapor heats up. It is also why most of them will not work at temperatures below about 50°F. (There are special types for instant lighting and low-temperature applications.)

Fluorescent lamps are economical because they produce very little heat to be wasted. They will last a long time in steady use—up to 3,000 hours—but they wear out more quickly when frequently turned on and off. They should not be used in any location where breakage is a hazard, because the vapor released from a broken tube is highly poisonous. For these reasons fluorescent lighting is mostly designed for ceilings and high wall valances. For a smaller space a thinner tube with a single contact pin at each end may prove to be more convenient.

When a fluorescent tube won't light, or if it blinks more than once or twice after being turned on, check the fixture in steps as follows:

1. Rotate the tube to make sure it is seated firmly in its sockets. The pins at each end are inserted by lining them up vertically, then pushing the tube into place and giving it a quarter turn.

2. Check the sockets for looseness. Tighten the mounting screws at either end that attach the sockets to the lamp housing.

3. If tightening doesn't fix it, remove the tube (being careful not to drop it), and take off the starter. This is a pillbox-shaped gadget usually located under the tube at one end or on the housing in back of the tube. Its function is to "start" the tube by heating up the filaments for a few seconds until the tube lights. Release the starter by pressing down and giving it a half-turn. Insert a new one.

4. If you still don't get proper lighting, insert the old starter and a new tube. In other words, determine first whether the starter is defective, then if the tube itself has burned up its mercury vapor. A defective starter is often indicated if the lamp has to be turned on and off several times to light it, or if the ends glow brighter than the center. Replace a starter promptly, since a bad one will shorten the life of a perfectly good tube.

A humming tube gets its noise from a sort of transformer in the fixture called the ballast. This should best be replaced by an electrician.

Note: A neon tube or lamp is not the same as a fluorescent (mercury vapor) lamp. It contains neon gas that glows when an electric current is passed through it—in effect the cold light of an electric spark jumping a gap. Since it consumes very little current, a neon lamp makes an ideal night light, stairway light, or fire exit light burning 24 hours a day. However, most neon tubes do not produce enough strong white light for good home illumination.

Chapter 9

PRESERVING THE PROPERTY

All four of our Ws conspire to keep a homeowner busy with the outside of his house and adjacent structures, such as the driveway, walks, and fences. They are exposed to Weather at all seasons, washed with Water, eroded by Wear, and vulnerable to even slight deficiencies in Workmanship. Exterior areas often may appear to be beyond nonprofessional repair skills, yet the fact is that the little things any individual can do often represent the difference between maintaining property in good order and inviting major repairs.

Any property should be inspected regularly for minor defects that could become major if neglected. The traditional inspection schedule coincides with the seasonal cycle, the basic changes in the weather that occur in spring and fall. In our climate where the ravages of winter can be severe, it is logical to take a systematic look at the exterior each April or May. Here is a suggested spring maintenance program followed by tips on repairing defective items.

Masonry. All masonry should be examined for any damage during the winter by the alternate freezing and thawing of infiltrated water. Loose brick- or stonework should be reset with mortar. Where the mortar has disintegrated in the joints, it should be removed with a hammer and chisel and the joints brushed clean. Then wet down the bricks and stones preparatory to refilling the joints with fresh mortar.

Examine the house foundation closely for any cracks in one area that could indicate a shifting of the footings. Minor cracks should be filled. Inspect the cellar and inside foundation walls for dampness and water leakage, which would call for the steps to improve drainage described in Chapter 7.

Paint. Inspect the paint on all exterior wood surfaces. If it is dirty, perhaps all it needs is a washing; but if the paint is chalky, blistered, or peeling in some places, a touching up or even a complete repainting may be due.

Actually, the best time to paint a house is not in the spring when the surfaces may be damp, and not in summer when the sun's heat could blister fresh paint, but in the early fall. At that season the moisture will have been extracted from the house surfaces by summer heat. The air will be relatively free from bugs and insects. Never paint when the temperature drops below 50 degrees, and wait at least three or four days after a rainfall.

Screens and storm windows. Remove and inspect the storm windows, looking for loose glass, warped frames, or other faults that should be repaired now. Store them in a dry place that has good air circulation; dampness during summer storage can do more damage to wooden windows than the winter storms. If they are self-storing aluminum windows, clean out and lubricate the grooves before sliding the glass into summer position. Similarly, inspect and repair all screens before installing them in place for the summer.

Roof. Inspect the roof for loose or blown shingles. Check the flashing around the chimney and roof valleys. Plan for necessary repairs as soon as convenient. Remem-

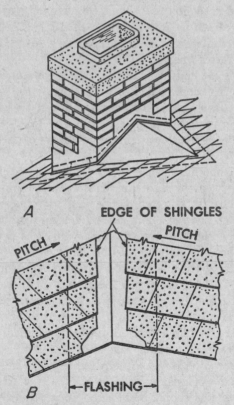

CORRECT FLASHING FOR A, CHIMNEY AND SHINGLES AND B, VALLEY

ber that failure to repair a single bad shingle can set in motion a process that may result in a costlier and major repair. Check the chimney and chimney cap, including the mortar around the chimney and between the bricks.

Examine the gutters and downspouts. Fasten sections that may have worked loose and replace broken sections. See if dry wells are accepting roof drainage without backing up; wet, saturated soil persisting around a dry well location may indicate the well needs cleaning out.

Siding and trim. Look for rotting wood, especially at the corners, swelled wood, rusted nails, blistered or water-stained trim, and other evidences of moisture infiltration into wooden parts of the structure. Plan to correct the cause before scheduling a paint job.

Paved areas. Inspect the driveway, sidewalk, flagstone paths for cracks, heaving, or sinking. Correct any drainage problems involved and schedule repairs, since concrete work and blacktopping are impractical in cold weather.

Seasonal Interior Inspections

Closely related to your spring inspection of the exterior are certain interior functions that are also affected by the seasons.

Plumbing. All traps, including some sink garbage disposers, should be cleaned because grease has a tendency to congeal in them during the winter. Examine the hot-water heater and check and lubricate the sump pump.

Heating. You would be well advised to consult your heating contractor or the service staff of your fuel oil company. An oil burner, gas burner, or electrical heating plant should be professionally inspected each spring. The controls should be checked and cleaned, filters replaced, and the furnace interior vacuumed and brushed. The combustion chamber, heat exchanger, fans, pulleys, and pumps should be inspected and all motors lubricated with SAE No. 20 oil. Smoke pipes, barometric draft regulator, and chimney interior should be carefully checked at this time.

Electrical wiring. Especially if you have had persistent trouble with blown fuses, your spring inspection should cover the entire wiring system. Start from the outside, where electricity enters the house via two, or more likely three wires from a utility pole to your meter. These wires then proceed to a master switch and a panel of fuses or circuit breakers covering each circuit in your home.

Examine all exterior outlets and exposed electrical cables; if there appears to be damage to the latter or tree branches have fallen on them, call the electric company. Throughout the house look for wires that have frayed ends, loose or chipped plugs, appliances that don't always work, temperamental switches, flickering lights, and the like. This is the time to repair or replace them. All major electrical repairs should be done only by a licensed electrician.

Closing Up a House

The fall season, heralding the near approach of winter, may require a different kind of procedure. You may be closing a summer cottage for the season, or leaving your permanent home for a long sojourn in the south. These suggestions should be helpful.

1. Clean the home completely. Remove all perishables, all liquid food in glass containers, all sugar and sugar products, all flour or cereals in paper containers or bags.

Wash the refrigerator interior, including all containers. Disconnect it and leave the door slightly ajar.

2. Lock all windows, secure all doors, and seal all openings. To prevent squirrels, chipmunks, and other animals from gaining entry, it would be wise to remove overhanging tree limbs (which could also cause damage to the roof or chimney). The fireplace chimney should be capped.

3. As further protection against insect and animal damage, scatter mothballs and crystals liberally through the house, especially on furniture fabrics. Store clothing, drapes, and blankets in heavily sealed cardboard or wooden containers with mothballs. Cover moth-protected furniture with heavy paper.

4. Remove screens along with all summer furniture and store in a weatherproof, dry place.

5. Turn off all electrical switches. Just before leaving the house, pull the main switch. Despite this cut-off of house current, disconnect all appliances individually by pulling the plug. The reason is that moisture, a defective wire or switch, or an invasion of mice or insects could cause a short circuit whenever the house current is restored.

6. Turn off the pilot light of *each* gas-operated appliance (kitchen range, hot-water heater, furnace, dryer, or refrigerator, etc.). Only then should you turn off the main gas valve. *This is very important.* Otherwise, when you turn on the main valve again in the spring, gas will escape through the open, unlighted pilots with a risk of serious explosions or, even worse, asphyxiation of the unwary homeowner. It would also be wise to place a metal tag at each pilot light and post a master list indicating where each is to be found.

7. Drain all water from the plumbing to prevent freezing. Most plumbing systems have a drain valve at the

lowest point of the system. If you open this drain, then close the main intake water valve and turn on all faucets in the house, the water should drain out. If it doesn't because of sagging pipe or inadequate pitch, these pipes will have to be opened and air pressure applied to rid the system of any remaining water.

8. Empty the pressure tank of your water pump and drain all water from the pump. Also drain the hot-water storage tank.

9. Remove all water in the drain line and in all traps. Dip out the water in the toilet bowl with a pan or a sponge. Refill the traps with automotive antifreeze (the "permanent" kind that does not evaporate). This will keep trap odors and sewer gas from entering the house.

10. Check your insurance to be sure it covers an unoccupied house.

Leaking Roofs

A leak in a roof can best be discovered by thorough examination of the underside during a rain. The point where water drips into the attic or upper story does not necessarily pinpoint the location of the leak, since water will often run for a considerable distance along rafters, joists, and other parts of the house structure before falling and becoming visible.

The path of the water should be successfully traced. When the actual leak is found, poke a thin wire or twig up through it so that you can find it from the outside.

If you have to climb on a roof, be extremely prudent —not only to protect yourself but to protect the roof. Wooden shingles can be crushed by tramping on them carelessly. Soft-soled rubber shoes or tennis shoes are advisable. On a pitched roof, hook a ladder over the ridge or use a cleating plank to distribute your weight and preserve your balance. Either the ladder or the plank can be secured by a rope over a ridge and tied to a tree.

Another way to locate a leak in dry weather is to soak the suspected area from above with a garden hose. Play the hose back and forth in such a manner as to simulate rain and wind velocity. Have someone stationed below the roof to let you know when dripping starts.

Look for shingles that have curled upward or have cracked, and for loose nails. Use asphalt roofing cement to flatten a loosened shingle against the roof, and to cover each nailhead after tapping it back into place.

When a shingle is badly damaged, try a patch of rustproof metal, such as aluminum, copper, or galvanized iron. Cut the piece a little wider than the shingle, and slide it upward under the shingle and as far as possible under the next higher row. You may have to remove some nails carefully to accomplish this, and replace them with equal care.

On a flat roof a patch of roll roofing material may be applied over the leaking area. Hold it down with a liberal amount of roofing cement and by nailing around the edges. Patching a flat roof may be worthwhile if a leak occurs in a vulnerable spot such as around a vent pipe, or where the roof meets the flashing around the edges, although the rest of the roof appears intact. In general, however, this type of roof has a tendency to perform perfectly for a number of years and then deteriorate more or less uniformly, rather than in spots. If the entire surface seems checked and crazed, it should be painted with an asphaltic coating. Eventually it will require replacement by a professional roofer.

On a metal roof, which has very great durability, a leak usually turns out to be manmade or due to accident —a puncture caused by a falling tree branch, antenna post, or a heavy pointed object dropped on the roof. If the hole is small, proceed as follows:

First, clean the metal down thoroughly around the hole with steel wool. Then apply putty, asphalt roofing compound, or one of the new synthetic sealers.

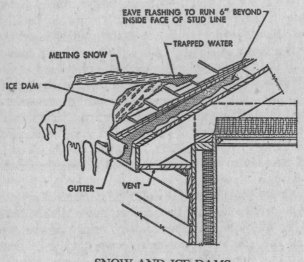

SNOW AND ICE DAMS

Ice on the Roof

In our climate, roof leaks often are caused by ice formation—a temporary condition that does not imply a damaged or defective roof. Water drips into the house through the soffits or vent strips, often running down a window in torrents. Look first for an ice dam (see illustration). It is usually created during a snowfall, when the outside temperature hovers just around freezing.

The roof, warmed by heat from the living quarters, melts the snow to water that then trickles down to the gutters and overhang and refreezes, forming a small dam. Additional water then cannot escape downward; a puddle forms and backs up under the shingles and through the insulation onto the ceiling.

You can prevent ice dams by keeping an eye on the roof when the temperature is just right (or wrong!), namely about 32 degrees, and ridding the roof edges of snow. If the problem is persistent, add several layers of roofing paper under the shingles of the overhang beyond the side wall. Some roofers recommend removing about three feet of shingles from the roof edge, and replacing them with a four-foot apron of galvanized metal overlapping the remaining shingles. Snow and ice would then slide off the roof on the metal, preventing the buildup of ice.

Another, possibly simpler, solution is to install an electric cable loop in a zigzag pattern under the lower shingles. Especially designed for the purpose, the copper cable is about 60 feet long and uses 500 watts of power to heat the roof edges slightly and so prevent freezing and creation of an ice dam.

Rain Gutters

Galvanized gutters should be periodically painted on the outside, because when the zinc coating wears off, the steel will rust. The inside should be coated with a thin application of roof cement, and recoated in any spot where bare metal shows through.

Aluminum gutters require no maintenance, even if left unpainted. After installation a thin coat of oxidation forms that protects the metal from further weathering.

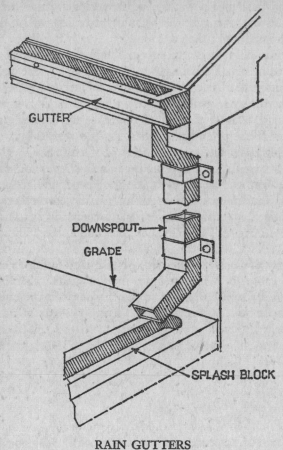

GUTTER

DOWNSPOUT

GRADE

SPLASH BLOCK

RAIN GUTTERS

Some have a baked enamel finish for a more colorful appearance. The half-round type carries more water than the box type. Corrugated downspouts are preferred over round ones in a severe winter climate.

Copper gutters do not rust, but will benefit by being coated periodically on the inside to slow down oxidation. Use roof coating or spar varnish. Coat wood gutters with linseed oil.

Periodically check the hanger straps and fastenings and tighten or renail any that have worked loose. If the gutter has been bent out of shape, pour a bucket of water into it to make sure the slope still permits proper drainage. A sag or reverse pitch can be corrected by adjusting the hanger straps or adding new ones where necessary.

When a gutter or downspout rusts through, plastic kits make the repair job simple. They contain a fiber glass cloth that is saturated in resin and applied over the hole to patch and seal it. The job may also be done with heavy aluminum foil or thin sheeting pressed over a layer of roof cement and covered with another layer.

Generally, however, one badly corroded spot indicates deterioration of the entire gutter, calling for replacement. Aluminum gutters are lightweight and easy to install. Follow manufacturer's instructions with special connectors for joining the sections and corners. The gutter is assembled on the ground, then lifted into place and propped up with boards while being nailed securely to the roof.

Pointing Up Mortar Joints

While brick, stone, and cement blocks are among the most durable building materials, the mortar that holds them in place is vulnerable to penetration by moisture and freezing. When a mortar joint crumbles or cracks, remove the loose pieces to a depth of about half an inch. Tap them out with a chisel and light strokes of a hammer, being careful not to loosen the bricks or blocks.

Then refill the joint with fresh mortar, which you can buy premixed. Or prepare it yourself with an aggregate of three parts sand, one part cement, and one part hydrated lime. An S-shaped tool called a pointing tool or tuck pointer is ideal both for removal and application of mortar. Be careful not to cover the weeping holes that are left in a brick veneer wall to dispel moisture collecting behind it.

Caulking Joints

Caulking compound is a putty-like blend of pigment and oils that never dries to brittleness but remains permanently flexible. Applied around cracks and joints where weather can force moisture or cold air into the house, it is a great boon to home maintenance. Caulking is applied with a pressure gun, or it may be bought in disposable cartridges. White and gray caulking will accept paint; the black type for roof work contains asphalt and should not be painted.

Caulking is a handy cure for minor leakage problems and preventive maintenance wherever masonry meets wood or metal, or wherever two boards meet and a tight seal is vital. It may also be used for filling fine cracks in stucco or wood siding. Here are some of the parts of the house where caulking should always be applied and renewed annually as necessary:

Flashing around chimney and in roof valleys.

Wood gutters.	Window frames and sills.
Door frames and sills.	Under porch posts.
Corner joints.	Wall joints.
Cracks in masonry.	Joint between steps and house wall.

238

Concrete Patching

Cracks do appear in solid concrete, despite its durability, especially in foundations and basement walls where the material is under constant stress from the weight of the house, or where it is subjected to repeated freezing and thawing. Patching should be done with care and attention to achieve professional results; a poorly applied patch will fall out before you know it.

Since you will need only a small amount of concrete, the ready-mixed kind is the most convenient. It comes in three formulas: sand mix for small patches or cracks; mortar mix for building a brick, stone, or concrete block wall; and gravel mix for paving and for foundations. The sand mix will probably suit your purposes best.

If you prefer to prepare your own mixture, combine three parts of sand with one part of Portland cement, adding a small amount of lime for better adhesion to a vertical crack. Add only enough water to bring the mixture to the consistency of putty.

1. Assemble all necessary tools: hammer, cold chisel, wire brush, whisk broom, small mixing board, trowel, bucket of water, and the mixed cement.
2. Chip the sides of the crack with the hammer and chisel to widen the opening for admittance of your patch. Undercut the edges.
3. Remove all loose mixture from the crack with wire brush and whisk broom.
4. Dampen the crack in order to prevent the water in your mixture from being extruded to the surface (water will tend to be attracted to a wet material but not to a dry one).

5. Apply the cement mixture into the crack with trowel. Tamp it into all corners, crevices, and depressions to make a uniform bond on either side of the crack.

6. When the crack has been packed tightly, smooth the surface with a wet trowel to conform neatly with the wall.

7. Allow the cement to set until it is stiff but *not* completely dry.

8. Wet a burlap bag or other piece of absorbent cloth and tape it to the wall to cover the patch. Keep the cloth moist for three or four days by sprinkling it with water, so that the concrete patch will harden very slowly. (Quick drying will cause fresh concrete to crack, thus nullifying all your work.)

Concrete Driveways

Follow the same procedure as above to fill small cracks or replace broken pieces on a concrete walk or driveway, but use gravel mix instead of sand mix. Take special pains to undercut the edges of the hole; they must not slope outward at any point (because the thin edge thus left will almost certainly crack in a short time). It is also a good idea to chop out enough old concrete to make the hole at least one inch deep. Roughen the bottom and sides before applying new concrete.

Level off the fresh patch by dragging a long board across it, then slick it down with your trowel. Cover it with wet straw or burlap for several days. Put a barrier around it to keep dogs and cats (and children) from immortalizing their footprints in the fresh cement.

New types of patching cement are available that eliminate most of the preparation of the surface, and which will adhere even in layers as thin as one sixteenth of an inch. One is a mixture of cement with liquid latex instead of water; the other contains a vinyl binder and is mixed with water.

Efflorescence on Brick

New brickwork sometimes will assume a whitened, frosty appearance in a relatively short time. Called efflorescence, it is the result of evaporation of moisture from the bricks and mortar, leaving lime and salt on the surface. Some people rather like this aging effect, like the green patina on bronze, but if it is undesirable, it can be removed as follows:

Mix one part muriatic (hydrochloric) acid to five parts water. Brush over the affected area. Wear glasses and gloves for protection from the powerful acid. If any contacts the skin, wash the skin immediately with large amounts of water.

The acid solution loosens the efflorescence, which may then be scrubbed off with a wire brush. Rinse the wall. Wash it again with a solution of one part ammonia and 16 parts water.

Efflorescence frequently disappears in a year or two. If it shows up in particular spots only, the cause may be improper drainage from roof gutters, downspouts, and windowsills, which can be corrected to prevent a recurrence. The frosty crust should be removed before painting the brick.

Blacktop Repairs

A hole in a blacktop driveway or road should be cleaned of all loose material before attempting to patch it. Although it would seem as if large stones in the hole would make the patch stronger and more resistant to traffic, the opposite is the fact. The patching material adheres unevenly to stones, which soon break loose again. However, the *bottom* of a deep hole may be partially filled with gravel (medium-size stones) to give the patch a more solid foundation than bare earth alone.

You can fill the prepared hole with patching compound, a specially prepared cold-mix asphalt. It requires no mixing or heating, but is simply poured out of the bag.

1. After preparing the hole, tamp the bottom of it firmly and as flat as possible.

2. Fill with patching compound to within one inch of the top. Tamp this down with a length of two-by-four or of four-by-four lumber.

3. Pour in more patching compound to a level about one-half inch higher than the driveway surface.

4. Tamp or roll the material to compress it down level with the surrounding surface. You can use a garden roller, or simply drive your car back and forth over the patch. It is now ready for application of a sealer.

5. If the surface has a great many small voids, it may be sufficient to fill them with sand instead of asphalt before sealing. Spread dry sand over the entire surface, then sweep it off the smooth areas without removing it from the crevices.

6. Apply a blacktop sealer (sold under that name) on a day when the weather is dry and warm, preferably when the sun is shining on the driveway surface. First sweep the surface absolutely clean to remove all dust, dirt, and foreign material. Greasy areas and oil slicks should be scraped up and scrubbed clean with detergents.

7. Wet down the entire cleaned surface to simplify spreading of the sealer and assure a good bond. Try to achieve a uniform wetting, and sweep away any puddles that form in low spots.

8. Stir the blacktop sealer thoroughly and pour it on while the surface is still damp. You may pour it only on the area of a patch, or on the entire driveway if you have filled small voids with sand as in Step 5 above. Use a long-handled push broom or a roofing brush to spread the coating evenly.

9. Let the sealer dry at least overnight, or longer as the manufacturer recommends, before opening the area to normal traffic.

10. If one coat of sealer doesn't appear to be enough, apply a second coat after the first one is completely dry. This is usually advisable if the surface is in very poor condition.

Stains on House Walls

A good job of house paint should last five years or more, and one should be in no hurry to repaint before that time. Adding more paint prematurely may cause cracking and peeling. Good paint wears out gradually by becoming chalky, which is washed away by the rain. Dingy siding may be simply encrusted with dust and grime. Often it can be washed away with a hose.

Stubborn stains such as appear on the parts of a house sheltered from rain can be washed with a solution of detergent and a long-handled brush. If this is not satisfactory, try a scrub brush and a solution of one pound of trisodium phosphate in a bucket of hot water. Wear rubber gloves to protect the hands. After scrubbing thoroughly, rinse with clean water.

Metal stains caused by drip from copper screens or gutters may be bleached off. Dissolve three-quarters of a pound of oxalic-acid crystals in one gallon of hot water and apply to the stained area with a sponge. Allow to dry for four or five minutes, then rub the stain with a cloth. Repeat two or three times, or until the stain is lightened enough to be unobtrusive. (You probably will not be able to eradicate it completely.)

Remove iron-rust stains from wood or masonry by soaking with a solution of one part sodium-citrate crystals in six parts of water. Dip a white cloth in the solution and paste over the stain for ten or fifteen minutes.

On a horizontal surface, such as a concrete walk, sprinkle a thin layer of sodium hydrosulfite, moisten with water, and cover with a paste made of whiting and water.

On a vertical surface, after removing the white cloth soaked in sodium-citrate solution, apply a paste of whiting that has been sprinkled with the hydrosulfite. Do not leave the paste in place more than one hour, since the stain may turn black. Remove and flush with clean water. Repeat the treatment if necessary.

Green or brown stains from copper or bronze may be removed (instead of bleached) with a dry mixture of four parts powdered talc and one part sal ammoniac or aluminum chloride. Add household ammonia to make a paste, observing all precautions when handling these chemicals. Apply the paste to the stain and allow to dry, then flush with clean water.

Mildew stains must be "killed," since the mildew is a living organism. Add two tablespoons trisodium phosphate to a gallon of water, then pour in eight ounces of household bleach or disinfectant. Scrub this over the surface and allow to soak for ten or fifteen minutes, then rinse with clear water. Immediate repainting with a mildew-resistant coating would be a good idea.

Smoke stains on masonry rarely can be completely removed, but can be lightened with a solution of one-half pound trisodium phosphate in one gallon of water. Soak the surface with this solution before scrubbing, and spot-treat stubborn spots by rubbing with powdered pumice on a cloth soaked in the solution.

While the chemicals specified above will be helpful, some good old-fashioned friction and elbow grease may also be required. For instance, try rubbing green stains with an abrasive household cleanser and steel wool. On brickwork, rub the stain with a brickbat of the same color.

Wobbly Fence Posts

The sagging of a fence nearly always can be traced to a post that has worked loose in the ground, because of alternate freezing and thawing that crumbles the soil.

The loose post may be tightened by driving either angle irons or two-by-four lumber into the ground alongside it. These supports should be hammered down about 30 inches and attached to the fence post with screws. A fence may also be propped up with diagonal wooden braces—but the only really solid and permanent fix is a new concrete base for the fence post.

1. Excavate the earth around the post with a garden spade, down to within a few inches of the bottom and at least 12 inches wide.

2. Brace the post temporarily by affixing it to stakes a few feet away. Check with a carpenter's level to make sure the post is held truly vertical.

3. Fill the hole around the post with gravel-mix fresh concrete. Pour in enough to rise slightly higher

than ground level. With the trowel, slope it all around so that the concrete base is narrower at the top and will shed water away from the post.

4. Let the concrete harden for several days. Remove the braces. There may be a slight space between the post and its new base; if so, seal with roofing cement or other waterproof compound.

Only rot-resistant wood should be driven into the ground for a fence post or bracing, notably cedar and redwood. Other woods may be factory treated to prevent rot, or you can soak them in a wood preservative such as zinc naphthenate or pentachlorophenol. The exposed upper end should be capped or at least trimmed bevel to facilitate runoff of water.

If a gate sags even if its supporting posts are solid, first check the hardware and tighten or replace if necessary. Bolt a strong wire diagonally from the top of the hinge side to the bottom corner of the outside edge. Insert a turnbuckle at the center of the wire; tighten it to draw the bottom edge of the gate upward until it is square.

Chapter 10

HOME PAINTING

Few improvements in your home can match the psychological uplift of a fresh coat of paint. The effect is dramatic and rewarding on any wall, both inside and outside. Because of these aesthetic values, we tend to concentrate upon the colors and decorative effects of painting; in fact, we call the work "redecorating." But from a functional point of view, paint is crucially important to the upkeep of your house.

When paint covers wood, metal, or masonry, it protects these materials from rotting, rusting, or other types of deterioration. Any surface will eventually wear out from usage, damage, and the weather. A new surface of fresh paint is a lot cheaper than a new wall or a new roof. By a happy circumstance, we can combine this purely practical need with making our homes more colorful and pleasant to the eye.

Until recent years, good house painting automatically implied a professional job. But new developments in coatings and painting methods have made it possible for any homeowner to put down a bright and shining finish, neatly executed, wherever he wants to make the effort. His principal problem, in fact, is to find his way through the bewildering variety of paints available on the market. With the right paint and the right brush, roller, or spray gun, he will have little trouble with proper technique.

The tips in this chapter will be helpful when the time comes to give a home its regular maintenance bath of a new surface coating. It includes facts from authoritative sources on the different types of paint, where they are used, how to apply them, and how to take care of brushes and rollers.

Preparation for Painting

The surface must be clean, smooth, and free from dust or old paint. Use sandpaper, a wire brush, or a scraper.

Oil and grease should be removed by wiping with mineral spirits. If a detergent is used, follow by a thorough rinse with clean water.

Chipped or blistered paint should be removed with sandpaper, a wire brush, steel wool, or a scraper.

Chalked or powdered paint should be removed with a stiff bristle brush, or by scrubbing with water mixed with household washing soda or TSP (trisodium phosphate). If the old surface is only moderately chalked and the surface is relatively firm, an oil primer can be applied. The primer rebinds the loose particles and provides a solid base for the paint.

Loose, cracked, or shrunken putty or caulk should be removed by scraping.

New putty, glazing compound, caulking compounds, and sealants should be applied to a clean surface and allowed to harden before paint is applied. If the caulk is a latex type, latex paint can be applied over it immediately without waiting for the caulk to harden.

Damp surfaces must be allowed to dry before paint is applied, unless you are using a latex paint.

Painters' Weather

You can easily ruin your paint job if you forget to consider the weather.

Unless you are using latex paint, you should not paint on damp days. Moisture on the painting surface may prevent a good bond.

If humidity is high, and you can feel a film of moisture on the surface, it would be better to wait for a better day. If the area is air-conditioned, however, neither rain nor humidity will affect the job.

Exterior painting is not recommended if the temperature is below 50 degrees or above 95 degrees Fahrenheit, since you may not be able to get a good bond. This is especially critical if you are using latex paint.

Good ventilation will help paint to dry. Allow more drying time in damp or humid weather. Test each coat by touch before you add another. When paint is thoroughly dry, it is firm to the touch and not sticky.

Wood Surfaces

Scrape clean all areas where sap (resin) has surfaced on the wood, and sand smooth prior to application of "knot sealer." Small dry knots should also be scraped and thoroughly cleaned, and then given a thin coat of knot sealer before applying wood primer.

Fill cracks, joints, crevices, and nail holes with glazing compound, putty, or plastic wood and sand lightly until flush with the wood. Always sand in the direction of the grain—never across it.

New wood surfaces to be stain-finished should first be sanded smooth. Open grain (porous) wood should be given a coat of paste filler of matching color. The surface should then be resanded.

Masonry Surfaces

Plaster, gypsum, cement, and drywall should be dry and clean. If the surface is cracked, sand it smooth and then fill with spackling compound or other crack filler. After the repaired surface is dry, sand lightly until smooth—then wipe clean.

Allow new plaster to dry for 30 days before painting.

Roughen unpainted concrete and stucco with a wire brush to permit a good bond between the surface and the paint.

Wash new concrete surfaces with detergent and water to remove any film from the compound used for hardening the concrete during curing.

Remove efflorescence on a brick wall.

Metal Surfaces

Clean new metal surfaces such as galvanized steel, aluminum, or tin with mineral spirits to remove the oil and grease applied to the metal as a preservative by manufacturers.

Remove rusted or corroded spots by wire-brushing or using coarse sandpaper. Chemical rust removers are also available. Paint will not adhere well over rusted or corroded surfaces.

Allow galvanized roof gutters to weather for about six months before painting. If earlier painting is necessary, apply a primer recommended specifically for galvanized surfaces.

There is now a new rust-proof paint for painting gutters and other exterior metal parts of a house subject to rusting. Unlike most metal paints this does not require a primer coat and can be applied directly on rusty spots that have been cleaned of any loose particles. Only one coat is sufficient in most cases.

Interior Painting

Previously painted surfaces usually do not require primer coats except where the old paint is worn through or damaged. Unpainted surfaces should be primed.

Wood Surface Primers

Unpainted wood to be finished with enamel or oil base paint should be primed with enamel undercoat to seal the wood and provide a better surface. If the unpainted wood is not primed, the enamel coat may be uneven.

Unpainted wood to be finished with topcoat latex should first be undercoated. Water-thinned paint could raise the grain of the bare wood and leave a rough surface.

If clear finishes are used:

Softwoods such as pine, poplar, and gum usually require a sealer to control the penetration of the finish coats. In using stain, a sealer is sometimes applied first in order to obtain a lighter, more uniform color.

Open-grain hardwoods such as oak, walnut, and mahogany require a paste wood filler, followed by a clear wood sealer.

Close-grain hardwoods such as maple and birch do not require a filler. The first coat may be a thinned version of the finishing varnish, shellac, or lacquer.

Masonry Surface Primers

Smooth, unpainted masonry surfaces such as plaster, plasterboard, and various drywall surfaces can be primed with latex paint or latex primer-sealer. The color of the first coat should be similar to the finish coat.

Coarse, rough, or porous masonry such as cement block, cinder block, and concrete block cannot be filled and covered satisfactorily with regular paints. Block filler should be used as a first coat to obtain a smooth sealed surface over which almost any type of paint can be used.

Unpainted brick, while porous, is not as rough as cinder block and similar surfaces and can be primed with latex primer-sealer or with an exterior-type latex paint.

Enamel undercoat should be applied over the primer where the finish coat is to be a gloss or semi-gloss enamel.

Metal Surface Primers

Unpainted surfaces should be primed for protection against corrosion and to provide a base for the finish paint. Interior paints do not usually adhere well to bare metal surfaces, and provide little corrosion resistance by themselves. Primer paints must be selected according to the metal to be painted.

An enamel undercoat should be used as a second primer if the metal surface is to be finished with enamel; that is, apply the primer first, then the undercoat, and finally the enamel finish. Most enamel undercoats need a light sanding before the topcoat is applied.

Paints for Light-wear Areas

Latex interior paints are generally used where there is little need for periodic washing and scrubbing; for example, living rooms, dining rooms, bedrooms, and closets.

Interior flat latex paints are used for interior walls and ceilings since they cover well, are easy to apply, dry quickly, are almost odorless, and can be quickly and easily removed from applicators.

Latex paints may be applied directly over semi-gloss and gloss enamel if the surface is first roughened with sandpaper or liquid sandpaper.

Flat alkyd paints are often preferred for wood, wallboard, and metal surfaces since they are more resistant to damage; also, they can be applied in thicker films to produce a more uniform appearance. They wash better than interior latex paints and are nearly odorless.

Paints for Heavy-wear Areas

Enamels, including latex enamels, are usually preferred for kitchen, bathroom, laundry room, and similar work areas because they withstand intensive cleaning and wear. They form especially hard films, ranging from flat to a full-gloss finish.

Fast-drying polyurethane enamels and clear varnishes provide excellent hard, flexible finishes for wood floors. Other enamels and clear finishes can also be used, but unless specifically recommended for floors they may be too soft and slow-drying, or too hard and brittle.

Polyurethane and epoxy enamels are also excellent for concrete floors. For a smooth finish, rough concrete should be properly primed with an alkali-resistant primer to fill the pores. When using these enamels, adequate ventilation is essential for protection from flammable vapors.

Clear Finishes for Wood

Varnishes form durable and attractive finishes for interior wood surfaces such as wood paneling, trim, floors, and unpainted furniture. They seal the wood, forming a tough, transparent film that will withstand frequent scrubbing and hard use, and are available in flat, semigloss or satin, and gloss finishes.

Most varnishes are easily scratched, and the marks are difficult to conceal without redoing the entire surface. A good paste wax applied over the finished varnish—especially on wood furniture—will provide some protection.

Polyurethane and epoxy varnishes are notable for durability and high resistance to stains, abrasions, acids and alkalis, solvents, strong cleaners, fuels, alcohol, and chemicals. Adequate ventilation should be provided as protection from flammable vapors when these varnishes are being applied.

Shellac and lacquer finishes are easy to repair or recoat. They apply easily, dry fast, and are also useful as a sealer and clear finish under varnish for wood surfaces. The first coat should be thinned as recommended on the container, then sanded very lightly and finished with one or more undiluted coats. Two coats will give a fair sheen, and three a high gloss.

Wax Finishes

Liquid and paste waxes provide a soft, lustrous finish to wood and are particularly effective on floors, since they are washable. Waxes containing solvents should not be used on asphalt tile; wax emulsions are recommended.

Wax should be applied to smooth surfaces with a soft cloth. Rub with the grain. Brushes should be used to apply liquid wax to raw-textured wood.

A wax finish is not desirable if a different type of finish may be used later, for wax is difficult to remove.

What to Use And Where
(Interior Surfaces)

Surface	Latex Gloss & Semi-gloss	Latex (Wall) Flat	Metal Primer	Sealer or Undercoater	Aluminum Paint	Floor Paint or Enamel	Floor Varnish	Wood Sealer	Stain	Wax (Emulsion)	Wax (Liquid or Paste)	Shellac - Lacquer	Interior Varnish	Gloss Enamel	Semi-gloss Enamel	Flat Enamel
MASONRY																
Asphalt Tile										X.	X.					
Concrete Floors						X	X			X.	X.					
Kitchen & Bathroom Walls	X.													X.	X.	X.
Linoleum										X.	X.					
New Masonry	X	X		X										X.	X.	X.
Old Masonry	X.	X		X	X									X.	X.	X.
Plaster Walls & Ceiling	X.	X		X										X.	X.	X.
Vinyl & Rubber Tile Floors										X	X					
Wall Board	X.	X		X										X.	X.	X.
METAL																
Aluminum Windows	X.	X.	X		X									X.	X.	X.
Heating Ducts	X.	X.	X.		X									X.	X.	X.
Radiators & Heating Pipes	X.	X.	X.		X									X.	X.	X.
Steel Cabinets	X.	X	X	X	X									X.	X.	X.
Steel Windows		X.	X											X.	X.	X.
WOOD																
Floors						X.	X.	X.	X.	X.	X.	X	X			
Paneling	X.	X.						X.	X.	X.	X.	X.	X.	X.	X.	X.
Stair Risers								X.	X.	X.	X.	X.	X.	X.	X.	X.
Stair Treads							X.	X.	X	X	X		X			
Trim		X.						X.	X.		X.	X	X	X.	X.	X.
Window Sills		X.		X.				X.	X.				X	X.	X.	X.

X. Black dot indicates that a primer or sealer may be necessary before the finishing coat (unless surface has been previously finished).

Table 10-1: Interior Paint Properties

Type	Properties	Typical Uses
Latex primer-sealer (water-thinned)	Simple to apply. Dries quickly and can be recoated in about two hours. Not flammable; almost odorless. One coat usually sufficient. Thinning unnecessary unless recommended.	Unpainted interior walls and ceilings of wallboard, plaster, masonry, and drywall.
Enamel undercoater (alkyd base—low-odor type)	Hard, tight film. Provides good base for enamel. Easy brushing, smooth leveling. Dries in about 12 hours.	Undercoater for interior enamels.
Latex wall paint (water-thinned)	The most popular interior paint. Durable, excellent coverage, good washability, quick-drying, and easy to touch up. Safe to use and store; nontoxic, practically no odor.	Primer-sealer and also finish coat for interior walls and ceilings of wallboard, wallpaper, plaster, and other porous, absorptive materials. Use on primed wood but not on bare wood.
Flat alkyd enamel	Made with alkyd resins. Has flat finish practically free of sheen. Used same as latex wall paint but has slightly better washability and abrasion resistance. Dries in about four hours. Practically no odor.	Primer-sealer and also finish coat on interior walls and ceilings of plaster, wallboard, masonry, and similar surfaces.

Type (cont'd.)	Properties (cont'd.)	Typical Uses (cont'd.)
Semi-gloss and full-gloss enamel (alkyd base)	Made with alkyd resins. Has good gloss retention, grease and oil resistance, and better washability and resistance to abrasion than flat alkyd enamel.	On primed plaster and wallboard, and on suitably prepared wood trim and metal. Very useful for kitchens and bathrooms, and for decorative use on properly primed woodwork.
Semi-gloss and full-gloss latex enamel (water-thinned)	Has most properties of alkyd enamels plus usual advantages of latex paints: easy application and cleanup, rapid drying, low odor, and nonflammable. Good leveling but lapping does not compare favorably with alkyd enamels.	Walls and ceilings of wallboard, wallpaper, wood, and plaster. Very useful for kitchens, bathrooms, and for decorative use on properly primed woodwork.
Epoxy enamel	Hard film, wide gloss range, low odor, ideal where vigorous and frequent cleaning is done. Has excellent adhesion and resistance to abrasion, water, solvents, greases, and dirt. Cost comparatively high but durability is excellent.	Highly effective in heavy-wear areas such as hallways, kitchens, bathrooms, laundries, and concrete floors.
Dripless enamel (special alkyd base)	Does not drip from brush or roller. Made with special alkyd resins to form a soft gel that liquefies with agitation but gels again on standing. Soft, buttery, easy brushing, low odor, self-sealing. Has excellent color retention; solvent- and water-resistant.	Decorative enamel for properly primed walls and ceilings of plaster, wallboard, and similar surfaces; also, for wood trim and primed metal.

Type (cont'd.)	Properties (cont'd.)	Typical Uses (cont'd.)
Interior floor and deck enamel	Alkyd and latex used successfully but polyurethane types provide harder, more flexible, and more abrasion-resistant surfaces. Follow manufacturer's instructions explicitly and also keep room well ventilated.	General application to properly primed floors and covered decks.
Clear varnish finishes for wood	Provide durable and attractive finish; seal wood better than lacquer; and form tough, transparent coat that will withstand frequent scrubbings and hard use. Tend to darken the wood surface and give impression of visual depth. Readily show scratch marks, which are difficult to conceal without redoing entire surface. Some turn yellow with age. Extra coat recommended on new work. Can be flat, satin, semi-gloss, or glossy finish.	For all interior smooth wood. Recommended for washrooms, kitchens, or other areas exposed to dirt, grease, and moisture and subject to frequent scrubbing. A rubbed-in coat of paste wax will provide some protection against scratches.
Shellac	Available in clear and "orange" finishes. Fast drying. Thinned first coat provides excellent seal for new wood. Can be overcoated in about 30 minutes. Should be lightly sanded between coats. Paste wax, as final coat, provides luster and some protection against scratches.	For wood walls, trim, furniture, or any wood surface requiring only occasional dusting. Unsuitable for kitchen, washrooms, or other areas exposed to dirt, grease, and moisture.

Type (cont'd.)	Properties (cont'd.)	Typical Uses (cont'd.)
Lacquer	Fast drying; can be overcoated in about 30 minutes. Provides gloss or sheen when two or more coats are applied. Paste wax, as final coat, provides luster and some protection against scratches. Available in clear and a variety of colors.	For wood walls, trim, furniture, or any wood surface requiring only occasional dusting. Unsuitable for kitchen, washrooms, or other areas exposed to dirt, grease, and moisture.
Stains	Available in a variety of colors. Several coats are required for bare wood, with light sanding between coats. Final coat of paste wax provides luster and some protection against scratches, particularly on furniture. "Thick" stains can be thinned with turpentine or mineral spirits.	For interior wood surfaces such as walls, trim, and furniture.
Aluminum paints	Resistant to water. Can be brushed or sprayed on new metal and wood surfaces. When brush is used, apply in one direction only for best results.	As a sealer for wood surfaces (especially knots) and as a primer for metal surfaces. Can be used as a finish coat if color is not objectionable. Particularly useful for aluminum and steel windows, heating ducts, and heating pipes.

Exterior Painting

Conditions must be right for exterior painting. The temperature should not be much below 50 degrees or above 95 degrees Fahrenheit, and surfaces must be free of moisture. Latex paints can be used even if the surface is not bone dry. The best time for exterior painting is after morning dew has evaporated.

Before you start on the job, make a thorough inspection tour and prepare the surfaces as described earlier in this chapter.

Wood Surface Priming

The tendency of wood to expand and contract during changes in temperature and humidity makes it imperative that a good exterior primer be applied to provide the necessary anchorage for the finish paint.

Painted wood usually does not need priming unless the old paint has cracked, blistered, or peeled. Defective paint must be removed by scraping or wire-brushing—preferably down to bare wood—and then primed. Scratches, dents, recesses, and raw edges should be smoothed and then touched up with primer.

Masonry Surface Priming

New masonry surfaces should be primed with an exterior latex paint, preferably one specifically made for masonry.

Common brick may be sealed with a penetrating type

of clear exterior varnish to control efflorescence and spalling (flaking or chipping of the brick). This varnish withstands weather, yet allows the natural appearance of the surface to show through.

Coarse, rough, and porous surfaces should be covered with a fill coat (block filler), applied by brush to thoroughly penetrate and fill the pores.

Old painted surfaces that have become a little chalky should be painted with an exterior oil primer to rebind the chalk. If there is much chalk, it should be removed with a stiff bristle brush or by washing with household washing soda or TSP (trisodium phosphate) mixed with water.

Metal Surface Priming

Copper should be cleaned with a phosphoric acid cleaner, buffed and polished until bright, and then coated before it discolors. Copper gutters and downspouts do not require painting. The protective oxide that forms on the surface darkens it or turns it green, but does not shorten the life of the metal. Copper is often painted to prevent staining of adjacent painted surfaces.

Zinc-chromate primers are effective on copper, aluminum, and steel, but other types are also available for use on metal.

Galvanized steel gutters and downspouts should be primed with recommended special primers since conventional primers usually do not adhere well. A zinc-dust zinc-oxide primer works well on galvanized steel. Exterior latex paints are sometimes used directly over galvanized surfaces, but not oil paints.

Unpainted iron and steel surfaces rust when exposed to the weather. Rust, dirt, oils, and old loose paint should be removed by wire-brushing or power-tool cleaning. The surface should then be treated with an anticorrosive primer.

What To Use And Where
(Exterior Surfaces)

Note: **X•** — Black dot indicates that a primer, sealer, or fill coat may be necessary before the finishing coat (unless surface has been previously finished).

Surface	Water Repellent Preservative	House Paint (Latex)	Metal Primer	Primer or Undercoater	Porch and Deck Paint	Trim Paint	Roof Coating	Wood Stain	Aluminum Paint	Exterior Clear Finish	Cement Powder Paint	House Paint (Oil or Oil-Alkyd)
MASONRY												
Asbestos Cement		X		X								X•
Brick	X	X		X								X•
Cement & Cinder Block	X	X		X								X•
Concrete/Masonry Porches And Floors					X							
Coal Tar Felt Roof							X					
Stucco		X		X								X•
METAL												
Aluminum Windows		X•	X•			X•			X•			X•
Steel Windows		X•	X•			X•			X•			X•
Metal Roof		X•	X•			X•			X•			X•
Metal Siding			X•									
Copper Surfaces										X		
Galvanized Surfaces		X•	X•			X•			X•			X•
Iron Surfaces		X•	X•			X•			X•			X•
WOOD												
Clapboard		X•		X•		X•			X•			X•
Natural Wood Siding & Trim								X		X		
Shutters & Other Trim		X•		X•		X•			X•			X•
Wood Frame Windows		X•		X•		X•						X•
Wood Porch Floor					X							
Wood Shingle Roof	X							X				

263

All exterior surfaces, properly primed or previously painted, can be finished with either exterior oil paint or exterior latex paint. *Never use an interior paint outdoors.*

Latex paints are easy to apply, have good color retention, and can be used on slightly damp surfaces.

Oil- or alkyd-base paints have excellent penetrating properties. They provide good adhesion, durability, and resistance to abrasion and blistering on wood and other porous surfaces.

If mildew, fungus, and mold growths are a problem, use paint that contains agents to resist bacterial and mold growth.

Exterior oil and latex paints can be applied by brush or by spraying; however, brush application generally provides a more intimate bond between surface and the paint film.

Colored exterior house paints must resist chalking so that colors will not fade and the erosion of the paint film will be minimized. The manufacturer's label will indicate whether the paint is a nonchalking type. Some white exterior house paints are expected to chalk slightly as a means of self-cleaning.

Table 10-2: Exterior Paint Properties

Type	Properties	Typical Uses
Oil-base primers	Good adhesion and sealing; resistant to cracking and flaking when applied to unprimed wood; good brushing and leveling; controlled penetration; and low sheen. Unsuitable as a top coat and should be covered with finish paint within a week or two after application.	As primer on unpainted woodwork or surfaces previously coated with house paint.
Antirust primers	Prevent corrosion on iron and steel surfaces. Slow-drying type provides protection through good penetration into cracks and crevices. Fast-drying types are used only on smooth, clean surfaces.	Priming of steel and other ferrous metal surfaces when good resistance to corrosion is required.
Galvanizing primers	High percentage of zinc dust provides good antirust protection and adhesion. Galvanizing zinc-dust primers give excellent coverage, one coat usually being sufficient on new surfaces. Two coats are ample for surfaces exposed to high humidity.	Priming of new or old galvanized metal and steel surfaces. Satisfactory as finish coat if color (metallic gray) is not objectionable.

Type (cont'd.)	Properties (cont'd.)	Typical Uses (cont'd.)
House paints (oil or oil-alkyd base)	Made with drying oils or drying oil combined with alkyd resin. Excellent brushing and penetration properties. Provide good adhesion, elasticity, durability, and resistance to blistering on wood and other porous surfaces. Often modified with alkyd resins to speed drying time. Apply with brush to obtain strong bond, especially on old painted surfaces.	General exterior use on properly primed or previously painted wood or metal surfaces.
House paints (latex type)	Exterior latex paints have durability comparable to oil-base paints. Resistant to weathering and yellowing, and so quick-drying that they can be recoated in one hour. Can be applied in damp weather over a damp surface. Easy to apply and brush or roller can be cleaned quickly with water. Free from fire hazard. White latex paints usually offer better color retention than oil or oil-alkyd exterior paints.	Covers properly primed or previously painted concrete, stucco, and other masonry and wood surfaces.
Trim paint	Usually made with oil-modified alkyds. Slow-drying (overnight). Made in high sheen, bright colors; have good retention of gloss and color. More expensive silicone-alkyd enamels are substantially more durable than conventional oil-alkyd enamels.	Applied over primed wood and metal surfaces such as aluminum and steel windows, metal siding, shutters and other trim, and wood frame windows.

Type (cont'd.)	Properties (cont'd.)	Typical Uses (cont'd.)
Porch and deck paints (for concrete and other masonry surfaces)	Many made with natural rubber base (chlorinated rubber resin). Good flow and leveling; good resistance to rain, moisture, and detergents. Coverage about 300 square feet per gallon. New concrete should age at least two months before painting. Three coats recommended, including thinned first coat. Good ventilation required if used indoors.	For both interior and exterior concrete and masonry porches and decks. Effective for swimming pools, shower rooms, and laundries.
Porch and deck paints (for wood surfaces)	A variety of alkyd-base and other types available. Tough, flexible, and abrasion-resistant. Good drying properties. Thin coats promote thorough drying. Allow ample drying time between coats.	Interior and exterior decks and porches.
Aluminum paints	Resistant to water and weather and provide excellent durability in marine environments. Can be applied on new metal or wood surfaces—in one direction for best results. Creosote-treated wood must age for about six months prior to application of aluminum paints.	Particularly useful in marine environments; as a sealer for wood knots; and as a combination sealer and finish coat for wood surfaces treated with creosote or other preservatives. Can also be used as a finish coat for metal and wood.

Type (cont'd.)	Properties (cont'd.)	Typical Uses (cont'd.)
Cement powder paint	Made from white Portland cement, pigment, and (usually) small amounts of water repellent. They are mixed with water just before application. Painted surfaces should be kept damp by sprinkling with water until paint film is well cured. This paint does not provide a good base for other types of finishes. Apply with a fiber brush.	Useful, low-cost finish for rough masonry surfaces, both interior and exterior, including brick, cement and cinder block, and stucco.
Wood stains	Semitransparent type available for exterior wood but not as durable as house paints. Improves appearance of wood by highlighting the grain and texture of the surface. Available in many colors, the most popular being cedar, light redwood, and dark redwood.	For smooth and rough wood surfaces. Can be used for staining house siding and wood fencing, but should not be used on surfaces that may soon be painted or on previously painted surface. Not recommended for frames, windows, and doors that need a high degree of protection against the weather.

Type (cont'd.)	Properties (cont'd.)	Typical Uses (cont'd.)
Clear finishes (for wood)	Not as durable as pigmented paint. Alkyd varnishes have good color and color retention but may crack and peel. Some synthetics such as polyurethane varnishes have good durability but may darken on exposure. Spar varnish (marine varnish) is quite durable but will also darken and yellow. Use thin penetrating coats on the bare wood, followed by the unreduced varnish.	For clear finish on wood surfaces where natural appearance is desired.
Roof coatings	Bituminous roof coatings are made of asphalt (chosen for good weather resistance), dissolved in a solvent. Asbestos and other fillers are added to prevent sagging on sloping roofs and, to permit application of relatively thick coatings. Basically made in gray and black; however, addition of aluminum powders provides for other colors. Asphalt-emulsion roof coatings can be applied over damp surfaces. Special application techniques are usually required and manufacturer's instructions must be followed carefully.	Used primarily for coal-tar felt roofs.

Type (cont'd.)	Properties (cont'd.)	Typical Uses (cont'd.)
Water-repellent preservative (silicone type)	Silicone water repellents are transparent liquids that help repel water without changing the surface appearance. Must be applied strictly in accordance with instructions to ensure adequacy of film and water repellency. Should not be topcoated with paint until surface has weathered for at least two years.	For wood shingle roofs, brick walls, and other surfaces where some degree of water repellency is desired.

Paintbrushes

A brush assures good contact of paint with pores, cracks, and crevices. Brushing is particularly recommended for applying primer coats and exterior paints.

In selecting a brush you should choose one that is wide enough to cover the area in a reasonable amount of time. If you are painting walls or a floor, you will want a wide brush—probably four or five inches in width. If you are painting windows or trim, you will want a narrower brush—probably one to one and one-half inches in width.

The bristles should be reasonably long and thick so that they will hold a good load of paint; and flexible, so that you can stroke evenly and smoothly.

Paint should be brushed up and down, then across for even distribution. On a rough surface, vary the direction of the strokes so that the paint will penetrate thoroughly.

The brush should be held at a slight angle when applying the paint, and pressure should be moderate and even. Excessive pressure or "stuffing" the brush into corners and cracks may damage the bristles.

Always start painting at the top and move downward. For interior painting, do ceilings and walls first, then the doors, windows, and trim areas. If floors are to be painted, they should be last.

Always work toward the "wet edge" of the previously painted area, making sure not to try to cover too large a surface with each brushload.

Clean brushes immediately after use with a thinner or special brush cleaner. Use turpentine or mineral spirits to remove oil-base paints, enamels, and varnishes; alcohol to remove shellac; and special solvents to remove lacquer. Remove latex paints promptly from brushes with soap and water. If any type paint is allowed to dry on a brush, a paint remover or brush-cleaning solvent will be needed.

How to Clean Brushes

1. After removing excess paint with a scraper, soak the brush in the proper thinner, and work it against the bottom of a container.

2. To loosen paint in the center of the brush, squeeze bristles between the thumb and forefinger, then rinse again in the thinner. If necessary, work the brush in mild soap suds, and rinse it in clear water.

3. Press out water with a stick.

4. Twirl the brush—in a container so you won't get splashed.

5. Comb the bristles carefully—including those below the surface. Allow the brush to dry by suspending it from the handle or by laying it flat on a clean surface. Then wrap the dry brush in heavy paper to keep the bristles straight. Store it suspended by the handle or lying flat.

Paint Rollers

On large, flat surfaces, roller painting is easier than brush painting for the average do-it-yourself painter. Try several dry sweeps across the surface until you get the hang of it.

A new roller comes with a sloping metal or plastic

tray. Pour paint into the tray until approximately two-thirds of the corrugated bottom is covered. Dip the roller into the paint in the shallow section of the tray, and roll it back and forth until it is well covered. If the roller drips when you lift it from the tray, it is over-loaded. Squeeze out some of the paint by pressing the roller against the upper part of the tray above the paint line.

Apply paint by moving the roller back and forth over the surface being painted, first up and down in long, even strokes, then across. Reload the roller with paint as needed.

Rollers used with alkyd- or oil-base paints should be cleaned with turpentine or mineral spirits. When latex paint has been used, soap and water will do a satisfactory cleaning job. If any kind of paint has been allowed to dry on the roller, a paint remover or brush-cleaning solvent will be needed.

How to Use a Roller

1. First use a brush to paint a strip of color just below the ceiling line for a width of two feet. Also paint next to corners from the ceiling to the floor.

2. With a newly loaded roller, always begin by rolling upward. Start a short distance from the finished area and work toward it.

3. After an area about two feet wide and three feet deep has been coated with up-and-down strokes, roll the coater back and forth.

4. At the bottom of the wall, brush paint onto areas the roller couldn't reach. Use a cardboard guard when brushing next to woodwork.

Paint Sprayers

Paint sprayers are particularly useful for large areas. Spraying is much faster than brushing or rolling and although some paint will likely be wasted, the savings in time and effort compensate for any additional paint cost.

Surface areas accessible only with difficulty to the brush or roller can readily be covered by the sprayer. All coats can be applied satisfactorily by the spray technique *except for primer coats*. Spraying should be done only on a clean surface since the paint may not adhere well if a dust film is present.

Pre-preparation of the paint is of critical importance. Stir or strain to remove any lumps, and thin carefully. If the paint is lumpy or too thick it may clog the spray valve; if it is too thin the paint may sag or run after it is applied. Follow the manufacturer's instructions for the type and amount of thinner to be used.

For best results, adjust the width of the spray fan to the size of the surface to be coated. A narrow fan is best for small or narrow surfaces; a wider fan should be used to spray table tops or walls.

Before spraying, test the thickness of the paint, the size of the fan, and the motion of the spray gun. Excessive thickness can cause rippling of the wet film or lead to blistering later.

Hold the nozzle about eight inches from the surface to be painted. Start the stroke while the spray is pointed slightly beyond the surface to be painted. This assures a smooth, even flow when you reach the surface to be coated.

Move the sprayer *parallel* to the surface, moving with

an even stroke back and forth across the area. Spray corners and edges first. Avoid spraying in an arc.

Use a respirator to avoid inhalation of vapors.

Cover everything close to the work area with drop cloths, tarps, or newspapers. The bounceback from a sprayer may extend several feet.

Clean sprayer promptly before the paint dries. After using oil-base or alkyd paints, clean the sprayer with the same solvent used to thin the paint. After using latex paint, clean with detergent and water. Fill the sprayer tank with the cleaning liquid and spray it clean.

If the fluid tip becomes clogged, it can be cleaned with a broom straw. Never use wire or a nail to clear clogged air holes in the sprayer tip.

Condition of Paint

When you buy new paint of good quality, it is usually in excellent condition. After stirring the paint thoroughly (if it is a type that should be stirred), examine it for lumps, curdling, or color separation. Do not use paint if there are any signs of these conditions.

Old paints that release a foul odor (especially latex paints) or show signs of lumps or curdling are probably spoiled and should be discarded.

If there is a "skin" on the surface of the paint, remove as much of the hardened film as possible with a spatula or knife and strain the paint through a cheesecloth or wire mesh such as window screening. Unless you do this, bits of the skin will show up with exasperating frequency to spoil the appearance of your paint job.

Always read paint labels carefully and follow instructions exactly as recommended by the manufacturer. Take nothing for granted, since modern paints are highly specialized products.

New paints usually require no thinning except when applied with a sprayer. *Check the label before you mix or stir.* Some manufacturers do not recommend mixing as it may introduce air bubbles.

If the pigment has settled, use a clean paddle or spatula and gradually work the pigment up from the bottom of the can, using a circular stirring motion. Continue until the pigment is thoroughly and evenly distributed, with no signs of color separation. Another way is to pour off the top liquid into another container, then pour back a little at a time as you stir. Many paint shops will mix paint for you with a machine.

If the settled layer should prove to be hard or rubbery, and resists stirring, the paint is probably too old and should be discarded.

Between jobs, even overnight, cover the paint container tightly to prevent evaporation and thickening, and to protect it from dust. Oil-base and alkyd paints may develop a skin from exposure to the air.

Clean the rim of the paint can thoroughly and put the lid on tight. Cover the rim with a cloth or piece of plastic film (to prevent spattering) and then tap the lid firmly into place with a hammer.

Avoiding the Mess

More homeowners would do their own painting and save large amounts in maintenance costs if they did not dread the messy job of cleaning up, and the anguish of the lady of the house. This can be largely avoided by proper planning before applying the first drop of paint.

Professional painters always cover everything in sight

with large canvas drop cloths or tarpaulins. You can duplicate them for much less cost by purchasing 9-by-12-foot paper or plastic cloths, which can be folded after painting and stored for future use.

Paint mixing is less messy in cardboard containers, from one and a half to five quarts in size, which cost only a few cents apiece and may simply be discarded after use.

When using a paint roller, cover the bottom of the tray with wrapping paper. You can then clean the tray afterward simply by peeling off the paper lining and wiping any oily residue with a dry rag.

Protect the edges of the painted surface—that is, keep the paint from smearing window glass, woodwork, etc.—with masking tape or masking paper. The latter is adhesive only along one edge, and comes in widths up to nine inches.

Wear clothes you won't need for any other purpose—old overalls, old gloves, an apron—and protect the hands, arms, and face with protective cream. This washes off afterward with soap and water.

Better than taking paint off the skin with irritating solvents is a cream-type waterless hand cleaner. It removes even dry paint spots without difficulty, simply by massaging vigorously and wiping off with a clean cloth.

Clean up as you paint. Wet paint is easy to remove; dry paint is difficult. Use turpentine or any other thinner on a cloth to wipe up oil paint; use water to remove latex.

Do not use solvents to remove a paint spill on an asphalt tile floor, since mineral spirits or turpentine can damage the tile. Wipe off wet paint with a dry cloth; whatever is left should be allowed to dry, then be scraped off.

A razor blade in a protective holder is an ideal instrument for scraping dry paint off glass, porcelain, ceramic tiles, or other impervious surfaces (not wooden), or for trimming a painted edge that comes out a bit irregular or fuzzy.

Painting Problems

Following are some common types of unsatisfactory paint jobs. Nearly all of them could be caused by using the wrong kind of paint for the particular situation, or paint of poor quality, or spoiled paint. Others are traceable to poor preparation of the surface to be coated. Occasionally some more deep-rooted problem is involved, the paint failure being merely a symptom. In such cases the cause should be eliminated before repainting is attempted.

Blistering results from inside or outside moisture, high humidity either from leaking and dripping water or from cooking, bathing, dishwashing, or laundry. After eliminating the cause of the dampness, scrape blisters and repaint with blister-resistant paint.

Chalking other than the normal slow chalking of aging paint results if paint is applied too thin, or applied in rain, fog, or mist. Remove chalk with stiff brush and repaint with nonchalking paint.

Alligatoring will occur when a hard coating has been painted over a soft oil-base paint, or when there has been insufficient drying time between coats. Scrape and sand smooth; apply new paint.

Checking may be a sign of excessive paint (as from repainting a house too soon), improperly mixed paint, or unevenly applied paint, as well as from oil-painting over

278

a damp surface. Scrape clean and start over again with a primer.

Mildew is a fungus growth associated with dampness; it will not grow where sunlight hits the painted surface. Damp areas that cannot be kept dry require a mildew-resistant paint containing zinc oxide and a fungicide.

Peeling indicates a damp surface under oil-base paint, or oily spots under any type of paint. Apply new paint with a brush (not a roller) after scraping and sanding the peeled surfaces.

GLOSSARY OF GENERAL INFORMATION

Temperature

Temperature measures hotness or coldness, not the amount of heat, in any substance. What we call "one degree" is a difference in temperature calibrated on a specific scale.

A typical thermometer calibrates the expansion of mercury or alcohol that occurs as temperature rises. Other measuring rods include the expansion of metals (as in a thermostat) and change in electrical resistance. Temperature scales differ basically in the size of each degree and the placement of the zero point (0 degrees).

The oldest scale illustrated, *Reaumur*, places zero at the freezing point of water and divides the temperature rise from freezing to boiling into 80 degrees. It is rarely seen today.

The next oldest, *Fahrenheit* (abbreviated F), places zero at the coldest temperature the inventor knew, a mixture of snow and salt. His calibration put the freezing point of water at 32 degrees and the boiling point at

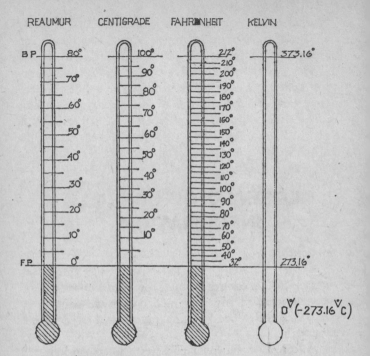

REAUMUR   CENTIGRADE   FAHRENHEIT   KELVIN

MERCURY LIQUID
BP BOILING POINT OF WATER
FP FREEZING POINT OF WATER

212 degrees, a difference of 180 degrees. Fahrenheit is in general use in English-speaking countries for everyday purposes and in engineering.

The *Centigrade* scale (abbreviated C) is also called Celsius after its inventor. Like Reaumur he placed zero at the freezing point of water, but counted 100 degrees to the boiling point. This calibration gives heat units a more convenient relationship to the metric system of measures. Centigrade is standard wherever the metric system prevails and for scientific work in all countries.

The *Kelvin* or Absolute scale (abbreviated K or Abs.) is the most modern scale, derived from Centigrade for the purposes of theoretical physics. One Kelvin degree measures the same difference in temperature as one Centigrade degree, but the zero is placed at a point where theoretically a substance has no molecular motion and no heat. This *absolute zero* occurs at minus 273.16 degrees Centigrade. Hence 0 degrees Centigrade equals approximately 273 degrees Kelvin and 100 degrees Centigrade equals approximately 373 degrees Kelvin.

To convert Centigrade to Fahrenheit, multiply degrees C by 9, divide by 5, add 32.

To convert Fahrenheit to Centigrade, subtract 32, multiply by 5, divide by 9.

$0°F = -17.8°C$ (cold day)	$32°F = 0°C$ (freezing)
$70°F = 21.1°C$ (room)	$90°F = 32.2°C$ (hot day)
$100°F = 43.3°C$ (bath)	$212°F = 100°C$ (boiling)

Units of Heat

One British thermal unit (BTU) is the amount of heat required to raise the temperature of 1 pound of water 1 degree Fahrenheit. The BTU content of fuels is measured at about 60 degrees, for the technical reason that water attains its greatest density at 62–63 degrees.

One calorie (cal) as used in heat engineering and food valuation is the amount of heat required to raise the temperature of 1 kilogram (1,000 grams) of water 1 degree Centigrade.

Note: Do not confuse this "great calorie" with the "small calorie" of your school chemistry classes. A small calorie is the amount of heat required to raise the temperature of 1 *gram* of water 1 degree Centigrade. Hence 1 cal = 1,000 small calories.

1 BTU = 251.67 calories. 1 therm = 100,000 BTU's
= 25,166,667 cals.

Number of degree days = 65 degrees minus day's mean temperature (F).

Insulation Ratings

A new consumer yardstick for insulation materials makes their selection a bit more scientific than hearsay Called the "R" value, it appears on most packagings of these materials. "R" measures the resistance of the material to the passage of heat. The *higher* the "R" value, the more effective the insulation.

Another measuring tool, the "U" value, measures the heat-transfer resistance of all the materials in a wall or some other exterior part of the house. It is a technical figure used by architects and engineers. The *lower* the "U" value, the more effective the insulation.

Here are recommended "R" values in various parts of a house in a cold climate, with approximate equivalents in thickness of the material.

Location	Minimum "R" Value of Insulation	Approximate Thickness
Over ceilings or under attic	19	5–7 in. of mineral wool
Exterior walls	11	3 in.
Floor over crawl space	13	3–3½ in.

WEIGHTS AND MEASURES

TABLES OF CANADA AND U.S. CUSTOMARY WEIGHTS AND MEASURES

LINEAR MEASURE

12 inches	= 1 foot
3 feet	= 1 yard (0.9144 meter)
5½ yards	= 1 rod
40 rods	= 1 furlong = 220 yards
8 furlongs	= 1 statute mile = 1,760 yards
3 miles	= 1 league
5,280 feet	= 1 statute or land mile
6,076.11549 feet	= 1 International Nautical Mile (1852.0 meters)

DRY MEASURE

2 pints	= 1 quart
8 quarts	= 1 peck
4 pecks	= 1 bushel (2150.42 cubic inches)

ANGULAR AND CIRCULAR MEASURE

60 seconds	= 1 minute
60 minutes	= 1 degree
90 degrees	= 1 right angle
180 degrees	= 1 straight angle
360 degrees	= 1 circle

SQUARE MEASURE

144 square inches	= 1 square foot
9 square feet	= 1 square yard
30¼ square yards	= 1 square rod
160 square rods	= 1 acre
640 acres	= 1 square mile

TROY WEIGHT

24 grains	= 1 pennyweight
20 pennyweights	= 1 ounce
12 ounces	= 1 pound, Troy

CUBIC MEASURE

1,728 cubic inches	=	1 cubic foot
27 cubic feet	=	1 cubic yard

LIQUID MEASURE

4 gills	=	1 pint
2 pints	=	1 quart
4 quarts	=	1 U.S. gallon (231.0 cubic inches)
	=	1 Imperial gallon (277.42 cubic inches)

AVOIRDUPOIS WEIGHT

27¹¹⁄₃₂ grains	=	1 dram
16 drams	=	1 ounce
16 ounces	=	1 pound (0.45359237 kilogram)
100 pounds	=	1 short hundredweight
20 short hundredweights	=	1 short ton (907.2 kgs.)
2240 pounds	=	1 long ton (1016 kg.)
2204.6 pounds	=	1 metric ton (1000 kg.)

THE METRIC SYSTEM

LINEAR MEASURE

10 millimeters	=	1 centimeter
10 centimeters	=	1 decimeter
10 decimeters	=	1 meter
10 meters	=	1 dekameter
10 dekameters	=	1 hectometer
10 hectometers	=	1 kilometer

LIQUID MEASURE

10 milliliters	=	1 centiliter
10 centiliters	=	1 deciliter
10 deciliters	=	1 liter
10 liters	=	1 dekaliter
10 dekaliters	=	1 hectoliter
10 hectoliters	=	1 kiloliter

SQUARE MEASURE

100 sq. millimeters	=	1 sq. centimeter
100 sq. centimeters	=	1 sq. decimeter
100 sq. decimeters	=	1 sq. meter
100 sq. meters	=	1 sq. dekameter
100 sq. dekameters	=	1 sq. hectometer
100 sq. hectometers	=	1 sq. kilometer

WEIGHTS

10 milligrams	=	1 centigram
10 centigrams	=	1 decigram
10 decigrams	=	1 gram
10 grams	=	1 dekagram
10 dekagrams	=	1 hectogram
10 hectograms	=	1 kilogram
100 kilograms	=	1 quintal
10 quintals	=	1 ton

CUBIC MEASURE

1,000 cu. millimeters	=	1 cu. centimeter
1,000 cu. centimeters	=	1 cu. decimeter
1,000 cu. decimeters	=	1 cu. meter

TABLES OF UNITS OF MEASUREMENT

Canada/United States Customary and Metric

UNITS OF LENGTH

Units	Inches	Feet	Yards	Rods
1 inch	1	0.083 333 33	0.027 777 78	0.005 050 505
1 foot	12	1	0.333 333 3	0.060 606 06
1 yard	36	3	1	0.181 818 2
1 rod	198	16.5	5.5	1
1 chain	792	66	22	4
1 mile	63 360	5280	1760	320
1 centimeter	0.393 700 8	0.032 808 40	0.010 936 13	0.001 988 388
1 meter	39.370 08	3.280 840	1.093 613	0.198 838 8

Units	Chains	Miles	Centimeters	Meters
1 inch	0.001 262 626	0.000 015 782 83	2.54	0.025 4
1 foot	0.015 151 52	0.000 189 393 9	30.48	0.304 8
1 yard	0.045 454 55	0.000 568 181 8	91.44	0.914 4
1 rod	0.25	0.003 125	502.92	5.029 2
1 chain	1	0.012 5	2011.68	20.116 8
1 mile	80	1	160 934.4	1609.344
1 centimeter	0.000 497 097 0	0.000 006 213 712	1	0.01
1 meter	0.049 709 70	0.000 621 371 2	100	1

UNITS OF AREA

Units	Square Inches	Square Feet	Square Yards,	Square Meters	Acres
1 square inch =	1	0.006 944 444	0.000 771 604 9	0.000 645 16	0.000 000 159 422 5
1 square foot =	144	1	0.111 111 1	0.092 903 04	0.000 022 956 84
1 square yard =	1296	9	1	0.836 127 36	0.000 206 611 6
1 acre =	6 272 640	43 560	4840	4046.856 422 4	1
1 square mile =	4 014 489 600	27 878 400	3 097 600	2 589 988.110 336	640
1 square meter =	1550.003	10.763 91	1.195 990	1	0.000 247 105 4
1 hectare =	15 500 031	107 639.1	11 959.90	10 000	2.471 054

Units	Square Miles	Hectares
1 square inch =	0.000 000 000 249 097 7	0.000 000 000 064 516
1 square foot =	0.000 000 035 870 06	0.000 000 009 290 304
1 square yard =	0.000 000 322 830 6	0.000 000 083 612 736
1 acre =	0.001 562 5	0.404 685 642 24
1 square mile =	1	258.998 811 033.6
1 square meter =	0.000 000 386 102 2	0.000 1
1 hectare =	0.003 861 022	1

UNITS OF VOLUME

Units		*Cubic Inches*	*Cubic Feet*	*Cubic Yards*
1 cubic inch	=	1	0.000 578 703 7	0.000 021 433 47
1 cubic foot	=	1728	1	0.037 037 04
1 cubic yard	=	46 656	27	1
1 cubic centimeter	=	0.061 023 74	0.000 035 314 67	0.000 001 307 951
1 cubic decimeter	=	61.023 74	0.035 314 67	0.001 307 951
1 cubic meter	=	61 023.74	35.314 67	1.307 951

Units		*Cubic Centimeters*	*Cubic Decimeters*	*Cubic Meters*
1 cubic inch	=	16.387 064	0.016 387 064	0.000 016 387 064
1 cubic foot	=	28 316.846 592	28.316 846 592	0.028 316 846 592
1 cubic yard	=	764 554.857 984	764.554 857 984	0.764 554 857 984
1 cubic centimeter	=	1	0.001	0.000 001
1 cubic decimeter	=	1 000	1	0.001
1 cubic meter	=	1 000 000	1000	1

UNITS OF CAPACITY LIQUID MEASURE

Units	Fluid Ounces	Liquid Pints	Liquid Quarts	Gallons
1 fluid ounce	1	0.062 5	0.031 25	0.007 812 5
1 liquid pint	16	1	0.5	0.125
1 liquid quart	32	2	1	0.25
1 gallon (U.S.)	128	8	4	1
1 gallon (Imp.)				
1 cubic inch	0.554 112 6	0.034 632 03	0.017 316 02	0.004 329 004
1 cubic foot	957.506 5	59.844 16	29.922 08	7.480 519
1 milliliter	0.033 814 02	0.002 113 376	0.001 056 688	0.000 264 172 052
1 liter	33.814 02	2.113 376	1.056 688	0.264 172 052

Units	Cubic Inches	Cubic Feet	Milliliters	Liters
1 fluid ounce	1.804 687 5	0.001 044 379	29.573 53	0.029 573 53
1 liquid pint	28.875	0.016 710 07	473.176 473	0.473 176 473
1 liquid quart	57.75	0.033 420 14	946.352 946	0.946 352 946
1 gallon (U.S.)	231	0.133 680 6	3 785.306	3.785 306
1 gallon (Imp.)	277.4			4.546 0
1 cubic inch	1	0.000 578 703 7	16.387 064	0.016 387 064
1 cubic foot	1728	1	28 316.846 592	28.316 846 592
1 milliliter	0.061 023 74	0.000 035 314 67	1	0.001
1 liter	61.023 74	0.035 314 67	1000	1

UNITS OF CAPACITY DRY MEASURE

Units	Dry Pints	Dry Quarts	Pecks	Bushels
1 dry pint	1	0.5	0.062 5	0.015 625
1 dry quart	2	1	0.125	0.031 25
1 peck	16	8	1	0.25
1 bushel	64	32	4	1
1 cubic inch	0.029 761 6	0.014 880 8	0.001 860 10	0.000 465 025
1 cubic foot	51.428 09	25.714 05	3.214 256	0.803 563 95
1 liter	1.816 166	0.908 083	0.113 510 37	0.028 377 59
1 dekaliter	18.161 66	9.080 83	1.135 103 7	0.283 775 9

Units	Cubic Inches	Cubic Feet	Liters	Dekaliters
1 dry pint	33.600 312 5	0.019 444 63	.550 610 47	.055 061 047
1 dry quart	67.200 625	0.038 889 25	1.101 220 9	.110 122 09
1 peck	537.605	0.311 114	8.809 767 5	.880 976 75
1 bushel	2150.42	1.244 456	35.239 07	3.523 907
1 cubic inch	1	0.000 578 703 7	0.016 387 064	0.001 638 706 4
1 cubic foot	1728	1	28.316 846 592	2.831 684 659 2
1 liter	61.023 74	0.035 314 67	1	0.1
1 dekaliter	610.237 4	0.353 146 7	10	1

RULES PERTAINING TO A CIRCLE

To find circumference:

Multiply diameter by	3.1416
or divide diameter by	0.3183

To find diameter:

Multiply circumference by	0.3183
or divide circumference by	3.1416

To find radius:

Multiply circumference by	0.15915
or divide circumference by	6.28318

To find side of an inscribed square:

Multiply diameter by	0.7071
or multiply circumference by	0.2251
or divide circumference by	4.4428

To find side of an equal square:

Multiply diameter by	0.8862
or divide diameter by	1.2840
or multiply circumference by	0.2821
or divide circumference by	3.5450

Square:

A side multiplied by 1.1442 equals diameter of its circumscribing circle.

A side multiplied by 4.443 equals circumference of its circumscribing circle.

A side multiplied by 1.128 equals diameter of an equal circle.

A side multiplied by 2.547 equals circumference of an equal circle.

Square inches multiplied by 1.273 equal circle inches of an equal circle.

To find the area of a circle:

Multiply circumference by one-quarter of the diameter, or multiply the square of diameter by	0.7854
or multiply the square of circumference by	0.07958
or multiply the square of one-half the diameter by	3.1416

To find the surface of a sphere or globe:

Multiply the diameter by the circumference, or multiply the square of the diameter by	3.1416
or multiply four times the square of the radius by	3.1416

Meter Reading

Nearly all gas and electric meters use a series of four or five small "clock" dials to record consumption. Each dial is numbered from 1 to 0 (10). There are also one or two small test dials that are not used.

Start at the right-hand dial and write down the number that the pointer is *closest* to. Proceed to the next dial and write down the number that the pointer has just *passed*. (Notice that each succeeding dial turns in the opposite direction to the preceding dial.)

Continue reading the dials from right to left, noting the number that each pointer has passed.

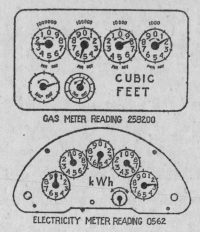

GAS METER READING 258200

ELECTRICITY METER READING 0562

If you wish to find out how much electricity or gas was used in a certain period, simply subtract the reading taken at the beginning of the period from the last reading.

Gas meters show the number of cubic feet of gas used. Regardless of whether they have four or five dials, the dial on the right is numbered in 100s of cubic feet, the next one in 1,000s, etc. To get the total number of cubic feet used, add two zeros to the dial reading.

TYPE OF EXTINGUISHER	FOR WHAT KINDS OF FIRE	CONTENTS	HOW TO START	RANGE AND DURATION
SODA-ACID	CLASS A (Wood, paper, textiles, etc.)	Water solution of bicarbonate of soda and sulfuric acid.	Turn over	30 to 40 feet 50 to 55 seconds (2½ gallon size)
PUMP TANK		Plain water	Pump by hand	●
GAS CARTRIDGE	CLASS A ("Loaded stream" model is also good on Class B)	Water and cartridge of carbon dioxide	Turn over and bump	●
FOAM	CLASS A and CLASS B (Oil, gasoline, paint, grease, etc.)	Water solution of aluminum sulfate and bicarbonate of soda	Turn over	DANGER: Do not use these water base extinguishers on electrical fires.
CARBON DIOXIDE	CLASS B and CLASS C (Live electrical equipment) ● NOTE: If nothing else is available, these extinguishers may have some effect on small Class A fires.	Carbon dioxide	Pull pin and open valve	6 to 8 feet about 42 seconds (15 lb. size)
VAPORIZING LIQUID		Carbon tetrachloride and other chemicals. CAUTION: Avoid breathing vapors from extinguisher, especially in small, closed places.	Turn handle, then pump by hand	20 to 30 feet 40 to 45 seconds (1 quart size)
DRY CHEMICAL		Bicarbonate of soda with other dry chemicals and cartridge of carbon dioxide	Pull pin and open valve (or press lever), then squeeze nozzle valve	About 14 feet 22 to 25 seconds (30 lb. size)

FIRE EXTINGUISHERS

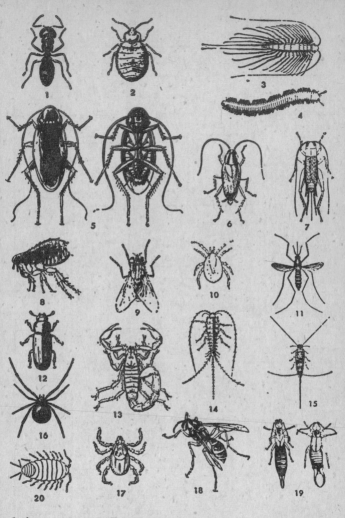

1. Ant	6. German	11. Mosquito	16. Black widow
2. Bed bug	cockroach	12. Flour beetle	spider
3. Centipede	7. Cricket	13. Scorpion	17. Brown dog tick
4. Millipede	8. Flea	14. Silverfish	18. Wasp
5. American	9. Housefly	15. Firebrat	19. Earwig
cockroach	10. Mite		20. Sowbug

HOUSEHOLD INSECTS

Penny Size	Length in Inches for Common, Box and Finish*	Common Nails			Box and Casing Nails		
		Gauge	Thickness in Thousandths	Number per Pound	Gauge	Thickness in Thousandths	Number per Pound
2d	1	15	.072	876	15½	.069	1010
3d	1¼	14	.083	568	14½	.078	635
4d	1½	12½	.102	316	14	.083	473
5d	1¾	12½	.102	271	14	.083	406
6d	2	11½	.115	181	12½	.102	236
7d	2¼	11½	.115	161	12½	.102	210
8d	2½	10¼	.131	106	11½	.115	145
9d	2¾	10¼	.131	96	11½	.115	132
10d	3	9	.148	69	10½	.127	94
12d	3¼	9	.148	63	10½	.127	88
16d	3½	8	.165	49	10	.134	71
20d	4	6	.203	31	9	.148	52
30d	4½	5	.220	24	9	.148	46
40d	5	4	.238	18	8	.165	35
50d	5½	3	.259	14	——	——	——
60d	6	2	.284	11	——	——	——

*Coated nails are ⅛ inch shorter.
Note: Flooring nails are similar in appearance to the casing nail but are about 1½ gauge thicker for each size. They are made in sizes from 6d to 20d. Wire nails are gauged by the old standard Birmingham wire gauge.

COMMONLY USED NAILS, THEIR SIZE, GAUGE, AND NUMBER PER POUND

Penny Size	Length in Inches for Common, Box, and Finish*	Coated Nails			Finish Nails		
		6d Coated			6d Finish		
		Gauge	Thickness in Thousandths	Number per Pound	Gauge	Thickness in Thousandths	Number per Pound
2d	1	16	.065	1084	16½	.062	1351
3d	1¼	15½	.069	848	15½	.069	807
4d	1½	14	.083	488	15	.072	584
5d	1¾	13½	.088	364	15	.072	500
6d	2	13	.095	275	13	.095	309
7d	2¼	12½	.102	212	13	.095	238
8d	2½	11½	.115	142	12½	.102	189
9d	2¾	11½	.115	130	12½	.102	172
10d	3	11	.120	104	11½	.115	121
12d	3¼	10	.134	77	11½	.115	113
16d	3½	9	.148	61	11	.120	90
20d	4	7	.180	37	10	.134	62
30d	4½	6	.203	29	—	—	—
40d	5	5	.220	21	—	—	—
50d	5½	4	.238	16	—	—	—
60d	6	3	.259	13	—	—	—

*Coated Nails ⅛ inch shorter.

Note: Flooring nails are similar in appearance to the casing nail but are about 1½ gauge thicker for each size. They are made in sizes from 6d to 20d. Wire nails are gauged by the old standard Birmingham wire gauge.

COMMONLY USED NAILS, THEIR SIZE,
GAUGE, AND NUMBER PER POUND

Length, in inches	Am. Steel & Wire Co.'s Steel Wire Gauge	Approx. No. to lbs.	Nailings	Sizes and Kinds of Material	Trade Names	Pounds per 1000 feet B. M. on center as follows: 12"	16"	20"	36"	48"
						Pounds				
2½	10¼	106	2	1x 4 (I, II)	8d common...	60	48	37	23	20
2½	10¼	106	2	1x 6 (I, II)	8d common...	40	32	25	16	13
2½	10¼	106	2	1x 8 (I, II)	8d common...	31	27	20	12	10
2½	10¼	106	2	1x10 (I, II)	8d common...	25	20	16	10	8
2½	10¼	106	3	1x12 (I, II)	8d common...	31	24	20	12	10
4	6	31	2	2x 4 (I, II)	20d common...	105	80	65	60	33
4	6	31	2	2x 6 (I, II)	20d common...	70	54	43	27	22
4	6	31	2	2x 8 (I, II)	20d common...	53	40	53	21	17
4	6	31	3	2x10 (I, II)	20d common...	60	50	40	25	20
4	6	31	3	2x12 (I, II)	20d common...	52	41	33	21	17
6	2	11	2	3x 4 (I, II)	60d common...	197	150	122	76	61
6	2	11	2	3x 6 (I, II)	60d common...	131	97	82	52	42
6	2	11	2	3x 8 (I, II)	60d common...	100	76	61	38	34
6	2	11	3	3x10 (I, II)	60d common...	178	137	110	70	55
6	2	11	3	3x12 (I, II)	60d common...	145	115	92	58	46
2½	12½	189	2	Base, per 100 ft. lin...	8d finish......	....	1	....	....	....
2½	10¼	106	2	Byrket lath..........	8d common...	....	48	....	....	....
2½	12½	189	1	Ceiling, ¾x4.........	8d finish......	18	14	....	....	....
2	13	309	1	Ceiling, ½ and ⅝....	6d finish......	11	8	....	....	....
2½	12½	189	2	Finish, ⅞...........	8d finish......	25	12	....	....	....
3	11½	121	2	Finish, 1⅛..........	10d finish......	12	10	....	....	....
2½	10	99	1	Flooring, 1x3.........	8d floor brads.	42	32	....	....	....
2½	10	99	1	Flooring, 1x4.........	8d floor brads.	32	26	....	....	....
2½	10	99	1	Flooring, 1x6........	8d floor brads.	22	18	....	....	....
4	6	31		Framing, 2x4 to 2x16.	20d common..	20	16	14	....	....
3½	8	49		requires 3 or more sizes	16d common..	10	10	8	....	....
3	9	69		and varies greatly.	10d common..	8	6	5	....	....
6	2	11		Framing, 3x4 to 3x14.	60d common..	30	25	20	....	....
2½	11½	145	2	Siding, drop, 1x4.....	8d casing. (or 7d Siding Nails)	45	35	....	....	....
2½	11½	145	2	Siding, drop, 1x6.....	8d casing. (or 7d Siding Nails)	30	25	....	....	....
2½	11½	145	2	Siding, drop, 1x8.....	8d casing. (or 7d Siding Nails)	23	18	....	....	....
2	13	309	1	Siding, bevel, ½x4....	6d finish.. (or 7d Siding Nails)	23	18	....	....	....
2	13	309	1	Siding, bevel, ½x6....	6d finish.. (or 7d Siding Nails)	15	13	....	....	....
2	13	309	1	Siding, bevel, ½x8....	6d finish.. (or 7d Siding Nails)	12	10	....	....	....
				Casing, per opening...	6d and 8d casing.......	About ½ pound per side.				
1¼	14	568	12" o.c.	Flooring, ⅜x2.......	3d brads.......	About 10 pounds per 1000 square feet.				
1⅛	15	778	16" o.c.	Lath, 48"...........	3d sterilized blued lath...	6 pounds per 1000 pieces.				
⅞	12	469	2" o.c.	Ready roofing.........	Barbed roofing.	¾ of a pound to the sq.				
⅞	12	469	1" o.c.	Ready roofing........	Barbed roofing.	1½ pounds to the square.				
⅞	12	180	2" o.c.	Ready roofing........ (⅝ heads)	American felt roofing......	1½ pounds to the square.				
⅞	12	180	1" o.c.	Ready roofing........ (⅝ heads)	American felt roofing.....	3 pounds to the square.				
1¼	13	429	....	Shingles*............	3d shingle.....	4½ pounds; about 2 nails to each 4 inches.				
1½	12	274	....	Shingles.............	4d shingle.....	7½ pounds; about 2 nails to each 4 inches.				
⅞	12	180	4	Shingles.............	American felt roofing	12 lbs., 4 nails to shingle.				
⅞	12	469	4	Shingles............	Barbed roofing.	4½ lbs., 4 nails to shingle.				
1	16	1150	2" o.c.	Wall board, around entire edge..........	Plaster board nails flat head	5 pounds, per 1,000 square feet.				
1	15½	1010	3" o.c.	Wall board, intermediate nailings.......	2d...........	2½ lbs., per 1,000 square feet.				

I. Used square edge, as platforms, floors, sheathing, or shiplap.
II. When used D. & M., blind nailed, only ⅓ quantity named required.

*Wood shingles vary in width; asphalt are usually 8 inches wide. Regardless of width 1000 shingles are the equivalent of 1000 pieces 4 inches wide.
Courtesy American Steel & Wire Co.

WIRE NAILS, KINDS AND QUANTITIES REQUIRED

Screw Gauge American		Wire Gauge Old Standard Birmingham		Decimal Equivalents			
No.	Inch	No.	Inch	Fraction	Dec. Equiv.	Fraction	Dec. Equiv.
0	.060	17	.058	1/64	.015625	33/64	.515625
1	.073	16	.065	1/32	.03125	17/32	.53125
2	.086	15	.072	3/64	.046875	35/64	.546875
3	.099	14	.083	1/16	.0625	9/16	.5625
4	.112	13	.095	5/64	.078125	37/64	.578125
5	.125	12	.109	3/32	.09375	19/32	.59375
6	.138	11	.120	7/64	.109375	39/64	.609375
7	.151	10	.134	1/8	.125	5/8	.625
8	.164	9	.148	9/64	.140625	41/64	.640625
9	.177	8	.165	5/32	.15625	21/32	.65625
10	.190	7	.180	11/64	.171875	43/64	.671875
11	.203	6	.203	3/16	.1875	11/16	.6875
12	.216	5	.220	13/64	.203125	45/64	.703125
13	.229	4	.238	7/32	.21875	23/32	.71875
14	.242	3	.259	15/64	.234375	47/64	.734375
15	.255	2	.284	1/4	.25	3/4	.75
16	.268	1	.300	17/64	.265625	49/64	.765625
17	.281	0	.340	9/32	.28125	25/32	.78125
18	.294	00	.380	19/64	.296875	51/64	.796875
20	.320	000	.425	5/16	.3125	13/16	.8125
22	.346	0000	.454	21/64	.328125	53/64	.828125
24	.372	—	—	11/32	.34375	27/32	.84375
26	.398	—	—	23/64	.359375	55/64	.859375
28	.424	—	—	3/8	.375	7/8	.875
30	.450	—	—	25/64	.390625	57/64	.890625
—	—	—	—	13/32	.40625	29/32	.90625
—	—	—	—	27/64	.421875	59/64	.921875
—	—	—	—	7/16	.4375	15/16	.9375
—	—	—	—	29/64	.453125	61/64	.953125
—	—	—	—	15/32	.46875	31/32	.96875
—	—	—	—	31/64	.484375	63/64	.984375
—	—	—	—	1/2	.5	1	1.00

SCREW GAUGES, WIRE GAUGES, AND DECIMAL EQUIVALENTS

NUMBER OF SCREW	For Shank Clearance Holes		For Pilot Holes								NUMBER OF AUGER BIT
	Twist Bit (Nearest size in fractions of an inch) Slotted or Phillips	Drill Gauge No. or Letter (To be used for maximum holding power) Slotted or Phillips	Hardwoods				Softwoods				(To counter-bore for sinking head by 16ths) Slotted or Phillips
			Twist Bit (Nearest size in fractions of an inch)		Drill Gauge No. (To be used for maximum holding power)		Twist Bit (Nearest size in fractions of an inch)		Drill Gauge No. (To be used for maximum holding power)		
			Slotted	Phillips	Slotted	Phillips	Slotted	Phillips	Slotted	Phillips	
0	1/16	52	1/32	—	70	—	1/64	—	75	—	
1	5/64	47	1/32	—	66	—	1/32	—	71	—	
2	3/32	42	3/64	1/32	56	70	1/32	1/64	65	75	3
3	7/64	37	1/16	1/32	54	66	3/64	1/32	58	71	4
4	7/64	32	1/16	3/64	52	56	3/64	1/32	55	65	4
5	1/8	30	5/64	1/16	49	54	1/16	3/64	53	58	4
6	9/64	27	5/64	1/16	47	52	1/16	3/64	52	55	5
7	5/32	22	3/32	5/64	44	49	1/16	3/64	51	53	5
8	11/64	18	3/32	5/64	40	47	5/64	1/16	48	52	6
9	3/16	14	7/64	3/32	37	44	5/64	1/16	45	51	6
10	3/16	10	7/64	3/32	33	40	3/32	5/64	43	48	6
11	13/64	4	1/8	7/64	31	37	3/32	5/64	40	45	7
12	7/32	2	1/8	7/64	30	33	7/64	3/32	38	43	7
14	1/4	D	9/64	1/8	25	31	7/64	3/32	32	40	8
16	17/64	I	5/32	9/64	18	30	9/64	7/64	29	38	9
18	19/64	N	3/16	9/64	13	25	9/64	7/64	26	32	10
20	21/64	P	13/64	5/32	4	18	11/64	9/64	19	29	11
24	3/8	V	7/32	3/16	1	13	3/16	9/64	15	26	12

BIT SIZES FOR BORING PILOT HOLES AND SHANK CLEARANCE HOLES FOR WOOD SCREWS

	Sizes of Screws and Bolts*											
Diameter	2	3	4	5	6	8	10	12	1/4	5/16	3/8	1/2
Coarse thread	56	48	40	40	32	32	24	24	20	18	16	13
Fine thread	64	56	48	44	40	36	32	28	28	24	24	

*Machine screws both fine and coarse threads; stove bolts coarse threads only. Diameters of small screws indicated by number, larger sizes by fraction of an inch.

DIAMETER AND THREAD, MACHINE SCREWS AND STOVE BOLTS

Artificial*	Garnet	Flint	Grade
400–10/0	—	—	
360	—	—	
320–9/0	—	7/0	
280–8/0	8/0	6/0	Very fine
240–7/0	7/0	5/0	
220–6/0	6/0	4/0	
		3/0	
180–5/0	5/0	—	
150–4/0	4/0	2/0	
120–3/0	3/0	—	Fine
100–2/0	2/0	0	
80–0	0	½	
60–½	½	1	Medium
50–1	1	1½	
40–1½	1½	2	
36–2	2	2½	Coarse
30–2½	2½	3	
24–3	3	—	
20–3½	3½	—	Very Coarse
16–4	—	—	
12–4½	—	—	

* Includes *silicon carbide* and *aluminum oxide.*

COMPARISON OF GRIT NUMBERS FOR ABRASIVE PAPERS

MAJOR AREAS OF HEAT LOSS AND HEAT GAIN IN HOMES

	Heat Loss	Heat Gain in Summer
Walls	33%	34%
Ceiling	22%	24%
Floors	1%	4%
Glass and doors	30%	26%
Infiltration	14%	12%

Building Parts	Average Life Years	Annual Depreciation Per Cent
Plastering	20	5
Painting, outside	5	20
Painting, inside	7	14
Shingles	16	6
Cornice	40	2½
Weatherboarding	30	3½
Sheathing	50	2
Flooring	20	5
Flooring (entirely carpeted)	40	2½
Doors, complete	30	3½
Windows, complete	30	3½
Stairs and newels	30	3½
Base	40	2½
Building hardware	20	5
Outside blinds	16	5
Sills and floor joists	15	4
Dimension lumber	50	2
Porches	20	5

DEPRECIATION OF WOOD FRAME HOUSE—LIFE OF PARTS

Size	Length in Feet											
	12	14	16	18	20	22	24	26	28	30	32	34
1x 2	2	2 1/3	2 2/3	3	3 1/3	3 2/3	4	4 1/3	4 2/3	5	5 1/3	5 2/3
1x 3	3	3 1/2	4	4 1/2	5	5 1/2	6	6 1/2	7	7 1/2	8	8 1/2
1x 4	4	4 2/3	5 1/3	6	6 2/3	7 1/3	8	8 2/3	9 1/3	10	10 2/3	11 1/3
1x 6	6	7	8	9	10	11	12	13	14	15	16	17
1x 8	8	9 1/3	10 2/3	12	13 1/3	14 2/3	16	17 1/3	18 2/3	20	21 1/3	22 2/3
1x10	10	11 2/3	13 1/3	15	16 2/3	18 1/3	20	21 2/3	22 1/3	25	26 2/3	28 1/3
1x12	12	14	16	18	20	22	24	26	28	30	32	34
2x 4	8	9	11	12	13	15	16	17	19	20	21	23
2x 6	12	14	16	18	20	22	24	26	28	30	32	34
2x 8	16	19	21	24	27	29	32	35	37	40	43	45
2x10	20	23	27	30	33	37	40	43	47	50	53	57
2x12	24	28	32	36	40	44	48	52	56	60	64	68
2x14	28	33	37	42	47	51	56	61	65	70	75	80
3x 8	24	28	32	36	40	44	48	52	56	60	64	68
3x10	30	35	40	45	50	55	60	65	70	75	80	85
3x12	36	42	48	54	60	66	72	78	84	90	96	102
3x14	42	49	56	63	70	77	84	91	98	105	112	119
4x 4	16	19	21	24	27	29	32	35	37	40	43	45
4x 6	24	28	32	36	40	44	48	52	56	60	64	68
4x 8	32	37	43	48	53	59	64	69	75	80	85	91
4x10	40	47	53	60	67	73	80	87	93	100	107	113
4x12	48	56	64	72	80	88	96	104	112	120	128	136
4x14	56	65	75	84	93	103	112	121	131	140	149	159
6x 6	36	42	48	54	60	66	72	78	84	90	96	102
6x 8	48	56	64	72	80	88	96	104	112	120	128	136
6x10	60	70	80	90	100	112	120	130	140	150	160	170
6x12	72	84	96	108	120	132	144	156	168	180	192	204
6x14	84	98	112	126	140	154	168	182	196	210	224	238
8x 8	64	75	85	96	107	117	128	139	149	160	171	181
8x10	80	93	107	120	133	147	160	173	187	200	213	227
8x12	96	112	128	144	160	176	192	208	224	240	256	272
8x14	112	131	149	168	187	205	224	243	261	280	299	317
10x10	100	117	133	150	167	183	200	217	233	250	267	283
10x12	120	140	160	180	200	220	240	260	280	300	320	340
10x14	140	163	187	210	233	257	280	303	327	350	373	397
12x12	144	168	192	216	240	264	288	312	336	360	384	408
12x14	168	196	224	252	280	308	336	264	392	420	448	476
14x14	197	229	261	294	327	356	392	425	457	490	523	555

BOARD MEASURE

TOOLS FOR HANDYMAN AND HANDYWOMAN
FOR HOUSEHOLD OPERATION, MAINTENANCE, AND REPAIR

If you plan to do—	Minimum equipment	Desirable equipment	Supplementary equipment
Household or kitchen activities:			
open crates and boxes..........	crate opener or pry bar or 8" screw driver.	12 or 13 oz. claw hammer.	
open jars, can, etc.............. cut cardboard............... lubricate appliances, locks, hinges, etc.	jar and can openers. scissors and paring knife. high-grade oil suitable for small appliances.	combination opener. utility knife. powdered graphite. graphite in oil.	
measure and space items.......	ruler or yardstick or good-quality measuring tape.	6'-10' steel tape or folding rule.	25' or 50' tape.
attach items to walls............	paste-on tabs for light items. hangers with nails or screws for heavier items: 12 or 13 oz. curved claw hammer. hand drill and bits. screwdrivers.	Hollow-wall screw anchors and toggle bolts: hand or electric drill and twist drills ¼" and up. stud locator.	For masonry or concrete: screw anchors and screws. proper size star drill or electric drill and tungsten carbide masonry drill.
level items.....................	pan of water to level appliances. string with attached weight.	level as part of combination square.	9"-12" level.
Small repair jobs:			
tighten or loosen screws........	4" and 6" screwdrivers. Nos. 1 and 2 Phillips screwdrivers.	hex wrenches. special screwdrivers and wrenches.	ratchet screwdriver.
tighten nuts or hold small items.	6"-7" slip joint pliers. adjustable wrench.	locking-type wrench pliers. needle-nose pliers.	open-end and box-end wrenches.
drive or pull nails, etc.........	12 or 13 oz. curved claw hammer. 6" screwdriver.	hand stapler. pry bar.	staple gun. tack puller.
repair plastic items..........	plastic mending tape.	liquid mender for type of plastic.	plastic repair kit with strips and adhesive.
seal openings and joints........	special sealants and tapes.	calking gun. tape or cloth to place between wrench and polished fitting.	
replace ordinary faucet washers.	adjustable wrench. screwdrivers.	....	
open drains and pipes...........	force cup.	small wire. putty knife.	flexible drain auger.
other minor jobs..............	packaging material and string. polishes and waxes. cleaning supplies and equipment. step stool.	vacuum cleaner. stepladder.	glass cutter. fabric mending and fastening kits.
Small jobs with wood:			
measure and mark............	sharp pointed No. 2½ or 3 common pencil.	8" by 12" utility, steel combination, or try square.	dividers. rafter or framing square.

(NOTE.—Operations are listed in their usual sequence.)

Operation			
cut wood...............	ruler or yardstick, tablet back or drawing triangle may serve as a square, pencil compass, coping saw, friction vise or bench hook to hold wood.	6' to 10' steel tape or folding rule. 20"–22" 10-11 point hand saw, two 4" C-clamps.	hand ripsaw, miter box, electric hand and sabre saws, jack or smoothing plane, electric sander.
smoothen wood (may be repeated after assembly).	fine, medium, and coarse sandpaper, sandpaper block,	block plane, or multiblade wood smoothing tool, rasps and scraper,	
assemble pieces into unit......	assorted sizes of wire nails and brads, 12 to 13 oz. curved claw hammer, 3/16" nail set, 6d nails, white glue (not moisture resistant).	wood screws, countersink, 4" and 6" screwdrivers, hand drill with drills and bit brace with bits or light duty electric drill with bits, nails with heads cut off may be used as small drills, urea or plastic resin glue (moisture resistant).	gluing clamps, 8" or stub screwdriver, assorted sizes of common, finish, and special nails, set of combination drill and countersink bits for use with screws, resorcinol glue (waterproof).
fill holes in wood:			
nail holes...............	colored putty, wood dough, plastic wood, or surfacing putty.		
larger holes...............		spackling compound for surfaces to be painted.	
Work with metals:			
measure and mark...........	see measure and mark wood.	see measure and mark wood.	metal scribe, power grinder and safety goggles.
cut...........	utility saw or keyhole-type hacksaw.	tin snips, 3/4" cold chisel, vise. hacksaw with set of blades,	
drill holes...........	hand drill with twist drills.	light-duty electric drill with a set of twist drills,	high-speed drill bits desirable for frequent heavy use,
smoothen or sharpen...........	8" mill file, sharpening stone.	8" half round file, 8" round file,	emery cloth, grinder and safety goggles,
assemble...........	4" and 6" screwdrivers, Nos. 1 and 2 Phillips screwdrivers, 6"–7" slip-joint pliers.	locking-type wrench pliers, adjustable wrench.	small sets of open-end and box-end wrenches.
polishing...........		emery and crocus cloths,	
repairing...........	epoxy resin,	epoxy resin and fiber glass,	soldering equipment.

| Size of fireplace opening | | Depth | Minimum width of back wall | Height of vertical back wall | Height of inclined back wall | Size of flue lining required | |
Width	Height					Standard rectangular (outside dimensions)	Standard round (inside diameter)
Inches	Inches	Inches	Inches	Inches	Inches	Inches	Inches
24	24	16–18	14	14	16	8½ x 8½	10
28	24	16–18	14	14	16	8½ x 8½	10
30	28–30	16–18	16	14	18	8½ x 13	10
36	28–30	16–18	22	14	18	8½ x 13	12
42	28–32	16–18	28	14	18	13 x 13	12
48	32	18–20	32	14	24	13 x 13	15
54	36	18–20	36	14	28	13 x 13	15
60	36	18–20	44	14	28	13 x 18	15
54	40	20–22	36	17	29	13 x 18	15
60	40	20–22	42	17	30	18 x 18	18
66	40	20–22	44	17	30	18 x 18	18
72	40	22–28	51	17	30	18 x 18	18

FIREPLACE DIMENSIONS AND SIZES OF FLUE LINING

INDEX

INDEX

309

311

315